Year-Round Education

ECONOMIC, EDUCATIONAL,

AND

SOCIOLOGICAL FACTORS

JOHN D. McLAIN

McCutchan Publishing Corporation
2526 Grove Street
Berkeley, California 94704

©1973 by McCutchan Publishing Corporation
All rights reserved
Library of Congress Catalog Card Number: 72-14044
International Standard Book Number: 0-8211-1222-8
Printed in the United States of America

Contents

Preface

In all history, no better way has been found than the process of education for equipping citizens in a free society with the knowledge and understanding needed to make the decisions and to take the actions necessary to sustain and improve that society. Through this process, our nation has developed the science and technology of creating changes in the human environment and in ourselves at an ever-increasing rate and magnitude. We have the power now to intervene in the processes of nature with such great force that we can literally destroy ourselves and the life-sustaining capacity of the earth on which we live. That same power, used wisely, can enhance the quality of the environment and give greater meaning to the dignity and worth of the individual human being.

The powerful forces of technological development have generated such great inertia that there is no turning back. Our society and our world, like a giant brakeless vehicle rushing headlong down an obstacle-laden highway, must steer a precarious course to new horizons or crash into oblivion. The future of mankind literally hinges upon the choices that are made and the actions that are taken in the next few decades. As the late James Allen stated, "The key to human survival is education."

The American people expect much from our schools. It is the responsibility of the school to prepare our children and youth to live productively and intelligently in this technologically advanced, rapidly changing society. The schools are expected to discover and to cultivate the talents and capacities of each individual, and to assist his growth into a mature, creative, and productive adult capable of making choices and taking actions essential to self-fulfillment, to the progress of our society, and to the survival of the world. In the history of mankind, no other society has expected so much of its schools, nor has the success or failure of the schools ever had such profound and far-reaching impact on society and the future of man.

But the goals of survival and enhancement of humanity cannot be achieved through techniques, processes, and tools that were designed for a much lesser task. The schools that successfully educated less than five percent of our youth at the turn of the century, or half of our youth at mid-century—scarcely a generation ago—are far from being adequate to provide the quality and quantity of education we must have today and in the future.

The American school has made great strides since the beginning of this century, when formal education past the primary level was expected only for the elite few. The changes and improvements in our schools have been immense, in keeping with the changes in the ways we live and earn our livelihoods. Although some decry the failures of the school, the American education system has produced the generalized knowledge and skills that spawned the technology that offers us such great hope, as well as fear, for the future. In doing so, this also made our schools obsolete.

The rate and magnitude of change our society is now undergoing is unprecedented, therefore, so must be the rate and magnitude of change in our schools if the emergent educational needs of our society are to be met.

John D. McLain

1 * The Significance of the Taxpayers' Revolt

The public school today is on trial. The people are the jury, and they pass judgment at the polls as they vote on school budgets and bond issues. More and more frequently in recent years, the verdict is "guilty" as the people continue to "revolt" against higher school taxes. Guilty of what? What does a vote against the school budget really mean?

It does not mean that our society is economically unable to support good schools. A nation that spends more for cosmetics, more for alcoholic beverages, more for leisure time traveling, and far more on war than it does on its public schools *can* afford to pay for a quality education for its children. It is a matter of human values.

It does not mean the people are unwilling to support good schools. The American people have consistently demonstrated their belief that an investment in good schools is good business. The right to attain a quality education is considered an essential part of the American way of life, and the demand that this right be met is growing, not lessening. According to the National Education Association, the operating budget in 1969-70 for American public elementary and secondary schools totaled about $32 billion, with an

1

added $4.7 billion for capital investment. It has continued to increase at the rate of about 10 percent per year since that time.

Without a doubt, education is big business. It is only logical that the stockholders of this huge enterprise, the people, are demanding an accounting as to how the business is being managed. A "no" vote at the polls is the taxpayers' way of saying that there is a credibility gap between the way the people think the schools *are* being run, and the way they think the schools *should* be run. In essence, the taxpayers' revolt is an indication that the people believe the schools must be brought up to date, and they believe this can be done without continually increasing taxes. The stockholders of this great enterprise that is so paramount to the well-being of our society are asking the board of directors to reexamine current practices and priorities. They want to be sure that the useful and effective programs and practices are retained, while the obsolete and nonproductive ones are eliminated, making way for the new that is also needed.

Without dispute, the most important aspect of the school program is what the students learn, but the most conspicuous aspect is the school *building*. The school building, sitting idle all summer, infers economic inefficiency. Also conspicuous are the children under their mothers' feet and the youth on the hot city streets with nothing to do but get into trouble when they cannot get jobs, implying the obsolescence of the school calendar.

It may therefore be expected that in times of increasing enrollments, rising building costs, and tight money, people would consider the idea of operating the schools all year. This, in fact, did happen as an aftermath of the "baby booms" following the two world wars. The feasibility of year-round education was widely considered between 1924 and 1931, and again between 1947 and 1953. The idea generally was rejected at the planning stage; in the few schools where it was initiated, the program was usually abandoned within a short period of time.

In the past, the major objections centered around one or more of three factors: (1) the anticipated financial savings could not be achieved; (2) a mandated change in the school calendar required children to be in school at times when their parents wanted them to be out, and out of school when their parents wanted them to be in school; and (3) there were scheduling problems in offering the regular course of study in proper sequence when student attendance was rotated.

In spite of these previous experiences, the concept of year-round education came to the fore again in the late 1960s and has reached an all-time high level of interest among both educators and the general public today. This emerging development is reflected in the growth of the National Seminars on Year-Round Education. The first such seminar, conducted in Arkansas in 1969, attracted a handful of dedicated educators who were convinced the school calendar must be restructured. The numbers in attendance have steadily increased at the Second National Seminar on Year-Round Education in Pennsylvania in 1970, the third in Florida in 1971, and the fourth in California in 1972. At the Fourth National Seminar on Year-Round Education, it was evident to the thousand educational and lay leaders in attendance that a movement to reexamine the school calendar is under way in every state in the nation. On that premise, they organized the National Council on Year-Round Education.

The underlying forces in our society that have caused this movement to emerge are significantly different from the relatively simple problem of overcrowding that triggered consideration of year-round education during the postwar eras. The empty schoolhouse in the summertime symbolizes the obsolescence and inefficiency of the system, but the tax revolt is a demand by the people for a renaissance in the total American way of life and for the school to help lead the way to a better world. Far more significant than the empty schoolhouse is the fact that the rigid time schedules of the traditional school calendar inhibit the development of flexibility in the curriculum, essential if the school is to undergo the necessary reformation.

People will continue to judge the public school. Their judgments will be based upon what they know, or do not know, about the school and its operation. The electorate can make wise choices about the operation of the schools only if it is adequately informed about the educational needs of the community and society, as well as the alternative ways by which these needs may be met. Their decisions will continue to be expressed by their support, or lack of support, of the school budget.

It is not uncommon for professional educators to proclaim their interest in year-round education as a concern for quality education, not economics, while at the same time they are working under pressure from their local constituency to attain optimum use of school buildings for economic reasons.

Public concern about alternative ways to structure the schools provides educational leaders with a unique opportunity, as well as a responsibility, to help the people gain a better understanding about the role of the public school in a democratic society. The professional educator should not feel apologetic about examining the operation of the school in terms of economic efficiency; he would be remiss in his duty if he were not cognizant that the financial resources of any community, any state, and the nation are limited and are allocated on a priority basis. Priorities are determined, at least in a broad sense, by the people on the basis of their value systems and felt needs.

If the only concern of our society were to save money or cut taxes, the most efficient and effective way to reduce to a minimum the operating costs of the schools would be simply to close them, but our society does value a quality education for its children and youth.

The people are not only concerned about economic efficiency and quality education. They are also concerned about *when* the students are taught. Again, if our prime concern were economic efficiency, an easy way to increase the use of school facilities would be to operate the school in two shifts. An even fuller use of school buildings could be attained with three shifts, using the facilities twenty-four hours of the day. The standard school year is 180 days, but there are 365 days in a calendar year. A school district could schedule *six* times as many students in its existing school facilities, without reducing the number of hours each student attended school, simply by operating three shifts 360 days instead of 180 during the year. Of course, no community would consider such a schedule because the school schedule must also be compatible with family life-styles and the community living patterns.

Logically, the time structure of the American public school should be based on the answers to these three questions:

1. What school time patterns or schedules will provide optimum economic efficiency?

2. What school time patterns or schedules will provide quality education, with equality in educational opportunity, for all children and youth?

3. What school time patterns or schedules are acceptable to the people in terms of sociological needs—their personal, family, and community living patterns?

Each of these questions is interrelated with the other two. Adults want the school schedule to meet their convenience, but will give up some convenience for quality education and economy. They want quality education for their children but will make some "sacrifices" for economy and convenience. They want economy but are willing to pay extra for convenience and quality education. As our society reacts to these value-oriented questions, they give shape to the American public school and the school calendar.

The task of improving education is the business of everyone concerned with the future; in a free society, the citizens bear ultimate responsibility for the choices that are made and the actions that are taken. With so much of fundamental importance at stake, a people with the advanced theoretical knowledge, practical know-how, and economic affluence that we have, can and must find ways to develop the schools that will fulfill the emergent educational needs of our society.

2 * The Meaning of Year-Round Education

Ask almost any student if he favors year-round schools and the chances are he will answer with a resounding "no!" and add some comment that he does not want to go to school all year because he needs to earn money during the summer, or that he is opposed to the idea of spending his vacation in school "getting more of the same old stuff." Some, however, will answer "yes" and explain that they like school, there is nothing else to do, or that it gives them a chance to catch up or learn about things they could not study otherwise.

One concerned taxpayer may quickly support the idea of operating schools all year with the expectation of reducing taxes, while another opposes the idea of extending the school year because "we are spending too much money already."

Some mothers may see year-round education as an easy way to have their children cared for during the day without hiring baby-sitters, while others may see the all-year school as a threat to the family plan for summer activities of recreation, travel, and other leisure time pursuits.

The teacher seeking summer employment would probably welcome the opportunity to work a longer part of the year in his own profession, rather than taking a lower paying summer job for which he is not really prepared and in which he is not really interested. Another teacher, in contrast, may see the year-round operation of the schools as a threat to his freedom to go back to college during the summer for advanced study, refresher courses, or certification purposes, or simply to relax and do whatever he wants to.

The businessman with a shop near the school, who makes his money selling products or services to students and teachers during the school year, may think of year-round operation of the schools as a way to boost his sales; the resort owner, who depends upon the vacation trade, may see the year-round school movement as a basic threat to the success of his business enterprise.

A minister working with the youth on the hot city streets in the summer, trying to help them find worthwhile things to do instead of get into trouble, may welcome the opening of the schools in the summertime. On the other hand, the minister who conducts a summer Bible school may object on the grounds that "we cannot teach religion in the schools anymore, and now you want to take the children away from us in the summertime."

Obviously, the idea of operating the schools all year or an increased portion of the year means different things to different people. Even the terms "extended school year," "year-round education," "year-round school," and "all-year school" are used interchangeably by some people (as they were in the above paragraphs); but some people contend that they have separate meanings. To make it even more confusing, there are numerous plans for extending the school year or operating the school on an all-year basis.

Anyone seriously considering the feasibility of making changes in the school calendar should have a clear understanding of what he is talking about before he takes a position for or against any of the all-year school plans.

There are several basic issues involved that need careful consideration. The taxpayer who expects to save money by year-round operation of the schools probably assumes that the school facilities will be used all year or most of the year, but that each student will still go to school the same number of days as he does now. On the other hand, the mother who looks forward to having her children in school during the summer as inexpensive babysitting probably expects that these will be additional days, not as a way to get some compensatory time off during the regular school year. Either assumption may be correct or incorrect, depending on the plan.

Some plans *mandate* changes in schedules for students while others provide *options*. In some cases, teachers may have choices; sometimes the schedule may be imposed on them. And so it goes: almost any objection commonly raised to year-round education may be valid for some of the all-year school plans but not others; almost any claim of advantage may be valid for some plans but not others. Every plan thus far devised has its strengths and its weaknesses.

In an attempt to offset some of the confusion resulting from this ambiguity and to provide some constructive leadership for the all-year school movement, in 1969 the Pennsylvania Department of Education convened a three-day meeting for key leaders in year-round educational programs from various parts of the nation. They discussed basic issues and agreed to submit a Statement on Year-Round Education to the 1970 National Seminar on Year-Round Education as a guideline for considering all-year school plans. The Statement on Year-Round Education was unanimously adopted by the participants of the National Seminar[1] and is presented here in its entirety.

Statement on Year-Round Education

Adopted at the Second National Seminar on Year-Round Education
Harrisburg, Pennsylvania, April 7, 1970

It is recognized that the standard 180-day school year as it now prevails in most schools is not universally satisfactory, nor has any operating program for a year-round school yet proved to be universally acceptable.

It is recognized that a plan which may be appropriate in one community situation may not be acceptable in another situation, and that the extended programs which seem to have been most acceptable are those which provide flexibility or optional attendance.

It is recognized that every individual is unique; and, if each is to learn what he needs to know at his own best rate, the school curriculum must be individualized.

It is recognized that the time schedules of individuals and families are continuing to become more diverse and that a student's time in school must be adaptable to this changing situation.

It is recognized that financial resources of any community, state, and the nation are limited and must be allocated on a priority basis and that educational programs, including the school calendar, must be designed to obtain optimum economic efficiency.

It is, therefore, recommended that each state:

1. Take appropriate action to provide enabling legislation and/or policy permitting flexibility of programming so that various patterns of year-round education may be explored at the local level.
2. Take appropriate action to provide state school aid on a prorated basis for extended school programs.
3. Encourage experimental or exploratory programs for year-round education through financial incentive or grant.

It is recommended that each local school system:

1. Consider ways, including year-round education, in which the educational program can be improved in terms of (a) providing a quality education with equality in educational opportunity, (b) adapting to the community and family living patterns, and (c) attaining optimum economic efficiency.
2. Include representation of those who would be affected by the changes in the school schedule in the planning for a year-round education program, including teachers, parents, students, and other interested groups, and provide the public with adequate information about the proposed plan before it is adopted as a mandatory change.
3. Carefully assess the adequacy of the financial resources and current school facilities, including a careful analysis of comparative budgets, before adopting a new schedule.
4. Select and assign staff which will be both effective in terms of the school program and fair and equitable in terms of the demands placed on staff.
5. Carefully develop budgets that will adequately provide for initiating and operating the proposed program and assess adequacy of school facilities before adopting a new schedule. This includes

payment to teachers on a prorated basis for additional time worked.

6. Provide, in the initial planning, for the institutionalization of the program if it meets expectations (i.e., do not accept a state, federal, or other grant to initiate such a program unless the intent is to adopt it as the regular school schedule if it proves successful and acceptable).

It is recommended that the U. S. Office of Education and the Education Commission of the States:

1. Encourage experimentation in year-round education.
2. Rigorously examine all year-round education models which seem to be widely acceptable in terms of well-defined, established criteria.
3. Foster the adoption of those plans or models which have demonstrated their value and acceptability so that nationwide patterns may emerge that are compatible with each other.

The Statement on Year-Round Education did not attempt to describe the various all-year school plans or to define the terms commonly used to describe them. Rather, it attempted to establish the idea that there are various plans and that they offer pitfalls as well as promises.

The term *extended school year* is frequently used to include all programs that extend the academic offering of the school for a longer part of the year than the regular school year. This would include summer school as well as the various types of all-year schools or year-round programs.

Summer school usually does not last all summer and usually does not offer the same curriculum as the regular school does. An all-year, or year-round, school usually operates longer during the summer than does summer school, and its summer activity is usually more closely integrated with the regular school program than is summer school.

There are no precise definitions that would clarify what is meant when these various terms are used. It is essential, therefore, to understand each of the plans and how they work before making any decisions about their appropriateness for adoption in any particular community. Beginning with the "standard school year plan" as the base by which to compare, the most commonly considered all-year school plans are here described and collated. Some of the most common variations of these plans are also presented. Any local school planning committee should be able to adapt these plans to its own needs, thus developing a new plan if it wants to so label it (as many educators are inclined to do).

The Standard School Year Plan

The *standard school year* is generally thought of as nine months of school, beginning about September 1 and ending in late May or early June, followed by a summer vacation of about three months. Most states have a law or regulation that specifies the number of days that constitute a school year. This is commonly 180 days, particularly in the eastern United States, but tends to be a little shorter where agriculture still has an important influence on the living patterns of a community, and exceeds 180 days in some areas, particularly metropolitan areas.

The commonly conceived standard school year with its long summer vacation is illustrated in figure 2-1. Along with this concept of the standard school year is the standard school week of five days, Monday through Friday, and the standard school day of five to five and one-half hours, not counting lunch time. The primary grades are normally in school less time than the older students. In Pennsylvania, instead of specifying the number of days, the standard school year is 900 clock hours for elementary schools (180 days x 5 hours per day = 900 clock hours), and 990 clock hours (180 days x 5.5 hours per day = 990 clock hours) for secondary schools.

As a general practice in the United States, all students begin the school year in the fall at the same time and go on vacation at the same time in the spring. The course of study in each subject area is usually organized on a whole school year basis, with all students beginning a course at the beginning of the school year and pursuing it, in the preplanned sequence, at a rate so as to complete it at the end of the school year.

A student's progress is usually determined at the end of the school year, either passing or failing the whole year's work in a particular subject area at the secondary level, or the entire grade including all subject areas at the elementary level.

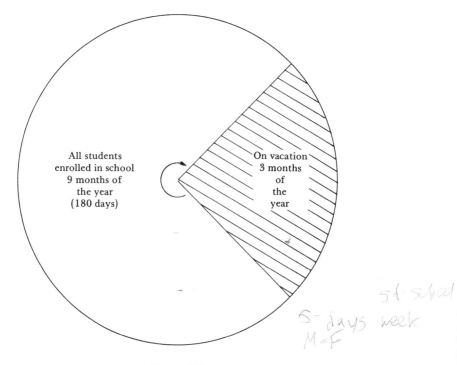

Figure 2-1

Standard School Year Divided into Semesters

Some school systems operate a standard school year using semesters to divide the course of study with a pass or fail determination at the halfway mark of the school year instead of the full year. (See figure 2-2.) This semester plan is common in colleges and universities throughout the country. At the secondary level, it is common to offer most of the "regular" courses on a full-year basis, while offering some of the electives or less basic subjects, e.g., speech and driver training, on a semester basis.

Standard School Year Divided into Quarters

Another deviation from the standard school year, while retaining its essential characteristic of the long summer vacation, is the school year organized into three quarters. (See figure 2-3.) This is a common plan at the higher education level. It is being introduced or considered at the secondary level as the first step of a transition to the

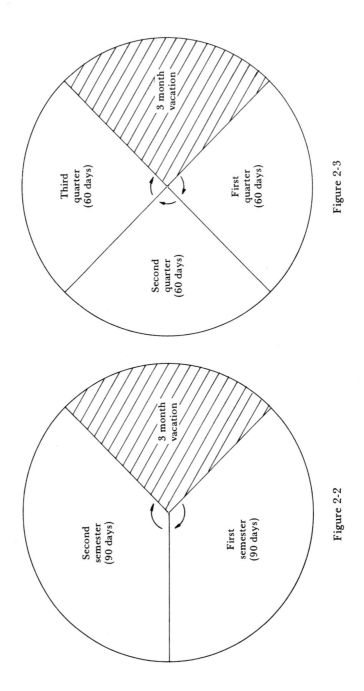

First quarter
(60 days)

Second
quarter
(60 days)

Third
quarter
(60 days)

3 month
vacation

Figure 2-3

First semester
(90 days)

Second
semester
(90 days)

3 month
vacation

Figure 2-2

four-quarter, all-year school plan, which will be described later. In this plan the length of the school year or vacation is not changed; the courses of study are simply organized into shorter units for the student to complete with a pass or fail at the end of each unit, rather than at the end of the school year.

Standard School Year with Summer Session

It is common practice for school systems to operate a summer school at the elementary or secondary level, or both, independent from the regular school year. In most cases, there is a short break of a week or two between the end of the regular school year and the beginning of summer school. Summer school is commonly four to eight weeks long, with a vacation of about a month before the next regular school year begins. This summer school plan, as illustrated in figure 2-4, operates with all the standard school year plans (shown in figures 2-1, 2-2, and 2-3).

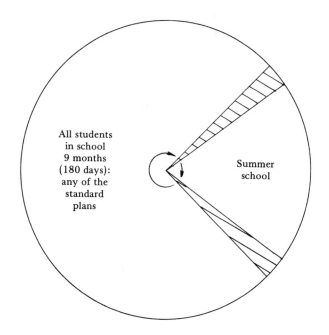

Figure 2-4

In the standard school year program with a summer school, all students attend the regular school year. Summer school attendance is almost always optional, but some students are encouraged to go to summer school to avoid repeating a course (at the secondary school level) or a grade (at the elementary level). Summer school usually includes the opportunity for remedial and make-up classes, enrichment activities, and advanced courses not generally offered during the regular school year. Opportunities for acceleration, with the possibility of earning extra credit for early graduation, are also often provided; but this generally is not considered a form of year-round education.

The Eleven-Month School Plan

It was common for the schools in American cities during the early and middle nineteenth century to be open all, or nearly all, year. School usually consisted of one, or possibly several, poorly paid teachers teaching the three Rs. The cost of operating the schools was minimal, and they were available for use at the convenience of parents whose children attended the schools. It was, of course, the growth in the size of the school and the number of teachers that led to the graded system, initiated in Boston in 1847, which in turn led to the graded textbook. The lock-step system of starting the student at the front of the textbook at the beginning of the school year and pacing him through the book to completion at the end of it led in turn to a compromise standard school year that became stereotyped as the nine-month school year.

A frequently considered plan is to operate the school eleven months (220 days) instead of nine months (180 days) for all students. Thus students could graduate in ten years instead of twelve (9 months x 12 = 108 months; 11 months x 10 = 110 months). This plan would save building space because the student body would be reduced about 16-2/3 percent, as the number of grades enrolled at a time would be reduced by one-sixth.

The *continuous four-quarter plan* is the same as the eleven-month plan (see figure 2-5) except that the school calendar is divided into four quarters. All students attend all four quarters and are thus in school eleven months a year instead of nine. A student could, therefore, complete twelve years of schoolwork in ten years.

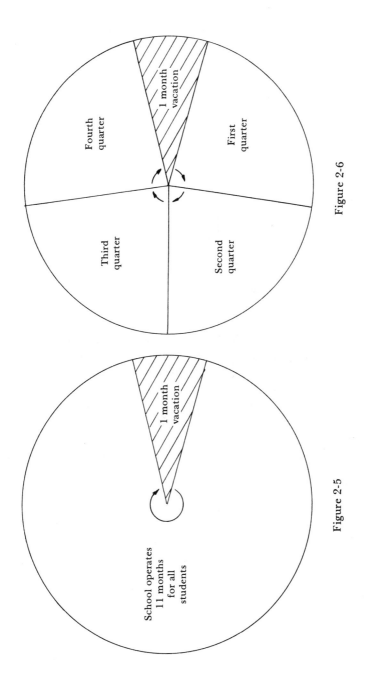

School operates
11 months
for all
students

1 month
vacation

Figure 2-5

Fourth
quarter

1 month
vacation

First
quarter

Third
quarter

Second
quarter

Figure 2-6

Two other eleven-month school plans are now under consideration by some school districts. One is a split day or a double shift, whereby half the student body attends school in the morning, the other half in the afternoon. This is different from the two-shift program frequently used by school districts faced with emergency housing conditions. In this eleven-month plan, the length of time each secondary student is in school is reduced from five and one-half hours per day to four and one-half hours, while the number of days he is in school is increased from 180 to 220. For example, school may operate from 8:00 a.m. to 12:30 p.m. for the morning section and 12:30 p.m. to 5:00 p.m. for the afternoon section. In this way, each student would be in school as many hours per year as he is now (180 x 5.5 hours = 990 hours; 220 x 4.5 hours = 990 hours). The length of the school day would likewise be shortened proportionately for elementary students. The specific number of hours per day or number of days per year may vary from state to state or from region to region, depending on what is currently considered the standard school day and year.

At least one vocational-technical high school (in Erie, Pennsylvania) is operating a split week; half the student body attends school on Monday, Tuesday, and Wednesday, and the other half attends school on Thursday, Friday, and Saturday. This introduces the concept of using the school facilities six days a week instead of five. Thus, in an eleven-month program of forty-four weeks, the school facilities would be used 264 days (44 x 6 days) instead of 220 (44 x 5 days). Each student is in school half of the six-day week, a total of 132 days. To attain the standard 990-hour school year (180 x 5.5 hours), he needs to attend school 7.5 hours per day (132 x 7.5 hours = 990 hours).

In each of these two cases, the split day and the split week, the amount of building space needed for classrooms would be reduced 50 percent based on the present school schedule.

The Mandated Four-Quarter Plan

The mandated four-quarter, or quadrimester, plan is designed to operate school in four equal quarters each calendar year. Students are divided into four equal groups, and each group of students attends school three of the four quarters each year. Based on a standard school year of 180 days, each quarter would be 60 days in length; therefore, any three quarters would be equivalent to the 180-day school year. Three sections of students are in school and one is on vacation each quarter, as illustrated in figure 2-7.

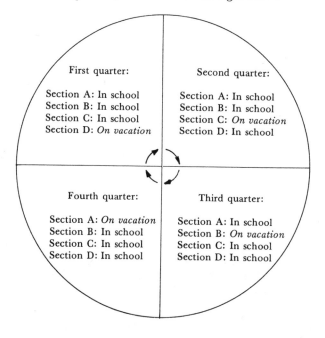

First quarter:

Section A: In school
Section B: In school
Section C: In school
Section D: *On vacation*

Second quarter:

Section A: In school
Section B: In school
Section C: *On vacation*
Section D: In school

Fourth quarter:

Section A: *On vacation*
Section B: In school
Section C: In school
Section D: In school

Third quarter:

Section A: In school
Section B: *On vacation*
Section C: In school
Section D: In school

Figure 2-7

In this plan, a student does not have a choice as to which quarter he is on vacation. He is assigned to a section, and, to ensure that only 75 percent of the students are in school at any one time, the schedule must be followed on a mandated basis. This works out mathematically in such a way that each section gets its vacation the same quarter each year. This may be fine for those who get their vacation during the summer quarter but objectionable to those who are scheduled for vacation in the fall, winter, or spring quarters. To offset this objection, a plan known as the *rotating four-quarter plan* has been devised. In order to give each student a chance to have his vacation in the summer his "share" of the time, the vacations of each section are shifted from year to year. This cannot be done so that there will always be three quarters of study between each quarter of vacation. Sometimes a student will have a vacation after two quarters of work, and sometimes he will go to school six quarters between vacations. This is also objectionable and is not being used by any school today. Table 2-1 illustrates a twelve-year schedule for one section of students showing how the vacations would be shifted from one quarter to another. Dovetailing schedules, following the same pattern, would need to be worked out for each of the other three sections making sure only one section of students is on vacation at a time.

Table 2-1. Four-Quarter Plan with Rotating Vacations

Quarter	Year											
	1	2	3	4	5	6	7	8	9	10	11	12
Fall	S	S	S	V	S	S	S	V	S	S	S	V
Winter	S	S	V	S	S	V	S	S	S	V	S	S
Spring	S	V	S	S	S	V	S	S	V	S	S	S
Summer	V	S	S	S	V	S	S	S	V	S	S	S

S: In school
V: Vacation

Two other plans closely related to the mandated four-quarter plan are the *trimester* and the *quinmester* plans, illustrated in figures 2-8 and 2-9.

In the trimester plan, school operates with three equal segments, each 90 days in length. Each student attends school two of the three sessions, a total of 180 days, while school facilities are used 270 days of the calendar year. Each section of students is on vacation at a different time; therefore, only two-thirds as much building space is needed for classrooms as would be needed with the present standard school schedule.

The quinmester plan operates on the same basic principles except that the school operates with five sections of students and five sessions, each forty-five days in length. Each section attends school during four of these sessions for a total of 180 days. School is in operation five times forty-five days, or 225 days, of the calendar year.

The Optional Four-Quarter Plan

The optional four-quarter plan has the same basic structure as the mandated four-quarter plan (see figure 2-8). The school operates four quarter sessions during a calendar year. Each quarter is generally

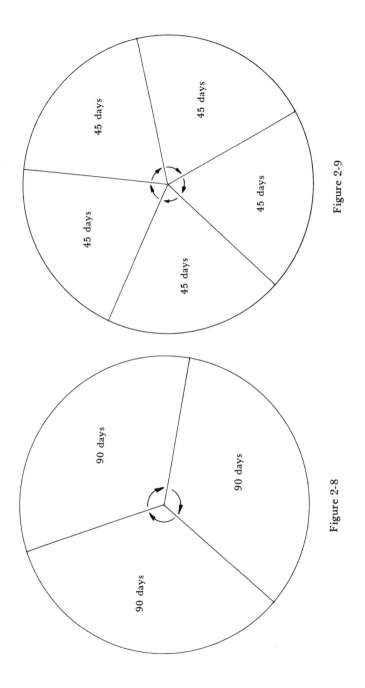

Figure 2-9

Figure 2-8

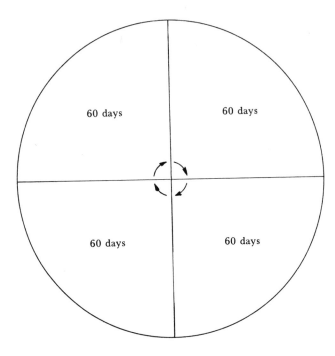

Figure 2-10

sixty days in length. The significant difference, however, is that each student may choose which three quarters he will attend and which one he will take as his vacation. (Three sixty-day quarters equal 180 days.) A school operating this plan may allow a student to choose to attend all four quarters in a year or it may limit attendance to three. A common deviation, particularly in the transition stages of development, is an optional *fourth* quarter plan. In this plan, a student *must* attend the three quarters during the regular school year but has the option of attending the fourth (summer) quarter. Students may attend the summer quarter for any of several reasons, such as acceleration, remedial, enrichment, or recreational activities. This, in reality, is an extended summer school (see figure 2-4).

The *optional trimester plan* is the same as the optional four-quarter plan except the school operates three ninety-day sessions instead of four sixty-day sessions. A student may select any two of the three sessions. (Two ninety-day sessions equal 180 days.) In the *optional quinmester plan* the school operates five forty-five-day sessions. A student may attend any four of the five sessions. (Four forty-five-day sessions equal 180 days.)

Four-Quarter Plan with Vacation Distributed between Quarters (Known as the Hayward, California, Four-Quarter Plan)

The Hayward four-quarter plan has the same basic structure as the other four-quarter plans in that the school operates four sessions during the calendar year (see figure 2-9). There are two basic differences from the other four-quarter plans, however. First, the students

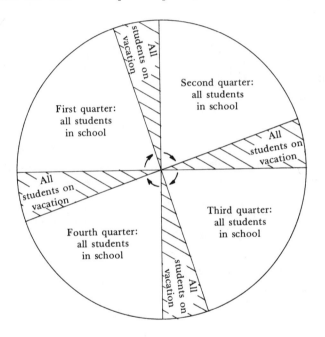

Figure 2-11

are not divided into attendance sections. All students *must* attend all four quarters, each of which is fifty days in length instead of sixty. Thus, students are in school 200 days of the year instead of 180 days. The 200-day school year is the standard length of the school year in the Hayward School System. (Not all the schools in the system are on the quarter plan.) The second significant difference is that the vacation from school is also divided into four equal parts, a three-week vacation after each quarter of study. The teachers, however, work one of these three weeks each quarter for additional pay.

The Mandated Four-Quarter Plan with Vacations Distributed between Sessions (Known as the 45-15 Plan and the 9-3 Plan)

This plan is usually referred to as the *45-15 plan*. It is a combination of the mandated four-quarter plan (see figure 2-7) and the Hayward four-quarter plan (see figure 2-9). School operates 240 days of the calendar year. Students are divided into four equal sections. Each section of students attends school four forty-five-day (or nine-week) sessions for a total of 180 days. Each section has four fifteen-day (or three-week) vacations, one after each session in school. Sections are rotated so that three of the four sections are in school and one section is on vacation at any one time while school is in operation.

A similar plan, based on the same principles, is the *12-4 plan*. School is in session 240 school days during the calendar year. Students are divided into four equal sections. Each section of students attends school three twelve-week sessions for a total of 180 days. Each section also has three four-week vacations, one after each session in school. Sections are rotated so that three of the four sections are in school and one is on vacation at any time while school is in operation.

The Flexible All-Year School Plan

The flexible all-year school plan is uniquely different from the other all-year school plans in that neither the students nor the school calendar is divided into segments (see figure 2-10). The school operates all year except for holidays and at other times when there is no demand for its use. When a student enrolls in school, he is expected to remain in continuous attendance (during regular school days) as long as he remains enrolled in the school, except when he has requested and is granted a vacation or leave of absence. A parent, or a student with parental consent, may request a vacation any time of the year and for any length of time provided that he meets the minimum time requirements of the state during the calendar year. This may be in the form of one long vacation or it may be in the

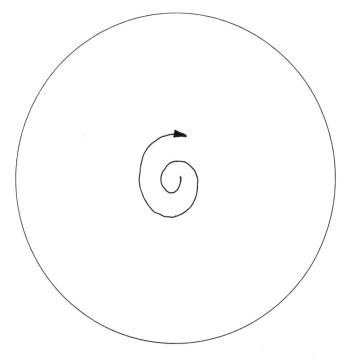

Figure 2-12

form of several shorter vacations. Under normal conditions, the school is expected to approve the request for vacation; but the request should be submitted enough in advance (except in emergencies or other unexpected situations) so that the exit and reentry can be planned and orderly. To provide this flexibility in the time structure to accommodate the needs of each student, the curriculum must also be flexible and based on the needs of the individual learner.

The essential characteristic of the flexible all-year school is that it operates the year around, as does the rest of society. Each student can take his vacation, or vacations, any time and for any length of time as are appropriate to his needs, provided that his schedule meets state requirements (normally 180 days of school enrollment).

There are numerous variations and combinations of these all-year school plans. It is obvious that *year-round education* means many different things to different people. Each person tends to see the issue of year-round education in terms of how it affects him or those

who are important to him. Two students may see the issue differ-
ently just as two parents, two teachers, two taxpayers, or any two or
more people may disagree with each other on this or any other issue.

Many questions are raised about the operation of all-year schools
or year-round education, in general centering around three major
categories of concern: economic efficiency, quality education, and
changing life-styles and community living patterns. An attempt has
been made to list the questions most frequently asked by students,
parents, teachers, administrators, labor, management, religious
groups, and others. The answer to each question obviously depends
on which plan is being considered.

Any school system seriously considering an all-year school operation for any reason should carefully consider as many of the following questions as may be pertinent to its specific situation:

I. **Economic efficiency**
    A. *Capital outlay*
        1. Will the plan eliminate the need to build?
        2. How many more students can our schools hold with this
            plan?
        3. How much money can we save in dollars? in tax rate?
        4. Is the need for new building(s) or more space temporary
            or will we need to build eventually anyhow?
        5. Is air conditioning necessary? If so, how much will it
            cost? Can it be installed in the old buildings? Will it be
            provided in the new buildings?
        6. Are other changes needed in building changes or capital
            goods to make the changeover?
    B. *Operating budgets*
        1. How much money can we save in dollars? in tax rate?
        2. How will this affect the cost of administration?
            a. Will administrators work a longer year?
            b. Will they get paid more?
            c. Will more administrators be needed?
            d. Will schedules have to be computerized?
            e. Will pupil accounting be more complex?
            f. Will more secretarial help be needed?
        3. How will this affect the cost of plant maintenance?

    a. How can the summer maintenance work get done with school operating all year?

    b. Will janitors do the maintenance work they usually do at times students are not in school?

    c. Will this require the employment of extra maintenance staff?

    d. Will different equipment or supplies be needed for continuous maintenance?

4. How will this affect costs for health, food, and other special services?

    a. Will the nurses work all year? Cafeteria help?

    b. Will as many nurses, cafeteria help, etc., be needed?

5. How will this affect the instructional staff budget?

    a. If fewer classrooms are needed, does this mean fewer teachers will be employed at one time?

    b. Can the employment of teachers on tenure be terminated?

    c. Will the savings in number of teachers be absorbed by reducing teacher-pupil ratio instead of reducing staff?

    d. Will teachers be paid on a prorated basis for additional time worked?

    e. Or will they be paid on a 12-month basis with a month of vacation with pay, like the administrators?

    f. Will this change in schedule have an impact on the cost of fringe benefits?

    g. Will teachers working four quarters a year get more sick leave? more retirement credit?

6. How will this affect the instructional materials and supplies budget?

    a. Will funds need to be provided for curriculum revision?

    b. Will new textbooks be needed or will the present ones fit a reorganized curriculum?

    c. Will other types of materials and equipment be used?

    d. Can the number of textbooks be reduced in the same way as classrooms and teachers?

    e. Can the amounts of other supplies or equipment be reduced by scheduling their use all year?

    7. How will this affect the plant operation budget?
- a. Will janitors be employed all year as janitors or will they do some of the maintenance?
- b. Can the custodial staff be reduced proportionately to compensate for the longer year?
- c. When will the custodial staff get their vacation?
- d. Will this cost more to hire temporary replacements for custodians on vacation?
- e. How much will it cost to keep the building air conditioned?

    8. How will the year-round operation of the school affect insurance?

    9. How will it affect the cost of pupil transportation?
- a. Will the number of buses and bus drivers be reduced to compensate for the longer year of operation?
- b. What effect will continuous (year-round) use of buses have on cost of maintaining buses? on the life expectancy of each bus?
- c. Will all bus schedules have to be maintained all year or will entire neighborhoods covered by a complete "bus run" be scheduled for vacation simultaneously?
- d. Will buses be provided for recreation activities during the regular school year for children not in school?

10. Will the school continue, delete, or expand its present recreation programs?
- a. Will the facilities currently used for recreational activities in the summer be available and operable on a year-round basis? If so, how much will it cost? If not, how can appropriate facilities be provided and how much will it cost?
- b. Will qualified staff be available on a year-round basis? Will it cost more or less?

II. **Quality of educational services**
  A. *Curriculum*
- 1. Does this schedule require a revision in the present curriculum?
- 2. Will the curriculum be organized into standard sixty-day

units of study (as compared to the common ninety-day units or semester units now used)?

3. If not organized into quarter units, how will it be organized?

4. Will the curriculum units be scheduled independently from each other or will they be provided in a sequence with prerequisites?

5. Will all courses commonly offered be equally available for all sections of students (if students are sectioned)?

6. Will a student who fails a course one quarter be able to reschedule it the next quarter? Will he have to shift sections to do this? If so, what happens to his other subjects?

7. Are appropriate curriculum materials available for the revised curriculum?

8. Will the students be given a greater choice or selection of courses or will the same courses simply be reorganized into three sixty-day (quarter) units instead of two ninety-day (semester) units?

9. Will the grading system or the report card system change?

10. Will "ability grouping" still prevail for each section or will the sections be organized on the basis of ability?

11. Can a student attend four quarters instead of three and graduate earlier?

12. How does this new structure provide for individual differences?

13. Will the same courses be taught all year or will new courses be added during the summer appropriate to that time of year?

14. What happens to summer school as it now exists? Will students be able to take enrichment and/or remedial courses? short-term courses?

15. How will students make up required courses?

16. How will credits be given? How many will be required to graduate?

17. How will extended absences due to illness or necessary vacation affect make-up of work for such a short course?

    18. How can specialized or advanced courses be offered each quarter?

    19. Do students get overfatigued by going to school longer than 180 days a year?

    20. Do they forget less when vacations are shorter?

B. *Extracurricular activities*

    1. Can students on vacation participate in interscholastic sports?

    2. Are they eligible players according to the athletic association?

    3. Can students on vacation also participate in band, drill team, cheerleading, etc.?

    4. Can students on vacation participate in school dances and other student activities?

    5. Can they participate in school plays, newspaper, yearbook, etc.?

    6. Can they visit school when they don't have anything better to do?

    7. Can they eat in the cafeteria with friends when their friends have to be in school and they do not? (If so, do they get federal subsidies?)

    8. How can the school prom and graduation be scheduled if there is no time when all the students will be in school together?

    9. Will students graduate each quarter?

    10. What "class" will they belong to?

    11. What will this do to school spirit?

    12. What will this do to class reunions?

    13. How can friends be scheduled into the same sections?

    14. Will boys be absent from school excessively at times when their girl friends are on vacation (and vice versa)?

C. *Special services*

    1. Will guidance, health, and other special services be provided all year?

    2. Will services be continuous to students while they are on vacation?

D. *Qualifications of teachers*

    1. How will teachers be helped to get ready for this change in the curriculum? Will they be allotted time (with pay)

to get ready? Will there be appropriate in-service programs?

2. Will colleges be preparing teachers for year-round education?

3. Will the college schedule coincide with the school schedule so teachers can take college courses during their
vacation quarter or three-week break (or other arrangements)?

4. If not, how will teachers meet their certification requirements?

5. When will new teachers begin? Will the change in schedule hamper recruitment of qualified teachers?

6. Will a teacher get overfatigued by teaching all year?

7. What will this schedule do to the teacher-pupil ratio?
What will it do to the number of courses taught by
teachers or the number of teacher preparations?

E. *Administrative procedures*

1. If classrooms are shared on a rotating basis, do students
change classrooms each quarter?

2. Will a teacher have a classroom to call her own?

3. How can a student change from one section to another?
Under what circumstances will this be allowable?

4. If a student transfers from another school during the
school year, can he begin school immediately or might he
be placed on vacation initially? If he moves in during the
summer, what will his schedule be? Might he miss his
vacation? Might he have to take an extra one?

5. How will students be assigned to a section initially?

6. Will brothers and sisters be on the same schedule?

7. When do children begin first grade or kindergarten? Might
they have to wait an extra quarter, or half year, or more?

III. Changing lifestyles and community living patterns

A. *Impact of school schedule on other scheduled activities*

1. What impact will the change in school schedule have on:
summer recreation programs?
summer camps (church, private, other)?
the summer labor pool (to replace workers on vacation)?

2. What impact will it have on family vacations?

    a. If parents have vacation in summer, can the children, too? How about other times of the year?

    b. Can parents split vacations (a growing practice)?

    c. How will the extended vacation (thirteen weeks) be managed?

3. Can married teachers have their vacations at the same time as their spouses—if they both work in the same school system? if only one works for the school?

4. What effect will the school schedule have on the schedules of working mothers?

5. What if parents' vacation schedules are changed? Can children change sections in school?

6. What changes in the work force schedules are taking place that might influence the school schedules?

7. How will Christmas, Easter, and other holidays be scheduled?

8. If students are already on vacation, will they get compensatory time in addition?

B. *Personal preferences in scheduling*

1. Will the student have a choice, initially, as to when he has his vacation or what section he is in?

2. Will parents have a choice?

3. Will brothers and sisters be in the same sections?

4. Will parents with only one child have a choice?

5. Will teachers have a choice as to the sections they teach?

6. Will they have a choice of teaching three quarters or four?

C. *Employment opportunities*

1. Will teachers be employed in recreation or other activities during vacation period(s)?

2. If teachers' vacations are broken up into small segments throughout the year, what will that do to their employment opportunities?

3. What will such schedules do to the employment opportunities of students?

4. What will the school schedule do to work force vacation schedules?

5. If fewer teachers are needed, what happens to those who are not needed?

6. Will the school schedule encourage the employment of youth by industry on a rotating, year-round basis (four students rotating to hold one full-time job)?

IV. Procedures for implementing change
A. *Making the decision to change*
1. Who will decide what schedule will be used? How?
2. How many need to approve it to get the schedule changed?
3. How many need to oppose it to prevent the change?
4. How will the opinions of people be obtained?
B. *Making the changeover*
1. Can we make the change immediately or what has to be done first?
2. Can the secondary change without the elementary or vice versa?
3. How is the changeover scheduled and when? during the school year or summer? Will some students miss their vacation in the changeover? or get extra time off?
C. *Feedback*
1. How will we know how the people like this system?
2. How soon can we change back if we do not like it?

V. Alternatives for the same objectives
A. *If a major objective is to house more children in existing buildings, are there other approaches that might be considered?*
1. How about double shifting?
2. How about a longer, but flexible, day?
3. How about a flexible week?
4. How about the "store front" concept?
B. *If an objective is to save money, are there other ways this can be done and still maintain quality education?*
1. How much does it cost to fail a student?
2. How much does it cost for remedial work? Could this be avoided by really adapting the curriculum to the needs of each student?
3. Do all students need to spend the same amount of time on each subject? Could money be saved by allowing each student to progress at his own rate?

    4. Are all subjects now being taught really useful? Is the way they are being taught really useful?

    5. Could some of the course work be combined with college and avoid duplication?

    6. Could some students earn a living and still earn high school credits "on the job"?

    7. Are there people in the community with valuable skills and talents who would gladly help out at school *without charge*?

C. *Are there ways that quality education can be achieved through other changes in the school structure?*

    1. Do all students need the same amount of time to complete a course? If not, how can it be scheduled?

    2. Do students of a given age or group need to learn the same things at the same time? If not, how can the schedules be adjusted to their needs?

    3. Do all students learn in the same way or need to use the same materials? Do they need to be in the classroom to learn or may they learn some things more effectively in camp, in a factory, in city hall, on a river bank, or someplace else? If so, how can schedules be adjusted to accommodate the needs?

    4. Is knowledge in organized disciplines taught best in fifty-minute capsules, or can students sometimes learn best by pursuing real problems over extended periods of time?

D. *If the need is to adapt to changing life-styles and living patterns, how is the school going to adapt to the following, any or all of which may develop?*

    1. A four-day work week, a three-day work week, a six-day work week?

    2. Extended and/or split vacations?

    3. A longer or shorter work day?

    4. A shift in time of day (or night) to attend school?

    5. Needs for lifespan education?

    6. The impact of other educational institutions such as television, computer services, etc.?

Whether a local community will benefit from an all-year school program at this time or not, and which all-year school plan would be most feasible, depends on the answers to questions such as these, many of which can be determined only by the people who must operate, use, support, and attend the school in their community. Any all-year school committee that seriously considers the questions on this list that are pertinent to its local situation should have a well-founded base on which to build its program and to select appropriate alternatives.

Notes

1. The Statement on Year-Round Education, based on the discussion of the Pennsylvania meeting, was prepared by John D. McLain with the assistance of the Pennsylvania Committee on Year-Round Education, and presented by him as director of the Second National Seminar on Year-Round Education.

3 * Economic Analysis of All-Year Operation of the Schools

"If I ran my business the way you operate the schools, closing down a fourth of the year, I'd go broke."

Many school administrators have been chided by such remarks over the past several decades by local businessmen and others who assume that substantial sums of money can be saved by the all-year use of the school facilities. How true is this assumption? Can taxes really be lowered or held down by shifting to an all-year school program?

The limited research currently available indicates that, under some circumstances, a substantial amount of money can be saved by a fuller use of the school facilities. However, the research also indicates that under other circumstances an all-year program will cost more money. There is no quick and easy answer that can be applied to all school districts. Current and future building needs, population growth trends, availability and cost of land, life-styles and value judgments of local people, state and local funding procedures and laws, and other complex factors determine the economic feasibility of year-round education.

In making an economic analysis of the feasibility of year-round education, three general categories of costs must be considered: (1) the capital outlay required to provide the school buildings, grounds, and other facilities to operate the schools; (2) the cost of operating the schools once the needed facilities are provided; and (3) the cost of changeover from the traditional nine-month school year program to an all-year school program.

Many local school districts need to build new schools or additions to schools now. In the future, other local school districts will also face this problem. A school district may be faced with a building-needs problem as the result of (1) increased enrollment, (2) school district reorganization, (3) obsolescence of present buildings, (4) a combination of these three.

Enrollment

The total enrollment in the public schools of a school district is determined by the number of school-age children in the district and what percentage of those children attend public school. The number of school-age children in a district is determined by the number of live births in that community and the migration of children at or below school age into or out of the school district.

The recent trend in America is toward a decreasing birth rate (ascertained by the number of live births per 1,000 women of child-bearing age). In 1972 the United States attained a replacement fertility level for the first time. However, the population of the United States is expected to continue to increase for the next seventy years because, even if the fertility level remains constant, the age distribution of our population is such that there is an increasing number of women of child-bearing age and the death rate is lower than the birth rate. It is safe to conclude that the numbers of children to be educated will continue to increase.

Another significant trend is the redistribution of the population. The migration of people from rural to urban or suburban areas, and from the urban to the suburban areas of the nation, continues. In general, it is the young and the aggressive who voluntarily leave the rural areas to seek a better way of life. They tend eventually to settle in metropolitan suburbs. Also leaving the rural areas are workers and their families who have been displaced by machines as our agriculture has shifted from small farming to mechanized agri-industry. These displaced persons tend to go to the urban areas seeking jobs and cheap housing.

The shift from urban to suburban is also a selective migration. Suburban areas seem to develop almost overnight as large tracts of open land are converted to housing projects to accommodate the market of dissatisfied families who want to leave the decaying inner city. The development projects that advertise "no down payment and low monthly payments" attract young families with children below or of early school age. Suburban communities often face a school building need without an adequate tax base to provide the necessary facilities. The wealthier suburbs tend to attract the families that have a larger savings for a down payment on a house and larger incomes to make higher monthly payments on the house. The children are often older and will therefore spend fewer years in school.

The population may be expected to continue to shift at an accelerated rate as Americans become more and more mobile. Mobility tends to create and sustain socioeconomic strata within the total population that have a major impact on the kinds of problems communities face, including school problems, and how the people in the community are able and willing to deal with them.

Public school enrollment is determined not only by the school population of the school district, but also by the percentage of that population attending public schools. Three significant trends have an influence on building needs today:

1. In 1900, less than 5 percent of the American youth completed high school. Now about 80 percent do. As dropout rates decline, school enrollments increase, and this is felt particularly at the secondary level.

2. Parochial and many other private schools are in a financial crisis due to rising costs of education, causing a shift in attendance from the private to the public schools. At the same time, a movement is developing for "alternative" schools. Disenchanted with the rigidities of the public schools, some are seeking alternative "free" or "open" schools.

3. Private enterprise is also eyeing the education industry as a possible lucrative market and is exploring performance contracting as an inroad. The combined weight of those supporting parochial schools, alternative schools, and performance contracting may have a

major influence on the financial structure of education in America and thereby a significant impact on the public school enrollment and building needs of public schools in the future.

School District Reorganization

School district reorganization has gone on since before the turn of the century and may be expected to continue in the future. In the first half of this century two major reasons for consolidation were to make high school available to all youth and to organize schools into systems that were large enough to achieve economic efficiency and quality education. Another significant argument in support of consolidation was to integrate the subculturally different rural and urban populations. The recent trend is to decentralize the schools because they have become too impersonal and too far removed from the people they serve. In contrast, however, is the emerging concept of the "educational park" as a means of integrating the subcultures of urban areas. Rural areas with declining populations may also reorganize into larger districts providing larger, more centralized, and more modern facilities.

Obsolescence of School Buildings

Schools, like other buildings, become obsolete because of age. Schools may need to be replaced because they are no longer safe or are so unattractive that the people choose to replace them. Schools in the past have been built for very rigid, classroom-oriented programs. As the curriculum changes and the practices of grouping students change, the types of building facilities to house the programs also change.

Considering all factors, it may be concluded that many school districts face the issue of planning and constructing new school buildings. The size and the design of those buildings will be influenced by the problems of each community as well as what the curriculum of the school is to be. The cost of a building and the programs that will operate in it are bound to be important, and a significant related factor will be the consideration of year-round education, in terms of both buildings and programs.

Capital Outlay

As an economic incentive, the greatest potential for the year-round school is in maximizing the use of school buildings when there is a shortage of space, particularly classroom space.

Any school district wishing to construct new classrooms should carefully consider the question, "Is this new construction really necessary?" If a new building or an addition really is necessary, the next logical question is, "How big does it have to be, and how should it be designed to meet the educational needs of the populations it is to serve?" For example, how much money could be saved by a school district that has adequate schools for 1,200 pupils but, due to increases in enrollment, must find a way to accommodate 1,600?

For the purpose of simple analysis, let us assume that the basic facilities already in existence have sufficient land space, with adequate athletic fields, parking areas, and space to build the addition to the school building. We will also assume that the gymnasium, cafeteria, and other special purpose areas would be adequate if a 400-pupil addition were constructed. The basic cost to the school district would be the cost of new classrooms.

If the rule-of-thumb method of figuring twenty-five students per classroom were used, there would be a need for sixteen additional classrooms to accommodate the additional 400 students. The "average" cost for constructing a classroom varies from region to region and depends on design, climate, materials used, size, labor market, etc.; but as illustration let us assume that the cost is $35,000 per classroom. If sixteen classrooms are needed, the basic cost of construction is 16 x $35,000, or $560,000.

A new school will normally be used by a community for thirty or more years. For the purpose of estimating per pupil costs, let it be assumed that the life use of this sixteen-room addition is thirty years. By the same token, we will assume that the costs (including interest) will be distributed equally over that thirty-year span by the sale of bonds.

Interest must be paid on the bonds. If the interest rate were 5 percent on the unpaid balance and the unpaid balance averaged one-half of the initial loan of $560,000, the total interest paid for the school would be 5 percent of $280,000 (one-half of $560,000) times thirty years, or $420,000. The actual cost for constructing the sixteen-room addition would be the initial capital outlay ($560,000) plus the cost of debt service ($420,000), for a total of $980,000.

A local community could theoretically save $980,000 by *not* building if a way could be developed to serve the total population of 1,600 pupils adequately in the already existing facilities. At least at first glance, the logical answer seems to be the all-year school. School is now used, on the average, three-fourths of the year. If the school could be used the other quarter of the year, and if students were scheduled so that only three-fourths of them would be in school at one time, the total enrollment could be served by the existing facilities.

Based on this hypothetical case, how much money could a community save in construction costs and interest by not building sixteen classrooms? The answer, of course, is $980,000. In terms of cost per pupil per year, how much would be saved? The building would serve 1,600 pupils for thirty years, or a total of 48,000 pupil-years. The amount saved, then, would be $980,000 divided by 48,000, or $20.42 per pupil per year.

The national average cost per elementary pupil in 1971-72 was $735.05, not counting capital outlay and debt service. (It is estimated that the cost at the secondary level is 1.3 times that of the elementary level, for an average per pupil cost of $955.56 in 1971-72.) The effect of such a savings on the total cost of school is that it would avoid adding $20.42 to $735.05 or $955.56 per pupil (per year for thirty years). Converted to savings in terms of the percent of the total budget, it would be 2.8 percent at the elementary level or 2.1 percent at the secondary level (savings divided by total cost).

What real effect this would have on the local millage rate, however, depends on who pays for the building. It is obviously the taxpayer, but if the state subsidizes the cost of construction, only that portion paid by the local school district will be reflected in the local millage rate. Assuming that the state pays no part of the cost, and that the millage rate to raise the current operating costs of $735.05 (national elementary average) is sixty mills, then the cost in mills to construct the sixteen rooms would be 2.8 percent of sixty mills, or 1.7 mills. (The millage rate is determined by the amount of money that is to be raised by taxes divided by the assessed valuation of the property to be taxed. If a local school district needed to raise $6,000,000 to operate the schools and the taxable property of the school district was assessed at $100,000,000, the tax rate would be 60 mills ($6,000,000 ÷ $100,000,000 = 0.060). A mill is one-tenth of a cent, or $0.001. Assessed value is not the same as actual or market value. The assessed value depends upon the assessment rate of the local community or state. It is a common practice to assess property at one-third of its actual value, in which case an $18,000 home would be assessed at about $6,000. If the tax rate on this property were 60 mills, the annual taxes would be $360 ($6,000 x .060 = $360).)

The above analysis was based on the assumption that the land and other facilities needed were already available and so were not calculated into the cost of this addition. If a community had to buy the land and start from scratch, it would cost more. The Northville public schools in Northville, Michigan, were awarded a grant by the Michigan Department of Education to conduct a feasibility study of year-round education. They are faced with the problem of an expanding enrollment and the need to acquire entirely new sites for additional school facilities. They calculated their cost per pupil as follows:[1]

1. Current available space including land and freestanding equipment	342,821 sq. ft.
2. Total value of capital investment	$8,704,062
3. Value per square foot (2 ÷ 1)	$25.40
4. Space currently utilized	289,000 sq. ft.
5. Current student enrollment	2,804 students
6. Space required per student (4 ÷ 5)	103 sq. ft.
7. Capital investment per student (3 x 6)	$2,616

Based on that calculation, the cost for 400 students (sixteen classrooms with twenty-five pupils per classroom), the cost of construction would be $1,046,400 instead of the $560,000 that was estimated by calculating the cost at $35,000 per classroom. The amount a community could save by building a 1,200-pupil school instead of a 1,600-pupil school, based on these figures, would be $1,046,400 plus interest on that amount. Calculating the interest at the same rate as in the previous example (5 percent for thirty years on the unpaid balance), the interest would be $784,800. The total savings to a community, then, would be $1,831,200 distributed over a period of thirty years. Expressed in cost per pupil, this would be the total cost ($1,831,200) divided by the number of pupils expected to use the facilities each year (1,600) for the life use of the building (thirty years), or $38.15 per pupil per year for thirty years. Converted to savings in terms of percent, it would be 5.2 percent; converted to mills (based on the example of sixty mills to raise $735.05 per pupil), it would be 3.1 mills (per year for thirty years). This is really a substantial savings in total dollars though it may not seem to be much in terms of the total budget when distributed over the thirty-year span. To realize this savings, however, an all-year school plan that will work in terms of the objective of three-fourths of the students attending school at any time of the year, and still be acceptable to the people in terms of the quality of education and changes in time schedules, must be put into operation *without* increasing the general operating costs of the school.

Operational Costs

There are two all-year school plans designed to guarantee accomplishment of the objective of having only three-fourths of the students in school at any one time during the year: (1) the mandated four-quarter plan and (2) the 45-15 plan (essentially like the mandated four-quarter plan except that the vacation period is divided into fifteen-day segments rather than a whole quarter of a year at a time).

The mandated four-quarter plan is frequently studied by local communities but has been almost universally rejected as inoperable. The 45-15 plan has received considerable acceptance, particularly at the elementary level. For purposes of analysis of costs, we will assume that one of these two plans is adopted by a community and put into operation to realize the savings in the above example. The basic question, from the cost analysis standpoint, is, "How much will it cost to operate compared to the standard 180-day school year?" The impact of the change on each segment of the budget has to be analyzed. So do the *transition* costs—the cost of modifying the building, if necessary, as well as the cost of redesigning the curriculum and retraining the teachers, if necessary.

The national average cost per pupil, as stated above, is $735.05 for elementary pupils and $955.56 for secondary pupils. These costs, and the analysis by category of expenditure shown in table 3-1, are based on data obtained from the Cost of Education Index.[2]

Table 3-1. Average Cost per Pupil, 1971-72

	Elementary	Secondary*
Administration		
Professional salaries	$ 12.07	$ 15.69
Clerks and secretaries	7.50	9.75
Other expenditures	6.70	8.71
Instruction		
Classroom teachers	425.84	553.59
Other professionals	59.94	77.92
Clerks and secretaries	15.40	20.20
Textbooks	6.93	9.01
Other teaching materials	18.56	24.13
Other expenditures	6.73	8.75
Health		
Professional salaries	3.50	4.55
Other expenditures	.70	.91
Operation	60.20	78.26
Custodial salaries	31.66	40.16
Heat	7.78	8.11
Utilities other than heat	12.15	15.80
Other expenditures	8.61	11.19
Maintenance		
Maintenance salaries	7.81	10.15
Other expenditures	12.10	15.73
Transportation		
Salaries	13.05	16.96
Other expenditures	18.78	24.41
Fixed charges		
Retirement fund	39.16	50.91
Other expenditures	15.20	19.76
Other services	2.88	3.74
TOTAL	$735.05	$955.56

*The cost estimates in the secondary level column were computed by multiplying each elementary category by 1.3, the differential between elementary and secondary costs.

Each of these categories will be considered separately, as will the cost of transition.

An estimation of how each of these budget categories is affected by a shift to a four-quarter operation with 75 percent enrollment at any one time will give some idea as to the impact the change will have on the total budget.

Administration

Professional salaries. In most school systems, the chief school administrator and other central staff are already employed on a twelve-month basis, so that a shift to a four-quarter plan should not change their salaries. The cost would be the same, probably, for the four-quarter plan as the regular school year plan. The way the time is used by the staff, however, may change.

Clerks and secretaries. Most clerks and secretaries in the central offices are already on twelve-month contracts so a change in schedule probably would not change this budget category.

Other expenditures. Other administrative expenditures include such items as office supplies, legal services, audits, printing, travel expenses, and other miscellaneous expenditures. Most of these items would not be affected by a change from a regular school year to a four-quarter plan. The one possible exception is travel expenses. If central staff (supervisors) spend a considerable part of their time during the school year traveling from school to school, they may be expected to do the same during the fourth quarter. However, with fewer classrooms per quarter to supervise, this should equalize with little or negligible effect on the budget. In summary, the cost of administration would be about the same under the four-quarter plans as the regular school year plan.

Instruction

Classroom teachers. If the teacher-pupil ratio remains constant and the total number of student-teacher contact hours remains the same, then the total cost for teachers' salaries should also remain constant, provided that the teachers' salaries on a per diem basis remain the same. For example, in a 1,600-pupil school with a teacher-pupil ratio of one to twenty-five, the total number of teachers would be sixty-four in a regular school year of 180 days. If in a four-quarter plan the number of students enrolled at any one time is 1,200, the number of teachers required would be forty-eight. If all teachers continued to teach three of the four sixty-day quarters, they would continue to teach 180 days a year and should receive the same salary. Since 1,200 pupils would be in school each of the four sixty-day quarters, an additional sixteen, or a total of sixty-four, teachers would be needed during the year to provide teaching while a fourth of the teachers, like the students, were on vacation. In other words, if the teachers followed the same schedules as the students, only three-fourths of the teachers (forty-eight in this case) would be on the job at any one time; but the total number would not change, and the total amount for teachers' salaries would remain the same.

If each of the teachers taught all four quarters instead of three quarters, the total number of teachers needed would be only three-fourths of sixty-four, or forty-eight. The total number of teacher-days taught would remain the same, however, provided of course that the quarters are equal in length. If forty-eight teachers taught four quarters or 240 days, it would be the same, in terms of total teacher time, as if sixty-four teachers taught 180 days. On a prorated basis the total budget for salaries should remain the same even though each of the teachers remaining on the job would receive a 33-1/3 percent increase in salary. For example, if the average teacher received $9,000 for 180 days and worked an additional sixty days (33-1/3 percent of 180 days), she would receive, on a prorated basis, an additional $3,000 or a total of $12,000.

$$64 \times \$ \ 9{,}000 = \$576{,}000$$
$$48 \times \$12{,}000 = \$576{,}000$$

Since it does not make any difference, from the total teacher salary budget standpoint, whether a teacher works three quarters or four quarters of the four-quarter plan, it would make no basic difference if some of the teachers worked four quarters and some worked three quarters. There may be a slight difference, however, as to where teachers were on the salary schedule if one teacher replaces another for a quarter.

In general, it can be estimated that there would be no change in the budget for teachers' salaries in a shift from the regular school year to a four-quarter plan. Some advocates of the all-year school as an economic measure, however, see two possible ways to save money on teachers' salaries.

Some economists have argued that teachers are getting paid in terms of their capital investment in themselves, the capital goods being the college degree. Since teachers are receiving greater income by working four quarters instead of three without increasing their capital investment, they should be willing to work at a lower rate of pay during the fourth quarter.

This is contrary to what most teachers are likely to consider fair. The National Education Association and the National Council on Year-Round Education have both adopted position papers recommending that teachers be paid on a *prorated* basis and should receive a "day's pay for an extra day's work."

A second possible way to save money, advocated by some, is to eliminate or reduce the teacher in-service days. For example, it is not uncommon for teachers to be under a 185-day contract, 180 of which are teaching days and five are for in-service. What happens to the five in-service days if the teacher goes to a 240-day (four-quarter) contract? If this is absorbed, as some economists think it might be, when will the teachers have time to do the things that they do now with those in-service days? It is likely that teachers will insist on these extra days and expect to be paid for them.

In summary, it is rather safe to assume that little or no savings can be realized in the teacher salary budget by shifting from the regular school year to the four-quarter plan. By the same token, it does not cost any more.

Other professionals. Other professionals in the instructional budget include principals, supervisors, consultants, substitutes, librarians, and guidance counselors. Some principals are already on a twelve-month contract, while some work the regular school year. Others are contracted for a week or two before and after the regular school year. The change in budget, on a prorated basis, would be zero percent if a principal is already on a twelve-month basis, and no additional administrative help is provided for him to do his work. If on the other hand his work year is changed from a three-quarter to a four-quarter year, the increase in budget, on a prorated basis, would be 33-1/3 percent. The same is true for all other personnel. If the library is staffed with four librarians under the regular school year plan and the work can be managed with only three librarians with a reduced number of students, the increase in salary per person would be 33-1/3 percent; but the budget would remain the same. Each local school would have to analyze the work load of each of these professionals and decide what changes in total personnel and salaries are needed.

In summary, the possible range of change in the budget for this category is from zero percent to an increase of 33-1/3 percent. Neither extreme is likely to occur. It is likely there would be an increase in total cost of this budget item, but the amount would be somewhere between 10 and 20 percent to operate the four-quarter plan.

Clerks and secretaries. The number of clerks and secretaries is likely to remain the same, although some schools add staff due to the increased paper work. Usually the secretaries work the same length of year as their principals so this will vary, according to the situation, from zero to +33-1/3 percent, with a probable range of 10 to 20 percent increase.

Textbooks. Some advocates of year-round education estimate a savings of 25 percent on textbooks since only three-fourths of the students will be in school at any one time. Others point out that the books will be used longer each year and will wear out sooner. The estimated change in the budget is a range of zero to -25 percent.

Other teaching materials. Consumable items such as paper, chalk, and pencils would remain the same. Nonconsumable items such as maps, globes, projectors, lab equipment, and physical education apparatus probably could be reduced 25 percent under the four-quarter plan. Library books, films, film strips, and other instructional materials may cost the same or less depending on the school holdings and the size of student body. The range of change may be from zero to -25 percent.

In summary, consumable items will cost the same under the four-quarter plan whereas other items may be reduced as much as 25 percent. The probable range of impact on this item of the budget is -10 to -15 percent.

Health

Professional salaries. The major cost of health services is the nurse's salary. In a school with only one nurse who is on a nine-month contract, the salary would have to be increased accordingly. On the other hand, if the system is large enough to have several nurses, the load may be redistributed so that no total increase is necessary. The range would be from zero to +33-1/3 percent to shift from the regular school year to the four-quarter plan.

Other expenditures. A major item in this budget is travel between schools and between school and homes. It is probable that this would need to be increased. The amount would depend on whether the nurse would actually make more home calls in four quarters than she did in three quarters. The total number of students would not change so if all the needed home calls were made the cost would not increase; but, if time were a limiting factor, a nurse may make a greater total number of home calls. A 15 to 25 percent increase in the budget would be likely.

Operation

Custodial salaries. If the custodial budget is based on cleaning the building when students are in attendance, then custodians would need to be on duty all year. If the staff were large enough that it could be reduced commensurately with the decrease of students on a four-quarter plan, the cost would be the same for the four-quarter plan as for the regular school year. If, on the other hand, the building is small and only one or two janitors are employed, their salaries would have to be increased accordingly. The range, then, would be from zero to +25 percent depending on the situation.

Heat. It is anticipated that in most instances there would be no increase in the heat budget since there is generally little or no need for heating the building in the summertime.

Utilities other than heat. The major change in utilities other than heat is the cost of electricity. There would be greater use of lights and appliances. If air conditioning were installed, there would be a very substantial increase in the utilities budget, perhaps as much as 50 percent.

Other expenditures. There probably would be negligible change in other expenditures.

Maintenance

Maintenance salaries. Since the number of classrooms needed would be 25 percent less under the four-quarter plan as compared to the regular school year, the actual impact depends on the total number of staff and how they are employed. The savings could be from zero to 25 percent.

Other expenditures. Some maintenance materials and supplies are already year-round expenses or are nonconsumable, whereas the consumable supplies based on number of days of operation would increase. The probable range of change is 10 to 20 percent increase.

Transportation

Salaries. Salaries may include supervisors, drivers, and mechanics. The supervisor's salary is likely to increase. The number of drivers and mechanics employed at one time should decrease under the four-quarter plan, along with the number of students, but the length of employment of these persons would increase commensurately, resulting in no change in the budgets. This is based on the assumption that bus routes would be organized so that buses would operate fully loaded.

Other expenditures. The number of buses needed at any one time would be reduced. However, each bus would be used longer each year and would wear out sooner. If the cost per pupil-mile remained constant, so would the cost of buses. Transportation insurance per bus probably would increase, but the number of buses would decrease so this item in the budget should remain the same.

Fixed charges

Retirement fund. There may be a substantial savings in social security. If the average teacher's salary is $9,000 under the regular school year plan, it would be, on a prorated basis, $12,000 on the four-quarter plan. Since social security is withheld only on the first $9,000, the additional $3,000 would not require social security payments by the school district. Since the number of staff would be reduced up to 25 percent, social security could be saved commensurately. If all teachers chose to remain on a nine-month contract, which is not likely, there would be no savings. Whether or not there would be any savings on the retirement program other than social security depends on the plan itself. The probable savings would be 10 to 15 percent under the four-quarter plan.

Other expenditures. There is likely to be a savings in health insurance commensurate with the decrease in staff. Liability insurance and other charges that are not keyed to the number of staff or days of operation would remain the same, except fire insurance; and other items keyed to the size of the buildings would be reduced commensurately. The probable savings would be 10 to 15 percent.

Other services

The impact on other services would depend on what was included in this category. In all probability, the change would be negligible.

The probable impact of the four-quarter plan compared to the regular school year is summarized in table 3-2.

The estimated cost for operating the four-quarter plan compared to the regular school year, based on the above item analysis, ranges from a possible per pupil savings of $3.83 to a possible increase of $26.05.

Another factor not considered in the above estimates is the cost of

Table 3-2. Estimated Impact of Four-Quarter Plan on Operating Budget

	Range of change (%)	Impact on elementary budget ($)
Administration		
Professional salaries	0	0
Clerks and secretaries	0	0
Other expenditures	0	0
Instruction		
Classroom teachers	0	0
Other professionals	+10 to +20	+6.00 to +12.00
Clerks and secretaries	+10 to +20	+1.54 to +3.08
Textbooks	-25 to 0	-1.73 to .00
Other teaching materials	-15 to -10	-2.79 to -1.86
Other expenditures	0	0
Health		
Professional salaries	0 to +33 1/3	0 to +1.17
Other expenditures	+15 to +25	+.10 to +.18
Operation		
Custodial salaries	0 to +25	0 to +7.92
Heat	0	0
Utilities other than heat	0 to +25	0 to +3.04
Other expenditures	0	0
Maintenance		
Maintenance salaries	0 to +25	0 to +1.95
Other expenditures	+10 to +20	+1.21 to +2.42
Transportation		
Salaries	0 to +5	0 to +1.59
Other expenditures	0	0
Fixed charges		
Retirement fund	-15 to -10	-5.88 to -3.92
Other expenditures	-15 to -10	-2.28 to -1.52
Other services	0	0
TOTAL		-3.83 to +26.05

operating smaller schools and the impact this would have on an all-year school program. The late Paul S. Mort of Teachers College, Columbia University, developed a "sparsity" correction to compensate higher cost per pupil in school districts with fewer than 316 elementary students or fewer than 695 secondary students. The formula is as follows:

If the district's elementary ADA (average daily attendance) is less that 316 and between:

1 and 22, use the figure 22;
23 and 44, use the actual ADA;
45 and 109, multiply ADA by 1.56 and subtract 25;
110 and 315, multiply ADA by .82 and add 57.

If the district's secondary ADA is less than 695 and between:

1 and 68, multiply the ADA by 1.68 and add 14;
69 and 391, multiply the ADA by 1.02 and add 59;
392 and 694, multiply the ADA by .78 and add 153.

If the school is actually divided into four schools within a school in the four-quarter and 45-15 plans, some of the factors considered by Mort are introduced as added costs. For example, if a 45-15 plan high school operated as four schools within a school, which basically it must, then a 16,000-pupil high school would, for scheduling purposes, really have four 400-pupil high schools. According to Mort's formula, the sparsity factor would be: $(400 \times .78) + 153 = 465$. The estimated per pupil cost would increase to the equivalent of having 465 students in each section instead of 400, or the cost would be for 1,860 students instead of 1,600, a 16-percent increase (or $117.60 per pupil based on a $735.00 total cost per pupil).

It should be pointed out that Mort's formula was not designed for measuring impact of a four-quarter plan with divided sections of students, so its application here is not really valid. It was used here simply to introduce the sparsity factor and the fact that it needs to be carefully analyzed because it will have an impact on the budget.

This generalized cost analysis (not yet considering transition costs) indicates that a school district can save on capital outlay (roughly, from $20.42 to $38.15 per pupil per year) by adopting the mandated four-quarter plan or the 45-15 plan. The change in the annual operating costs per pupil may be slightly less or more than the regular school year budget, ranging from $3.83 less to $26.05 more.

All the above figures are hypothetical and based on "averages" and "estimates." They serve to indicate the variables that must be taken into consideration. These variables must be considered in each situation before a conclusion can be drawn as to how much money, if any, can be saved by operating a four-quarter plan.

The conclusion reached by the Northville study is that the

community could save an estimated 6.22 mills per year per taxpayer in building costs and, after a transition period of four years, could break even on the operational budget and possibly even realize a cost savings.

Port Huron Area School District, another school system to undertake a feasibility study of year-round education under a Michigan State Department of Education grant, estimated that the mandated four-quarter plan would increase its operating budget 3.87 mills the first year and 2.5 mills in succeeding years. For the present, it would avoid the need to build new schools at a savings of 5.6 mills in construction costs, resulting in a savings of approximately 3 mills (on condition that the small schools were phased out). Port Huron's analysis of the actual operational budget compared to the estimated budget for operating a mandated four-quarter plan is presented in Appendix A.

Transitional Costs

There are several types of transitional costs that must be taken into consideration. The feasibility study itself, operating committees to analyze the various factors and informing the public of the progress and prospects of the study, entails considerable cost. No attempt will be made to estimate the cost of the study at this time. The allocations by the Michigan Department of Education to the six feasibility studies undertaken by eight school districts were approximately $20,000 per school district. (The school districts undertaking the studies in 1969 were Ann Arbor, Freeland, Northville, Port Huron, Utica, and a joint study by Okemos, Haslett, and East Lansing.)

Other major factors of transition are revision of the curriculum, if the local study concludes that it must be revised, and it usually does; and the cost of in-service training, to prepare teachers for the changeover. Neither of these expenses will be estimated here because so much depends on the current situation of the local school system.

The greatest transition cost, as far as the school plant is concerned, is air conditioning. This may or may not be necessary, depending on the climate and the location and construction of the building. Consideration may also be given to the type of program being operated and the time of day school is scheduled. For example, some schools operating a summer program capitalize on the community resources to a greater extent than at any other time of year, using the out-of-doors as a place to learn. Some schools reschedule the school day to complete the day's work before the buildings get too warm. Molalla, Oregon, reported, "Last summer, we proved that, at least in our beautiful Pacific Northwest, airconditioning is not a necessity to the year-round school. We started classes at 7:00 a.m. and turned out at 1:30 p.m. before the heat of the day."[3]

It would be difficult to make a generalized statement about the cost of air conditioning in local schools where it is decided that air conditioning is necessary. It depends on the existing wiring of the school building, the existing duct work in the building and the facility with which the necessary system could be installed, the size of cooling unit needed, etc.

Careful consideration should be given this issue. If air conditioning is considered essential, cost estimates should be obtained from local contractors. When making comparative cost studies, the installation of air conditioning and other changeover costs should be prorated over the period of the life-use expectancy of the installation.

This cost analysis is based on the assumption of a 240-day, or forty-eight-week, school year with only three-fourths of the students in attendance at any one time. It would be difficult to increase the use of the school to a greater number of days, considering the standard vacation periods of Christmas, New Year, Easter, Independence Day, and others. The savings projected in this study, then, present the *maximum* savings that may be anticipated by rescheduling the school year to the mandated four-quarter, 45-15, or any other similar plan based on the standard school day, the standard school week, and the standard 180-day school year for all students.

Summary

The conclusion that must be drawn, based on the above analysis, is that school systems faced with a need to expand building facilities may or may not find it to their economic advantage to operate on an all-year basis. School systems not confronted with the need to expand their building facilities, however, should not initiate an all-year school program with the expectation of attaining a major savings or increase in efficiency of the *operational* budget.

It should be pointed out again that this analysis is based on the assumption that the school operates four quarters of the year with each student scheduled to attend three of the four quarters in such a way that 75 percent of the students are enrolled each quarter. The two all-year school plans that meet this condition are the mandated four-quarter plan and the 45-15 plan.

The optional four-quarter plan, which permits each student to select the three quarters he will attend, cannot guarantee a reduced requirement in building size. Furthermore, the optional four-quarter program usually allows a student to attend all four quarters if he so wishes. Experience thus far has shown that most students attend school during the regular school year and a small percentage attend the summer quarter. The economic result is no savings in capital outlay, little or no change in the cost of operation during the regular school year, and an increase in the total budget equivalent to the total cost of the summer quarter, which would probably result in about a 10 to 15 percent increase in the regular school year budget. The actual increase, of course, would depend on the program offered and the number of students attending.

The flexible all-year school program is not designed as an economy program but may, in fact, be the most economical program in the long range. The flexible all-year school is designed primarily to break the lock-step in the traditional school program and to adapt the curriculum, the instructional process, and time structures to the real needs of the individual and the community.

This program, with no semesters, quarters, or other artificial segments, proposes that schools operate continuously with no beginning and no ending of the school year. With no beginning or ending of a school year, there is no time at which a learner must pass or fail, and no beginning of the year to be sent back to begin over. Thus, learning becomes continuously forward, without failure. This factor alone could reduce the budget in an amount equivalent to the percentage of students failing in school, since each year a student repeats a grade in school is an extra year's burden on the budget. A 10 percent reduction in "failures" would reduce the total number of students to be educated and hence the budget by an equal amount.

The only way the flexible all-year school program will work is for the instructional program to be flexible enough to adapt to the needs of the learner. With this flexibility a student may pursue any course at his own rate. A student may pass competency tests for credit without wasting his time or the taxpayers' money studying subjects about which he is already knowledgeable.

Another key concept of the flexible all-year school is that the total community is the classroom: some things can be learned better outside the classroom and from local people other than the classroom teacher. This has the potential for major impact on school costs in three ways:

1. If in an ongoing program a fourth of the students were learning in activities other than in the classroom during the regular school day, this would have the same effect on the *capital outlay* budget as would the mandated four-quarter or 45-15 plan.

2. If the community resources are used to provide learning experiences instead of buying instructional equipment and supplies to provide vicarious experiences, the cost of "displaced" equipment and supplies would represent a savings in the budget.

3. If the human resources of the community are used to help students to learn better, this may have a major impact on the teacher-pupil ratio. This is still an unresolved issue, but it is likely that as the role of teacher changes from a "disseminator of knowledge" to a "coordinator of learning experiences" the teacher-pupil ratio may shift significantly, particularly at the secondary level where the per-pupil costs are the highest.

In Pennsylvania the state laws and curriculum regulations have been changed, which makes such flexibility possible in all the public schools. A research demonstration model of the flexible all-year school is being put into operation at the Research-Learning Center of Clarion State College. The planners of this project are aware of the potential savings but are making no claims of a financial savings at this time. In fact, they estimate a 15 percent increase in costs, at least initially, *on the assumption that, given a choice, children will choose to attend school most of the year when school becomes a pleasant, exciting place for a student to spend his time.*

By far the greatest economic advantage of the flexible all-year school will not show up in the school budget itself, but rather in the impact the flexibility of the school structure will have on the time structures of the work force. Chapter 4 discusses the relationship between the school and maintaining full employment of the work force as productivity per man hour increases.

A local school system should be cautioned that the flexible all-year school cannot operate effectively unless the instructional program is very flexible, with a high degree of individualized instruction. The flexible all-year program *should not* be initiated as an economy measure unless and until the teachers of the school system have *already* become competent in the techniques of individualizing instruction. The matter of individualizing instruction will be discussed further in chapter 8 in regard to the transition to flexible all-year schools.

Notes

1. Northville Public Schools, *Year-Round School, Is It Feasible?* (Northville, Mich.: Northville Board of Education, 1971), p. 40.
2. "The Cost of Education Index," *School Management,* January 1972, pp. 21-56.
3. *Proceedings, Fourth National Seminar on Year-Round Education* (San Diego, Calif.: February 23-25, 1972), p. 6.

4 * Changing Life-Styles and Year-Round Education

Contemporary society has given little thought to the significant relationship between the school time structures and the way of life of the people the school serves. We have simply assumed that the long summer vacation is left over from the agrarian era when the children were needed to work on the farm in the summertime.

Such oversimplification has led many educators and others who plan all-year school programs to commit basic blunders that have caused their plans to be rejected by the people. A careful analysis of how people use their time and how this has related to the time structures of the school will show the logic of the school calendar as it has changed over the years. Such an analysis will even show the logic of maintaining the long summer vacation period in urban America up to this time. An analysis of the changing life-styles and living patterns of our society today, together with the technological forces that are causing these changes, will demonstrate that *major changes in our school time structures are inevitable* in the near future.

To make such an analysis we must begin with the concept of the role of the public school in society and how the public school emerged in the United States.

Man has always sought ways to adapt to a changing environment. We have sought to alter our environment through technological means, since the day man began to use his opposable thumb and fingers to grasp sticks and stones, to be used as weapons, tools, and to construct shelter. Along with this we developed systems to accumulate the knowledge about these techniques and to transmit them from one generation to the next. The accumulation of knowledge accelerated as man learned to exchange information through oral and recorded means, from one community to another and from one region of the world to another.

After thousands of years of slow and tedious progress, man accumulated enough technological know-how to spawn the industrial revolution. To be sure, there were concurrent social and political forces that helped bring forth the industrial revolution, just as there were many forces that brought forth the cybernetic revolution this past decade, but it was possible only through the accumulation, transmittal, and application of knowledge.

Every society develops many techniques and procedures to teach children what they need to know in order to live and to make a living in their social structure. In the relatively simple, slowly changing societies characteristic of life before the industrial revolution, most children learned through informal means. There were no schools, as we think of school today, for the common people. The United States had no public schools for the general population in our early history.

The idea of public school is a product of technological change and the resulting changes in the human environment. The term *human environment* we use to mean all of the external forces influencing the behavior of an individual person—the total environment, both natural and man-made, in which he functions. The public school emerged in our nation, as it did in other nations, as a system to teach members of our society what they need to know but would not learn adequately or conveniently without some formal structure to transmit this knowledge. School, then, was designed as a way to *augment* the learning processes already in operation, *not to replace them*. The more complex the society becomes and the more rapidly the way of life changes, the more dependent the society becomes upon the formal processes of school.

The era of the industrial revolution was marked by a rapid increase in the use of science and technology and by a commensurate increase in the complexity of society and in the rate of change in the way of life. It also marked the emergence of the public common school to help people adjust to these changes. *Need* has always determined *who* went to school, *when* they went to school, and *what* they were taught by the school. The *technologies* of education have largely determined *how* they were taught.

The common school, with the three Rs as the basic curriculum, grew out of real but newly developing needs of our society. When people spent their lives at the place they were born, the skills they needed to communicate with others were oral speaking and listening. As people migrated from Europe to the eastern seaboard of America and as they emigrated further west, the need for the common man to communicate in a new way emerged. In order for people to communicate with relatives and friends from whom they were separated and to keep them informed about life in the "land of opportunity," it was necessary to learn to read and write.

The ordinary family, before the industrial revolution, raised its own food, made for the most part its own cloth and clothing, its own furniture—all from the products of the farm on which it lived. Little trade was necessary, and this was done by direct barter. But as people migrated they needed to dispose of those belongings they could not take with them. They needed to buy anew, for a new start, when they reached their destination. They needed to be able to figure the price of things; they needed to be able to measure land, to calculate time and costs of clearing the land, constructing a house, barn, and storage areas for the produce: they needed to be able to do basic arithmetic.

Our society developed systems to meet these emerging needs—a postal system to carry the mail, a monetary system for a medium of exchange, and a school system to teach the three Rs. Before coming to America the need to learn the three Rs was not imperative for the common man, and most of the early settlers had not gone to school. Adults needed these skills in this new situation, but most of them did not have time to learn them. It therefore became the responsibility of those who were less needed on the farm or in the factory to acquire this knowledge for the whole family. These, of course, were the children, old enough to be somewhat independent but young enough to be of little use in much of the heavy work that needed to be done.

Need also determined when the children went to school, and need in the city was distinctly different from the need in the farm community. As the industrial revolution emerged, the production systems changed. The domestic system, whereby an entrepreneur distributed raw materials to workers in their homes and collected the finished product, gave way to the factory, in England initially the textile industry, which employed mostly children and women. As technology advanced the efficiency of production, the production rate increased and the number of workers needed was reduced. Children were a source of cheap labor, in competition with adults; frequently, children were the chief breadwinners for a family. This posed a problem for the unemployed adults, and pressure began to mount for this as well as humanitarian reasons to get the children out of the factories. The first child-labor law in England, passed in 1802, limited the work day of children to twelve hours and required the employer to teach them reading, writing, and arithmetic. Another law, in 1819, prohibited the employment in textile factories of children under nine years of age. The first child-labor law in the United States, passed by Connecticut in 1813, required the mill owner to provide children with instruction in reading, writing, and arithmetic.

The literature on year-round education frequently points out that in early American cities school operated all year, but no mention is made as to why. School provided a way to get the children off the labor market and a place for them to be while their parents worked in the factories—which was an all-year enterprise. As schools developed in the cities, they operated all year; this was standard practice at that time.

Children on the farm, however, were still needed to help with the planting, cultivating, and harvesting of crops as well as many other chores. They came to school when they had time, which was predominantly in the winter. In the early days of the common school children were taught from the readers and arithmetic books their family owned or could borrow. Each child was taught to read and compute from his own books, with the help of the slate and his teacher. He progressed "at his own rate." School attendance was irregular; a student was out of school when he needed to be out, and he picked up where he left off when he returned. He simply continued at "his own level" in his own books until he finished them, whether this took a few months or a few years.

As cities grew in size and population densities increased, so did the size of the school. As the number of students increased, it became necessary to divide them into groups. The idea of organizing them into levels of achievement, called grades, emerged in 1847, with the work organized so that a student would complete one grade in one year. Advances in printing technology made it economically feasible to print "graded" textbooks designed to cover one year's work in each subject. Rigid examinations were given at the end of the year to determine who completed the course satisfactorily and who had to repeat it. A great advantage of this new textbook system was said to be that anybody who could read and write could also teach, without teacher training, because the logical scope and sequence of instruction was already built into the textbook. Trained teachers simply were not available in those days.

This new graded system of the city was considered far superior to the older system that still prevailed in the rural schools. The movement to consolidate schools in America was based on the belief in the superiority of the graded system. The consolidated, graded school served both town and farm children and created a major conflict over the length of the school year. The lock-stepped system of starting all the students in a grade at the front of the book at the beginning of the school year, and pacing them through the book to its end by the end of the year, with a pass or fail examination at the end of the year, made it necessary for all students to begin at the same time, to be regular in attendance to keep up, and to remain in school until the end of the year. This created a great hardship on the farm child who could not always begin at the beginning or stay until the finish. He simply failed over and over again. The length of the school year, therefore, became a key issue.

Two changes were taking place to help resolve this issue, however. (1) In cities, the type of work being done in the factories with bigger machines was becoming "man's work." Labor laws were passed to prohibit both women and children from doing heavy and dangerous work, and social pressure developed for women to "stay at home where they belonged to take care of the children." As this became prevalent the *need* to operate city schools all year ceased to exist and so did the practice. (2) Technologies brought forth by the industrial revolution also greatly altered the way of life on the farm. Machinery like the gang plow, the cultivator, the planter, the mechanical harvester, released farm children from work so they could go to school longer. States began to establish a "standard" length for the school year. For example, in 1918 North Carolina established a standard school year of 120 days. It was changed to 160 days in 1933 and to 180 days in 1943. The close relationship between the public school and the society it is designed to serve has prevailed throughout history and shall continue to do so in the future.

As our nation expanded westward it also grew in complexity, becoming an industrialized nation. Factories in the east produced goods for immigrants as they arrived from Europe and moved west. Cities continued to grow around the ever-expanding factories. Transportation systems were built to haul the raw materials, finished products, and people wherever in this land they needed to go. Distribution systems and marketing systems were developed so people could use what was being produced. Local and state governments were formed and laws were passed to make this free enterprise system work.

The school curriculum was expanded to not only teach the three Rs but also to educate the young and those new to America about the way of life that was emerging—about the production, transportation, distribution, and marketing systems; about the opportunities people had in this new land; about the government and how it works in our society.

The dates of the North Carolina laws increasing the length of the school year are significant and reflect the trends of the nation. Nineteen eighteen coincides with World War I and the Smith-Hughes Act. During World War I our society developed new machines and vehicles, new ways to preserve foods, new machines to make clothes, all in the name of the war effort; but the technologies were applicable to consumers as well. Congress passed the Smith-Hughes Act in 1917 to encourage instruction about using farm machinery and keeping it in use, about the developing trades and industries in the cities, and about home economics—preparing and preserving foods and using sewing machines.

Nineteen thirty-three marks the beginning of the New Deal era and Roosevelt's attempt to recover from the Great Depression. Although tax dollars were scarce, the need to keep the youth off the labor market was more important, so efforts were made to keep the youth in high school. At the turn of the century, less than 5 percent of American youth were graduating from high school. (In 1900 the average American completed 5.4 years of school.) High school attendance expanded rapidly with the Smith-Hughes program, and, with the campaign slogan of "education for all American youth" in the 1930s, the number graduating from high school increased to 42 percent by 1940. This declined to 38 percent during World War II when jobs became plentiful and the youth were needed in the war effort. During the war, the school year was lengthened to give women, many of whom had children, more time to work in the defense factories.

The modern American industrial empire and whole American way of life have been built upon the concepts and techniques of mass production. Mass production is made possible through assembly line techniques, which are based on interchangeable parts. Mass production has changed our nation and our way of life, and it has changed the kinds of work people do. The craftsman or farmer took great pride in his work as he did a "whole job," but people working on assembly lines do the same repetitive task over and over again. There is little opportunity for an assembly line worker to take pride in a job well done because he doesn't do a "whole job" and may not even see the end product. The good worker is the one who works steadily to keep the assembly line going, does what he is told, and doesn't ask too many questions.

Schools also reflect the industrial development mood. School buildings were built in the image of the factories. Assembly line units were called "grades" as desks were neatly lined up in rows and screwed to the floor in factory-like fashion. Children were conditioned for industrial society by making them sit still, keep busy, and do what they were told. The "great American dream machine," including the lock-stepped school, rewarded the conformist to make the "system" work—a system which was and *had to be* organized on highly structured assembly line techniques mandating high degrees of conformity. (For example, Henry Ford once said that a person could have any color of Model T he wanted, as long as he wanted black.)

The tediousness of factory work caused physical and mental fatigue. The idea of vacations with pay developed in part as a technique for increasing production rates. During World War II both Franklin Roosevelt and Winston Churchill held that it was patriotic for defense plant workers to take vacations as a means to maintain high levels of production. Vacations with pay became a standard part of the labor contract. Workers wanted to take their vacations in the summer when their children were out of school; management wanted workers to take their vacations during the summer when schools were out. *This was the only time of the year when there was a labor pool of intelligent, adaptable, short-term workers—the teachers and older students on vacation.* As long as this pattern of the work-vacation schedule prevailed, the long summer vacation from school was needed by the industrialized urban area.

In the 1950s, as the post-World War II "baby boom" expanded the enrollments of our schools, the idea of operating schools all year on a four-quarter system to avoid constructing new schools was unanimously rejected because it was contrary to the living patterns of our society. The vacation schedules of the American work force in the cities had tied as tightly to the long summer vacation schedules of the school, as a source of temporary workers, as had the agrarian society of yesteryear. Furthermore, other segments of our society had developed programs to "fill the gaps" for students who didn't work. Churches developed summer church schools and camps. Private enterprise developed recreation facilities to occupy the time of those on vacation. Our society has developed life-styles and patterns of living keyed to the school schedule. The school cannot arbitrarily violate the way of life of the people. It is interesting to note that at the same time our society was exploring year-round schools as a way to save money in the 1950s, it was also striving for universality in education. Nineteen fifty marks the first year half of our youth were graduating from high school. It has increased about 1.5 percent per year since that time; about 80 percent graduate now.

A new era has emerged in the last few years. Russia's launching of Sputnik in 1957 shocked the world and triggered the United States into a technological speedup to "out-science" Russia. In 1960, for the first time in the history of mankind, a cybernetic system was put into operation—an automatic self-adjusting production system with sensors to monitor its own performance, with the data fed automatically into a computer that analyzes its activity and gives it directions for continued performance.

The cybernetic revolution will dwarf the industrial revolution, and indeed is already doing so. Richard Bellman of the RAND Corporation has predicted that "two percent of the population in the discernible future will be able to produce all the goods and services needed to feed, clothe, and run our society with the aid of machines."[1] Our society has already felt and reacted to the awesome power of this new revolution in many ways.

People who are displaced by machines must find a new way to live and make a living or die, and they will struggle to survive before they die. Many blacks and other minority groups who have been relegated to menial tasks in the past are faced with this problem now. The human rights revolution is a struggle for survival. *They must win today or there will be no tomorrow for our society.*

The problem of displacement is not limited to minorities, however. Forty thousand workers a week are being displaced by machines in the United States today. This includes many middle-aged people, too young to retire but "too old" to learn new trades. New jobs are being created, but they require higher levels of competency and the number of new jobs created is usually less than the number phased out. Continued technological advance places an absolute demand upon an ever-expanding quantitative growth, expressed in Gross National Product. This means the inevitable depletion of our natural resources and, thereby, self-destruction of our whole society; but the alternative appears to be economic stagnation and eventual decadence.

The instability of both our social and natural ecosystems is increasing at such an accelerated rate that disasters are inevitable if the trends continue much longer; but, as Gaylord Nelson said, we are not yet prepared to face the question of whether we have to destroy tomorrow in order to live today.

We did not need to be concerned about congested human settlements when man was sparse and predominately agrarian. We did not need to be concerned about depletion of natural resources when they lay before us in abundance. We did not need to be concerned about pollution when wastes were quickly diluted and lost among the abundance of fresh resources. But we must be concerned about all three now—the maintenance of human populations crowded into complex settlements, the use and depletion of the resources needed to sustain those growing populations, and the disposal of man-created wastes, which become pollutants when they contaminate man's resources and become harmful to man himself.

It is safe to say that our public schools will have a major responsibility in helping our society toil with these vexing problems; and in the process our schools will undergo major changes. Many of these changes are likely to have major impact on the structure of the school as well as on the curriculum. (The impact of these basic issues on the curriculum will be discussed in chapter 5, in analyzing the quality of education.)

Projecting Trends into the Future

Several generalizations can be made about the development of our society and schools in the past that can be used in projecting trends and probabilities into the future:

1. Technological change has continued to advance at an accelerating rate and is almost certain to continue this trend in the future.

2. Technological change has generally increased productivity per man-hour, reducing the number of man-hours that need to be worked to yield a given amount of product. Thus, as productivity per man-hour increases, our society must produce (and therefore consume) more goods and services, or the workers must work fewer hours, or a combination of the two (consume more goods and services, and work fewer hours.) Historically, our society has chosen the combination. Our economic standard of living has continued to rise (for the majority of our society), and the number of hours worked to make a living have continually been reduced.

3. The adjustment of man-hours worked has been made by reducing the number of hours each employee works per day, days per week, and the number of years worked in his lifetime. The work day has gradually been reduced from sixteen hours or more to eight hours or fewer. The work week has been reduced from seven days a week to five, and sometimes fewer. The number of years worked in a person's lifetime has been gradually reduced in two ways: first and foremost, by sending the children to school, thus keeping them off the labor market. Historically the length of the school year, and the number of years each child is expected to remain in school, have continually increased. Secondly, in more recent years the idea of retirement has been introduced, and the age for retirement is continually being reduced, thus removing the elderly as well as the young from the labor market.

4. Whether a child goes to school or not, and when he goes to school, have been dependent on three factors: the need to learn in a formal setting, the need to be on or off the labor market, and the

need to be occupied without parental care so the parent is freed (during school hours) to work or do other things society thinks important. This has been accomplished by our society in a number of ways: by legislation establishing child labor laws, compulsory school attendance laws, by adjusting the length of the school year, and by social pressure. Social pressure is exerted by emphasizing the need for education and relating it to the earning power of the worker, and by giving preference in employment to those who have completed high school and college even if the job itself does not make use of the education the worker received in school. These forces have acted in a flexible manner, changing as the needs of our society change, and it should be noted that they are generally compatible with each other. As technology advances, creating a need to reduce the work force, it creates a corresponding need to learn more in order to function adequately in the more complex, changing society.

5. The practice of giving workers a vacation with pay emerged because of the monotony of the assembly line, not as a way to maintain full employment by reducing the work force. Temporary workers are hired to replace the regular workers. Students and teachers on summer vacation were and still are used to replace regular workers on vacation *in the cities.* The school calendar therefore is integrally related to the work force schedule and cannot be changed substantially without disrupting that schedule. The degree to which this is true varies with the type of industry and labor contracts, and also varies from community to community depending on local industry.

6. Perhaps the most important concept in planning changes in the school calendar is the interrelatedness of time schedules of children in school with their parents' schedules and the schedules of community activities (churches, recreation departments, summer camps, various commercial enterprises), as well as the work schedules that involve both labor and management. In general, it may be concluded that the school schedule is subordinate to the basic schedule of the adult population, particularly the work schedule, and *will continue to adapt to the changing needs of our society as it has in the past.*

The Obsolescence of Summer Vacation

An examination of the issues or problems of our society today may show a significant relationship to work force time schedules or the schedules of major segments of our society, and should give some indication of the changes the school is likely to face and adjust to in the future.

One such problem is the vacation schedules of the work force, which, as was mentioned earlier, are closely tied to the school vacation schedule. Time away from the job with pay was initially sought by the labor unions to give the workers a chance for rest and relaxation from the monotony of the assembly line. It was pointed out that the tediousness of the job reduced worker efficiency and that vacations restored the rate of production. Thus vacations began as a necessary break from the repetitive assembly line. The concept of vacation as a necessity to rest has widely expanded to embrace the idea that the working man has a right to time away from the job for his own pursuits as a part of his share in the increased productivity per man-hour brought about by technological advancement.

When a worker takes a vacation someone else has to do his work or the work must go undone. To maintain production of goods or services, management needed a supply of adequate, temporary replacements for those on vacation. The habitually unemployed marginal worker would not do. Replacements would have to be people who were dependable, quick to adjust to new tasks, and who were willing to accept temporary employment. The best source for such workers was the schools—teachers and older students on vacation who were seeking employment for only a few months.

Society had already accepted the school's summer vacation to provide farm labor. It was only logical to keep the same schedule, making it possible to continue to provide farm labor to the extent it was still needed, and at the same time to provide a supply of temporary workers for industry. As the practice of providing vacations in industry became more widespread and the length of vacations increased, the need for temporary help became proportionately greater. As a result, urban society became committed to a summer school vacation, not so children could work on the farms but that workers in the cities could have their vacations.

How entrenched the summer vacation has been in American schools is reflected in the way problems relating to the schedule have been solved. In cities where the younger children had nothing constructive to do during the summertime, the need grew for an all-year school. Mothers, exasperated with children under their feet all day and apprehensive of the children playing in traffic-burdened streets, breathed sighs of relief when school finally began in the fall. As serious as this social problem was, it did not offset the need for school vacation as a resource for temporary workers.• Instead of having school all year as many mothers demanded, piecemeal recreation programs developed, as did remedial programs to help students who had failed basic subjects keep up with their classes. In recent years, particularly since the 1957 launching of Sputnik, summer school has been changing to include accelerated credit courses as well as enrichment courses. This provided a program for those whose services were not needed on the farm or in industry, and for others who find it to their advantage to register for summer school.

School administrators have frequently proposed extended summer school programs only to have the budget deleted. They have commonly concluded that the major factor causing the rejection was the cost. It may be argued, however, that the controlling factor was basically lack of public support for the program because, in the opinion of the populace, it did not meet their needs. *In fact, recent history indicates the willingness of the American people to expend huge sums of money to keep the school's summer vacation schedule.* Following World War II the sharp increase in the birth rate swelled school enrollments at a phenomenal rate. Most school districts were faced with the need for more classrooms. Tax-conscious citizens throughout the country pointed out that the school buildings were idle all summer, a fourth of the year—that present facilities could accommodate a 25 percent increase in enrollment simply by operating the schools all year on a staggered four-quarter basis. Each student could attend school a total of nine months, or three quarters, and have one quarter off, with a different fourth of the students on vacation each quarter. This, of course, not only would have disrupted the summer work schedule but also would have created new problems of having some students idle with no planned program each quarter of the year. The four-quarter plan was not given serious consideration by many school districts in spite of the clear-cut opportunity to save money. Instead, the American people chose to build new and expensive buildings, bonding their school districts and increasing their taxes, rather than adopt the staggered four-quarter plan.• They adhered to the long school vacation during the summer because it met societal needs that were more important than the money they could have saved.

Now, however, the school schedule that has served society more or less adequately for so long is rapidly becoming obsolete. Not only is the summer too short to schedule all workers' vacations but the school vacation schedule itself is becoming an inhibitor to other changes which society, in an era of cybernation, must adopt.

One of the causes for the change is the increasing demand for more specialized manpower. This is reflected in the present concern about the high school dropout. In the past, those who did not fit the patterns of education offered in the high school curriculum were able to drop out of school and find employment at the assembly line or some other unskilled or semiskilled job. Advancing technology continues to develop machines to do the work heretofore done by those laborers, and at the same time the newly created jobs require precise skills in communication, thinking, and exercise of judgment based on knowledge of the technology itself.

The teachers and older students who in the past served as the main source of temporary workers during vacations are not adequately trained for these new jobs. More time is needed to train them to use them as temporary replacements for workers on vacation, if at all. The need for precision is too great. The cost of error in high speed production or the cost of damage to complex, expensive equipment is too great to risk the use of untrained workers—even the untrained school teachers. New procedures must be, and are being, developed to solve the problem of staffing for vacations. Some industries already have sufficient numbers of highly trained personnel to relieve each other for vacations. Others are providing incentives such as longer vacations or cash bonuses to encourage workers to take vacations at times other than summer. This practice will be extended as the complexity of jobs continues to increase. Thus, the very problem that placed focus on the high school dropout is also eliminating jobs during the summers for teachers and those students who did not drop out. *By the same token, the schools are released from the need to maintain a long summer vacation schedule to provide labor for the world of work.*

Perhaps a more pervasive force for a new work schedule, and hence a new school schedule, is the need for job security. The need to reach full employment is recognized by the leaders of labor, management, and government as the number one domestic problem of this nation. The fear of machines replacing human beings is not new. Labor and management have contended with this problem since the beginning of the industrial revolution. As productivity per man-hour increases, either more goods and services must be consumed or fewer man-hours need to be expended. Throughout the history of the industrial revolution there has been a constant struggle for adjustment, seeking a balance between ability to produce and ability to consume, for there is no use to produce unless the product can be consumed. Ability to consume is directly related to having work and income. As the ability to produce increases, work must be divided somehow among all workers so they can also be consumers and survive. This struggle for adjustment has resulted in a division of the profits of increased productivity between labor and management. Labor's share has been reflected in a continued increase in the standard of living, as measured by goods and services consumed, and a continued reduction in the number of hours each worker must produce in order to make a living. Management's share has been used to develop new capital goods, which in turn encourage increasing productivity.

In 1850 the average American non-farm wage earner worked eleven hours a day, six days a week. In 1940 the forty hour workweek—eight hours per day, five days per week—became standard for all workers in interstate commerce, and quickly spread through most of the rest of the work force. Although the rate of productivity has continued to increase since 1940, labor has chosen to use its gains in other forms of economic advantages instead of reducing the workweek further. Chief among these are better working conditions, higher wages (hence greater consumption of goods and services), sick leave, health and life insurance, unemployment and severance benefits, portal-to-portal pay, coffee breaks, paid holidays, and vacations.

There is evidence that America is now entering an era in which the rate of productivity will increase very rapidly. This is the era of cybernation—the use of automatic, self-adjusting machines that receive their directions for operating from "thinking" computers. Their use is expanding as new and cheaper machine systems are developed and as the understanding of what they can do spreads. There seem to be almost unlimited possibilities in the kinds of work the machines can do and the amount of goods and services they can produce with little or no human labor. Commenting on this, former Secretary General of the United Nations U Thant stated: "The truth, the central stupendous truth, about developed countries today is they can have—in anything but the shortest run—the kind and scale of resources they decide to have. . . . It is no longer resources that limit decisions. It is the decisions that make the resources. This is the fundamental revolutionary change—perhaps the most revolutionary mankind has ever known."[2]

How rapidly cybernation will develop in the near future is not known but a continued rate of increase seems certain. To measure future changes by the past rate is almost sure to be a conservative estimate, but even that would present major problems of adjustment in the immediate years ahead. Since the beginning of cynbernation the rate of increase in productivity per man-hour has been about 3.5 percent per year. At this rate, if all of labor's share of increased productivity was used to shorten the workweek, ten years from now it would need to be only twenty-five hours. If it were used only to increase the number of vacation days, ten years from now the average worker could take a three-month vacation with full pay every year. It is not likely, of course, that all of labor's share of increased productivity will be used only to shorten the workweek or to lengthen the vacation, but the potential is there. Paramount, of course, will be the maintenance of high levels of employment and job security.

How will full employment be achieved? The total work to be done must somehow be distributed so that all workers will have sufficient incomes to consume the goods and services that are produced. As the rate of productivity increases each worker must spend less time producing goods or services, or more goods and services must be consumed, or a measure of both. Without a doubt it will be a combination, because the American people want more vacation time and they apparently have an insatiable thirst for more goods and services.

Some may argue that technological advance does not reduce employment—that it stimulates new employment, instead. It is clearly apparent that the number of farm workers needed to produce the food our society needs has greatly decreased. At one time our society was agrarian oriented, with the vast majority of the population working on farms. Now less than 7 percent of the work force is employed in agriculture. Our society shifted to an industrial-based society as the majority of the workers were employed in the production of manufactured or processed goods, and has now become a service-oriented society as the majority of the work force is employed in providing services rather than producing goods.

Immediately following World War II there was a critical shortage of consumer goods, which resulted from the channeling of our nation's production capacities into war goods. After the war the American people set about catching up with the need for new automobiles, new household appliances, new homes, as well as many other essential and nonessential items. For about a decade manufacturing output grew swiftly, adding 800,000 jobs per year in the manufacturing sector.

The launching of Sputnik triggered a technological speedup in America and the advent of cybernation. Since Sputnik, only 175,000 jobs per year have been added to our nation's economy in the manufacturing sector. Two-thirds of all new jobs since Sputnik have been in city and state government—and this has been mostly in *teaching*. The great demand for teachers resulted from the postwar baby boom. As the demand for teachers grew, the teacher training institutions expanded, enrolling more students (keeping them off the labor market four years), and producing more teachers. The birth rate now has leveled off and the teacher shortage has turned into a surplus of 110,000 teachers. New means must be found to maintain full employment.

Changing from a summertime vacation schedule to an all-year vacation schedule—which is needed as a result of increased demand for more highly skilled manpower—will in itself increase full-time employment while actually decreasing the cost of production. For example, if a company employed eleven workers and each worker took a one-month vacation during the summer, this would provide temporary work for four teachers or older students, but the job would support eleven full-time workers. However, if each of the eleven workers took his vacation at a different time this would provide eleven consecutive months of work, or full-time employment, for one additional worker who would take the twelfth month as his vacation time. The same job would then support twelve families instead of eleven. It would, of course, eliminate a commensurate amount of summer employment for teachers and older students. Such an all-year vacation schedule would decrease the cost of production by eliminating the cost of training temporary employees, the cost of paying double on some fringe benefits (for both the temporary employee and the worker on vacation), and the clerical costs involved in temporary employment.

Not only would the change to the all-year schedule increase full-time employment and decrease costs of production, it would also establish a new structure whereby any additional increases in vacations would result in increases in full employment. To use vacations as a means of employing workers full time they must be scheduled in such a way that during each month of the year—each week or day of the year—some workers will be taking their vacations. Otherwise replacement employment will not be full time.

For example, in 1964 most of the steel industry adopted the "extended vacation plan," which provided a three-month vacation every fifth year for the workers in the upper half of seniority, in addition to their regular annual vacations. This was adopted by labor and management as a means of creating 20,000 new jobs in the steel industry. However, in order for this to create new full-time jobs, some of the workers have to be on vacation at all times of the year. Workers objected to taking vacations when their children were in school so the plan resulted in increased moonlighting, with workers replacing themselves (drawing double pay for working and being on vacation at the same time) instead of creating new jobs.

The shifting of vacation schedules to an all-year basis is a vehicle for job security—for a means of distributing work through the use of increased vacations, which the people want—but *the school stands as a major obstacle to the change.* Most parents do not want to take vacations when their children are in school. Some are already faced with the unpleasant choice of staying home during their vacation time, leaving their children with a baby-sitter or friend, or simply taking them out of school for a few weeks. Almost every community is experiencing the impact of this now. Some parents choose to take their children out of school. It is no longer unusual for children to be out of school a few weeks to travel, and in most instances the schools have willingly cooperated. The practice will continue to grow until a substantial number of children are out of school at any time of the year and the school will, by necessity, shift to an all-year operation. This will provide all-year employment in their own profession for teachers who are being displaced in industry during the summer.

College students who cannot find summer employment will probably want to stay in school the year around, so colleges will need to operate all year. College students are generally independent from home, so their schedules can be independent from their parents'. A trimester or four-quarter plan will still suffice. However, below the college level the student's schedule will have to be dependent upon his parents' schedule.

Society needs to develop an all-year school program that will make it possible for any child to take his vacation any time of the year, for any length of time needed, then return to school and resume his pursuit of learning without loss of continuity. The long school vacation during the summer, designed to meet the needs of society in the agricultural era and continued to meet the needs of society in the industrial era, is now obsolete. Not only does the need no longer exist but it is rapidly becoming a major block to a smooth transition of society from the industrial era into the era of cybernation. As the American people become aware of this the school will have to shift to a continuous, all-year operation with flexible scheduling of student and teacher vacations.

The Impact of Ecological Issues

Two other major issues facing our society that may be dealt with in ways that change the living patterns of our society and the time structures of our schools are air pollution and the problems of urban transportation. Both are related to the time schedules of the work force. Every workday there is a mad rush by millions of people to get into the cities, either driving their cars or using public transportation. The major cause of air pollution in the cities is the automobile. The Environmental Protection Agency's air quality standards go into effect in 1975, recognizing that the automobile must be made less polluting or must be used less. City mayors are asking for billions of dollars in federal and state support to build new mass transit systems to handle the peak loads.

A technique that may be used in the future to deal with both of these problems is the thirty-six-hour workweek, twelve hours a day, three days a week, splitting the work force basically into two work shifts. One shift could work three days, for example, Monday, Tuesday, and Wednesday, and the other shift could work Thursday, Friday, and Saturday. (Lipton Tea Company and several small operations in various parts of the country are experimenting with this schedule now.)

The immediate impact on the problems of air pollution and mass transit would be great. The number of cars rushing into the cities each morning and returning home each evening would theoretically be reduced 50 percent. With less traffic the vehicles will not stand and idle in congestion so much so the amount of pollution caused by this source would also be reduced. The number of commuters using the public transportation system to go to and from work at a time could also be reduced 50 percent, thus existing systems may be able to handle the load without building new rapid transit systems in obsolete cities. This may not, and probably would not, be the ultimate answer to either of these problems, but it would give the American society some breathing space until better solutions can be developed.

A three-day workweek would have major impact on many other social problems and on the American way of life. First of all, the number of workers going to work at the same time would be reduced by half while the hours of operation of stores, offices, factories, etc., that now operate forty hours a week would be increased to seventy-two hours per week. (This increase in operation time would not apply to factories like steel plants that are on continuous operation, but the split shift could operate just as well.) The same rationale used about the increased economic efficiency of operating the schools all year can be applied to the extended operation of the private sector. The longer operating week could increase production by adding new employees, if needed, and by reducing capital investment in buildings and equipment.

In terms of public use of the stores, offices, etc., a seventy-two-hour week would give the users a wider choice of time, also tending to distribute public transit and automobile use of the cities over a wider range of time.

Working three days a week instead of five would have several major effects on the individual workers. First, it means a four-day weekend every week. A big question is how our society would adjust to that. In all probability it would mean a considerable increase in moonlighting, unless some means were taken to prevent it. But what would people do with a four-day weekend? For parents with children in school it would create a problem because the children are in school five days.

A possible approach would be a flexible work year whereby workers can restructure their nonwork time into more usable modules. For example, two workers doing the same job, one working the first three days of the workweek and the other working the last three days of the workweek, could trade with each other. One could work six days a week for several weeks or even months while the other was on vacation (with pay since his work is being done for him by the other worker), then they could shift, taking turns to even up the amount of time worked per year. With many workers working together in the same plant or office, it would provide an opportunity for each worker to be off work almost anytime desired while still working the total number of hours for the year. Flexible scheduling has been a common practice of the railroads for train operators (engineers, firemen, brakemen, etc.) for many years, except that they work on the basis of a month instead of a year.

Another idea that is growing and is likely to be accepted more quickly than the three-day week is the four-day week—ten hours a day, four days a week. Many workers prefer a longer weekend to a short workday with little to do in the evening but sit home and watch television.

This is not an attempt to predict that our society will shift to a three-day week, a four-day week, or a flexible work year. It is probable that no single work schedule will be appropriate for all of the work force. The point is that our society is faced with severe economic, social, and environmental problems and will adopt new life-styles to deal with them. One of the key characteristics of adaptability is *flexibility*. Our society is becoming more and more affluent, with a growing demand for flexibility in time structures. The major block to increased flexibility in the time structures of the work force and our society as a whole is the school. It seems almost inevitable that as pressure grows the school will yield and give greater options to the students and their parents as to when the children are in school and when they are out of school.

The eleven-month school plan would provide each student with a one-month vacation with all students on vacation at the same time. Instead of increasing flexibility in time structures it would make them more rigid. It is not likely that this plan will be adopted by a society seeking greater flexibility.

The mandated four-quarter plan, the optional four-quarter plan, the 45-15 plan, and the quinmester plan would all provide some increase in flexibility as far as the vacation schedules of the parents are concerned. The mandated plans (four-quarter and 45-15) place the burden on the parents to adapt their schedules to that of the students, whereas the optional plans (the optional four-quarter and the quinmester) give students options as to which sections they attend, therefore the students' schedules can be adapted to that of their parents. All of the plans that divide students into separate groups (all the quarter, trimester, quinmester) are based on the assumption that the basic school year for each student will remain 180 days. History, however, indicates it is gradually increasing. Such segmented schedules also inhibit the freedom of classmates and friends scheduled in different tracks to plan out-of-school activities together.

The flexible all-year school plan is designed specifically to meet the changing life-styles of our society and the potential flexible work year. It would be adaptable to any time patterns that may emerge for the work force and our society as a whole since it is based on an *individually scheduled educational program*. It provides opportunity for flexibility in scheduling in terms of length or time of day, week, or year. It could adapt to any changing patterns or life-styles as our society struggles for survival and to give greater meaning to the dignity and worth of human life.

Notes

1. "Ten Keys to the Growth of Economic Productivity in America," *Productivity Digest* (Tokyo, Japan: Asian Productivity Organization) 4, no. 2 (June 1968): 1.

2. "Cybernation: Its International Implications," *Productivity* (New Delhi, India: National Productivity Council) 8, no. 3 (winter 1967): 406.

5 * Quality Education with Equality in Educational Opportunity

Our society in general agrees that the public school should provide for all students a quality education with equality in educational opportunity. There is no common agreement, however, as to what *quality education* and *equality in educational opportunity* mean or how they are to be achieved.

The intent of this chapter is not to define these terms, but to analyze how they would be affected by the various all-year school plans. To do this, it is necessary to establish some understanding of the key characteristics of each and how they may be affected by changing time structures.

Quality Education

Quality education is a variable term; it really depends on the educational needs of the people and will vary as circumstances change. How it is defined by each individual depends on his perception as to what is needed.

We will assume here that a public school is doing a quality job when it is performing well those functions it is expected to perform by the society that sustains it. We will also assume that the role of the public school in a free society—or at least in this society—is to provide the student population with the opportunity to attain those learning experiences most people need but could not acquire conveniently if they did not go to school. This assumption has three significant implications:

1. People learn much of what they know from experiences outside of school: school *augments* a person's general learning environment. The functions of the school, therefore, are variable and depend on what the total educational needs of the people are, and, in terms of that, which educational needs are being met in some other way and which are relegated to the school. It might be said that the school is the educational ombudsman for the society it serves, making sure that the people learn what is needed for that society to sustain and improve itself and, in a democratic society, what is needed for the individual to sustain and improve himself.

2. By its very nature, the public school is an integral part of the community and the society it serves, not an entity unto itself. If the school is to serve its purpose, what a person learns in school must relate integrally to the real needs of society and the real life of the learner. Furthermore, the school facilities belong to the people and should be used to the greatest possible advantage to help meet their educational needs and other needs as may be deemed appropriate by the community and society.

3. The public school must be a viable, ever-changing institution, continuously adapting to the changing needs of the society it serves. The detailed functions of the public school are therefore variable. The learning experiences the school provides under one set of circumstances may not be adequate or even appropriate under another set. Quality education can be described or measured only in relative terms, based on the contemporary needs of society. There are, of course, more enduring values and needs that change very slowly, but human value systems are based on human needs and are subject to change.

Since change in institutional structure is a process of adapting to changing society, an attempt will be made here to identify some of the changing educational needs of our society that result from changes in the major characteristics of our society.

When the way of living is relatively simple and remains relatively constant, children can learn how to live and how to make a living from their parents; little formal schooling is required. A farmer's son, for example, can learn all he needs to know about farming from his father, if the way of farming does not change. If new ways of farming are developed, however, ways must also be developed to disseminate this new knowledge. (Providing information about using farm machinery and new farming techniques was an important function of the high school under the Smith-Hughes Act after World War I.) If the way a child will live or make a living is radically different from that of his parents, he must learn much from other sources; and the basic role of the public school, as previously stated, is to provide the opportunities for such education as well as communicating the enduring values which give stability to society. The more technologically advanced a society becomes, the more literate and skilled must be its work force. The more rapidly change takes place, the more difficult it becomes for society to pass the accumulating knowledge and skills to the next generation, and even to acquire and assimilate them as they develop—and the more dependent society necessarily becomes on the public school and other forms of formal education. It is apparent that the way of life and the way of making a living are changing so rapidly that *public education through the secondary level must become universal* in our society, and continuing education must become available on a life-span basis.

In the past the best way to have knowledge at hand when one needed it was to *keep it in his own mind,* because there was no other way to store and classify knowledge and have it readily available when needed. The school, therefore, selected what were considered the most important bodies of knowledge for all to know from the various disciplines (subject areas), and had each learner *memorize* the information. Today, however, there is an explosion of knowledge, with so much being discovered and developed that no individual could begin to learn all that is important to know, or to keep up with new developments, new techniques, new knowledge, even in one discipline, much less the broad spectrum of knowledge an individual will need to draw on in a lifetime. Nor is there any way to predict which aspects of the body of knowledge each individual will need in the future. New methods of storing and retrieving information are being developed that make virtually all knowledge readily available, if one knows how to retrieve it. In this situation the most appropriate technique is to teach skills of communication, computation, and other basic skills, but also to develop in each learner the ability to *use retrieval systems* to acquire the background and information needed in dealing with specific issues and problems, rather than have him memorize many facts he may never use.

Historically, our society has needed a major work force of common and semiskilled laborers who would work hard and steadily, doing what they were told without asking too many questions. Schools conditioned children for this role by making them sit still, keep quiet, do what they were told, and keep busy. Now machines are rapidly displacing the common and semiskilled workers. There are still many low-skill jobs to be done, but they are being eliminated more rapidly than the workers who hold them are dying, retiring, or being upgraded into more complex jobs. As a result there is "no room at the bottom" of the employment ladder for the unskilled youth entering the labor market. Man's role in the future is likely to be working *with* machines, using his thinking capacity to make decisions about their operation and maintenance rather than doing heavy physical labor or repetitive, nonthinking tasks in competition with machines. The appropriate teaching technique, then, is to help children learn *how to think, how to analyze situations,* and *how to make decisions on a reasonable, rational basis.*

In a slowly changing society, one generation (parents, teachers, and other adults) can teach children how to solve the problems they are likely to face as they grow up, since the problems are much the same as those already faced by the adults. The teaching technique is to have the children *learn the solutions to the problems;* and such techniques still permeate our formal education programs. Under conditions of rapid change, one generation cannot predict many of the problems that will be faced by the next generation, much less solutions to the problems. The most appropriate teaching technique in this situation, then, is to help children learn *how to solve problems* rather than memorizing solutions to problems of the past.

For several decades many employers have given preference to youth who have completed high school, with highest preference to those receiving good marks on their report cards, even though the subject matter taught in high school had little or nothing to do with the job itself. This was done in part as social pressure to keep youth in school and therefore off the labor market, but mainly it was due to the significant relationship between the high school diploma and social conformity. A high school graduate was more likely to be a good worker (i.e., work hard and steadily, do what he was told, and not make trouble) than the high school dropout. What was taught in high school was not that important; what counted was the attitude of the individual. High schools commonly offer three somewhat different courses of study: the college preparatory course for the "academically inclined" students who plan to go to college, the business and vocational course for those who plan to do clerical work, farming, or a few other selected vocations, and the general course for the "average" students whose main objective is to receive a high school diploma and enter the labor market without specialized training. Generally, the public school has simply graduated students after twelve years of satisfactory work and relinquished all responsibility for their success or failure in future life. As long as jobs were available that required only physical strength and endurance or persistence in mass production efforts, the transition from school to work was relatively simple and it was each individual's responsibility to shift for himself. Most available jobs today, and in all likelihood in the future, require specific skills and competencies that must be learned. Our society must develop some system to provide these skills. It is likely that the school in the future will focus more on helping students *develop occupational skills* and *make the transition from school to work* or to a training program leading to employment.

In a simple, relatively unchanging situation a person can become oriented to his environment and understand his own relationship to it rather easily. The school has taught basic skills and what were considered the important areas of knowledge, but left to the individual the integration, generalization, and application of this knowledge to life situations. In a complex, rapidly changing environment it is difficult to understand one's own role in or responsibility to that environment, or to see the relationship between the segmented bodies of knowledge taught in school and their application to real life problems faced by the individual or by society in general. This can lead to frustration and even chaos. A good understanding of basic principles and relationships helps one develop broad generalizations applicable to real problems, helps him to see the order and direction inherent in change and understand better the role of his own life in society. The appropriate technique is to teach each student the basic skills, concepts, and principles needed to understand interrelationships and how *to draw conclusions and make generalizations about the solution of broad societal problems and understand his total environment*. To do this, the focus of study should be more on the significant issues and problems faced by our society, drawing on all the disciplines as appropriate in analyzing these problems and seeking alternative solutions, rather than teaching narrow disciplines as separate entities, as is common in school today.

Equality in Educational Opportunity

Like quality education, equality in educational opportunity is a variable term, at least in interpretation though it may not be so in the absolute sense. Educators and the rest of society should clearly recognize that the American system is imperfect and that the American dream of "liberty and justice for all" still remains to be achieved. It is just as important to recognize that our society has made continuous progress toward those idealistic goals, and is probably closer to achieving them than any other society in history.

We cannot achieve the American dream by denying or glossing over the shortcomings. To be overcome they must be brought out into the open and analyzed. One of the key instruments of our society for this is the public school, by providing the learners not only an equal opportunity to learn the basic skills of communication, arts, and sciences, but also equal opportunity to grow as persons and to understand the societal structures and how their operations affect the lives of all segments of society.

The ideal of freedom and justice for all was forged in America before the concept of free public education emerged, so our earliest concern for equality related to the right of the individual to personal freedom and self-government. As school developed as an instrument of society, a quality education was early recognized as a prerequisite to equality:

The increasing demand for freedom and self-government can be seen clearly at work in Massachusetts in the very first decade of the Puritan settlement. The Puritan leaders had led their hosts of several thousand into the wilderness with the intention of being free to worship as *they* chose and to escape from political and economic conditions in England. The leaders had brought with them to Massachusetts the original charter, intended to be that merely of a trading company, and by a skillful interpretation of its clauses they made it into a sort of constitution for a self-governing state . . . but they had no intention of allowing democracy in their government or liberty in worship. The American dream owes more to the wilderness than to them.

Almost at once the influence of conditions in the new and empty land began to make itself felt. The demands and protests of the men of Watertown in 1634 showed clearly that the plain man with his farm cleared by his own labor was going to insist upon a voice in making rules to govern himself.[1]

One of the fundamental needs in America—to expand its economy —was the accumulation of capital, or resources greater than those consumed in daily living. It was to no avail for a man to obtain large land holdings if he could use only that small part which he could till himself. In the absence of machinery the only way an ambitious man could expand his wealth-producing power was through the labor of other men. But free men were not available for hire when they could easily get land for themselves and build their own farms.

For several generations colonial landholders turned to the use of indentured servants, who were bound to work for a specified number of years to the man who had paid their passage to America. Indian slavery was tried in all the colonies but was unprofitable because the Indians were not adjusted to settled life. The importation of Negro slaves was also explored, and they proved to be excellent workers as house servants and at repetitious farm labor, notably in the South in the cultivation of tobacco and later cotton, particularly after Eli Whitney invented the cotton gin. It was more profitable in the North to continue to use white indentured servants for diversified work (though black slaves were used as house servants in the North as well as in the South). (It is interesting to note that Thomas Jefferson, who drafted the Declaration of Independence and was the major champion of the American dream of life, liberty, and the pursuit of happiness, was a slaveholder. Another slaveholder, George Washington, led the American army in the Revolutionary War and became the first president of the United States. And Alexander Hamilton, who professed no belief in the capacity of the common man to rule himself or others and stood for a strongly centralized government controlled by a monied class built up by special privileges, provided the economic and political doctrines on which the American industrial empire is built.)

As already mentioned, the need for public schools—with the three Rs as basics for communication by reading and writing and computation in trade—developed as migration to this new land and the westward movement expanded. In general the monied class almost everywhere opposed the movement for free education. It was the working class, who wanted but did not have those educational skills, who pressed for a public school system.

In 1830 a workingmen's meeting in Philadelphia unanimously resolved that "there can be no real liberty without a wide diffusion of real intelligence . . . , that until means of equal instruction shall be equally secured to all, liberty is but an unmeaning word, and equality an empty shadow." Within the next two decades the present system of free education in the lower grades was established. . . . Unfortunately, just as our modern system originated among the people and continued to be largely controlled by them, so it bore some of the marks of its sponsors. Not only were instruction and intelligence considered more or less synonymous, as in the above quotation, but the aim and content of education tended to be limited in cultural standards and outlook of the class which had brought it into being. It was aimed at safeguarding economic and political democracy rather than the development of the individual, and its content was selected accordingly. To a great extent, largely because our national aims are even yet obscure to ourselves, this original confusion in our educational system has never been resolved.[2]

It was the workingman then, not the monied class, who pressed for social reform that brought about the free public school system. It should be pointed out that the workingmen were free men, men who had cleared land and gained for themselves a small farm, and later the factory workers, but not the indentured servants or slaves. But it was the monied class who had to help finance the program and furthermore, through the system of electing a local school board to govern the school, it has been predominantly the wealthy or influential "kingmakers" in each community who have controlled the local school boards. Thus two significant factors have permeated our schools: (1) the concept that less educated people are less intelligent —and this has influenced how we treat students in school; and (2) the influence of the monied class upon the curriculum, which has been used to sustain their social and economic power.

This concept of intelligence (and its impact on society and the public school) is aptly described by Boyer and Walsh:

The democracies of the new world . . . brought a new, radical, equalitarian outlook. In principle, if not always in practice, man became equal before the law, and the idea of "the worth of the individual" established a principle of moral equality. Yet legal and moral equalitarianism did not necessarily mean that men were intellectually equal. So the assumption upon the public schools and the American marketplace developed was that democracy should mean *equal opportunity for competition among people who are genetically unequal.*

This creed has satisfied the requirements of modern wisdom even for the more liberal founding fathers such as Thomas Jefferson, and it equally fit into the social Darwinism of an emerging industrial society.

In contemporary American education many of these assumptions remain. People are usually assumed to be not only different in appearance, but also innately unequal in intellectual capacity and therefore unequal in capacity to learn. The contemporary creed urges that schools do all they can to develop *individual* capacities, but it is usually assumed that such capacities vary among individuals. Ability grouping is standard practice and begins in the earliest grades. Intelligence testing is standard practice and begins in the earliest grades. Intelligence tests and the burgeoning armory of psychometric techniques increasingly facilitate ability tracking, and therefore the potentially prosperous American can usually be identified at an early age.[3]

In the past few decades our schools have given a great deal of lip service to the concept of adapting the instructional program to the needs of the individual learner. Considerable effort has been put into finding ways to determine whether a child is "working up to capacity" and, if he isn't, how to get him to do so. This is based on two assumptions, *both of which are probably erroneous.* It is assumed first, that students in general are coming close to using their maximum capacities, and secondly, that this is the primary factor in determining academic achievement of the individual student. We seem to think of human capacity as if some children have pint-sized capacities, some have quart-sized capacities, some have half-gallon-sized capacities, and some even have a gallon-sized capacity, and the responsibility of the school in each case is to "fill the tank." It is therefore assumed that if the school does its job adequately some children, as they are destined, will receive a pint of education, some will receive a quart, perhaps the "average student" will get a half-gallon of education, while the "more blessed" will be able to get a gallon of education—and thus their roles in life are cast in our social structure by nature.

The public schools were never designed to provide equality in educational opportunity. In fact, in most public schools there are many practices that mitigate against equality in educational opportunity. For example, the usual methods of reporting pupil progress on report cards tend to work against some children, particularly the poor, minorities, and the nonconformists. Grades or marks on the report card are generally based on the comparison of students in the class, somewhat on a normal curve basis, rather than on *the specific amount accomplished by each student.* Grading is primarily subjective, based on the teacher's general opinion of the student and his competencies rather than on objective testing based on specific criteria that were established on goals for attainment in the course. These two factors together leave a wide range of opportunity for discrimination or misjudgment even though most teachers would not knowingly do this, or be aware of it when they do.

Closely related to the factor of teacher judgment or personal evaluation in assigning report card grades to students are the grading of daily work and the pass-fail decisions at the end of the course, which generally coincides with the end of the semester or the year. These too are very subjective, generally depending upon teacher opinions or results of tests that really were not adequate measures of the skills, competencies, or knowledge presumed to be taught in the course.

Historically, schools have been taught by middle-class teachers and governed at the local level by middle-class school boards, while the textbooks were written by middle-class professors. The courses are designed for "pint-sized, quart-sized, and even gallon-sized" capacities. The gallon capacity student gets an A; the half-gallon capacity student gets a B; the quart-capacity student gets a D; and the student who doesn't fit the middle-class norm at all gets an F. There is a high correlation between grades and dropout, juvenile delinquency, and social and economic success in life—of the parents and of the child when he grows up. Low income earners raise children in poverty, with limited opportunities to learn, producing educationally disadvantaged children, who in turn become low income earners. *Thus the cycle of poverty is sustained by our school and social systems.*

Title I of the Elementary and Secondary Education Act was specifically designed to become a vital factor in breaking this poverty cycle by providing equality in educational opportunity, but it is not succeeding because it does not reach the roots of inequality.

Recognizing there may be and presumably are genetic differences in individual capacities, what if the capacities came in barrel sizes instead of pint, quart, and gallon sizes? How could the rationale of the school of varying individual capacities be used to justify the passing out of pint, quart, and gallon educations to learners with barrel capacities?

Speaking of this undeveloped capacity to learn, the renowned pathologist, René Dubos, stated:

It has now been demonstrated by the most convincing techniques that in any living cell, any living organism, only a very small percentage of the genes are active, not more than ten or fifteen percent, probably less. All the other genes are depressed, do not manifest themselves, through all sorts of mechanisms that have their origin in the environment. . . . I think all educational techniques in the future would benefit from increased knowledge of the brain's development and of the responses of the genitive equipment to the stimulators and the repressors set in motion by the environment. . . .

Now, seen from this broad point of view, the educational process includes two different but complementary aspects. One of them has to do with the supplying of the kind of information, the kind of raw material, which the child or adult encounters, assimilates, and out of which he creates his own personality. . . . Human beings are different, . . . each and every one of them has different potentialities and will function better and develop better in a certain kind of environment or when exposed to a certain kind of stimuli. As far as I can judge, there is no indication at present that machines can ever have the wisdom, the sensitivity, to recognize the diversity of human beings, and this is the reason why an effective educator is so much more than a teaching machine. He is sensitive to the diversity of human beings and he knows how to encourage the development of all kinds of mental gifts, endowments, by taking advantage of the mind's unexpressed potentialities and plasticity.[4]

Since each individual is unique in potentialities and will function better and develop better in a certain kind of environment or when exposed to certain stimuli, equality in educational opportunity *cannot* mean that all students are taught the same things at the same time in the same way. To the contrary, it *must* mean that all students have an equal chance to learn what they need to know, when they need to learn it, in ways and in an environment that are conducive to learning.

The significance of the individual's personal feelings in relation to equality in educational opportunity is reflected in the U.S. Office of Education civil rights studies. The Civil Rights Act of 1964 directed the commissioner of education to conduct a survey on the availability, or lack of it, of equal opportunity for individuals by reason of race, color, religion, or national origin in public institutions at all levels. In compliance with this act, the Office of Education conducted a comprehensive survey to assess the answers to this broad question and has published a report on the findings. A very significant factor is the relationship between a pupil's attitude and his achievement.

This analysis has concentrated on the educational opportunities offered by schools in terms of their student body composition, facilities, curricula, and teachers. This emphasis, while entirely appropriate as a response to the legislation calling for the survey, nevertheless neglects important factors in the variability between individual pupils within the same school; this variability is roughly four times as large as the variability between schools. For example, a pupil's attitude factor, which appears to have a stronger relationship to achievement than do all school factors together, is the extent to which an individual feels that he has control over his own destiny.[5]

If segregation between schools is unconstitutional and inherently unequal, what of segregation within schools? How does the child who is taken out of his regular classroom for special remediation feel? Does this give him the feeling that he can achieve as others do, that he has control over his own destiny? What about ability grouping and other forms of comparing students? The Task Force on Education, Committee on Children and Youth of the Governor's Council for Human Services of Pennsylvania, responded:

Since one's self-concept is so important a factor in how he learns, the learning environment and how it makes the individual learner feel is significant in providing equality in educational opportunity. It means that each child and youth needs to grow in an environment where he has an opportunity to explore new ideas, live new experiences on the growing edges of learning (for him) in a situation where he (a) feels accepted and is, in fact, accepted by his peers, teachers and others with whom he has personal relationship; (b) succeeds in the activities he is expected to do to the extent that he expects to be successful as a person; and (c) the activities in which he succeeds are important to him and to the people who are important to him.

Can any program under Title I of ESEA which separates the disadvantaged from the advantaged really provide equality in educational opportunity? Can ability sectioning as commonly practiced in the junior and senior high schools or ability reading groups in the elementary grades really provide equality in educational opportunity? Can the traditional practices of placing approximately 30 or 40 students in a box-like classroom, staffing this unit with one teacher, and equipping it with a set of textbooks for each subject to be taught ever achieve equality in educational opportunity?

The lock-step must be broken. The curriculum and the time schedule must be adapted to the needs of the individual. Learning experiences must truly become individualized and personalized if the human right of equality in educational opportunity is to be achieved.[6]

The influence of the monied class on the social and economic studies in the school curriculum also has many implications. Some have been perceptively spelled out by Robert J. Havighurst[7] and by Maurice P. Hunt and Lawrence E. Metcalf in their description of "closed areas of culture."[8] These are defined as "areas of belief and behavior characterized by a relatively large amount of irrationality, prejudice, inconsistency, confusion, and taboo."

These "closed areas," according to Hunt and Metcalf, are ones in which reflective treatment of the problems involved has largely been excluded in contemporary schools. Six areas which these writers judge to be closed in varying degrees are:

1. Economics. While "open" to professional economists and laymen, this field is so affected by taboos, confusion, and emotion that schools tend to avoid it as a subject for rational study.
2. Race and minority group relations. In recent years this field has become more open to reflective inquiry in schools, but in some places fears, tensions, and confusion continue to make it a closed area.
3. Social class. Here is a truly closed area in the writers' judgment, "neatly ignored as a result of the widespread belief, 'There are no social classes in America'."
4. Sex, courtship, and marriage. This area is more open to inquiry than it was a few years ago, but critical analysis of contradictions and problems is not usually encouraged.
5. Religion and morality. Morality is somewhat more open to reflective inquiry than are religious beliefs, but both tend to form a closed area as far as schools are concerned.
6. Nationalism and patriotism. This area is one in which it is difficult to question traditional beliefs, even if they are inconsistent with real behavior, or the requirements of national survival.[9]

The National Council for the Social Studies points out further that:

If there is controversy about alternative values in a society, it is also unlikely that education [school] will be used as a vehicle of change, judging from our experience.

In terms of citizenship education and the future of a free society, [this] concerns us deeply. It is precisely in the arena of competing social values, conflicting policy choices and difficult decisions that citizens of a free society must be prepared to operate, today and for the indefinite tomorrow. The dimensions of change noted earlier affect all of social life in the present and foreseeable future. To the extent that citizens are equipped to recognize, appraise, and consciously play a rational democratic part in shaping change, the society stands a chance of remaining free. In more stable eras this requirement, by definition, was not of the critical importance it is now. The perpetuation of stable values and social patterns remains a need. But the explosive present and future demand a high capacity on the part of citizens to invent new solutions adequate to an incredibly great and growing array of new problems, while retaining the essential orientation of a free society.[10]

This set of prejudices and limitations that are built into and permeate the American public education system greatly influences the attainment of quality education, or even what is meant by quality education, as well as the attainment of equality of educational opportunity and the recognition of the many ways in which the school fosters *un*equal educational opportunity.

In summary, if we are to attain quality education with equality in educational opportunity, the public school must provide:

1. *A humane learning environment.* Each learner needs to have the opportunity to function and to grow in a learning environment in which he: (a) is on the "growing edges of learning" with opportunities to experience new challenges, new situations, new ideas, new people (rather than a static environment with predominantly repetitive and meaningless tasks); (b) is accepted and feels that he "belongs" with his peers, teachers, and others with whom he has regular contact; (c) is successful enough to learn to expect success rather than failure in his general life's endeavors and aspirations; and (d) feels that the things he succeeds in are important to him and to the people who are important to him.

2. *A relevant curriculum.* If the curriculum is to be relevant to the real needs of the individual learner and of society, it must change: (a) from the same for all students to a curriculum adjusted to individual needs; (b) from rote learning of solutions of problems, to learning how to solve problems; (c) from simply learning to "do as you are told," to learning to make decisions based on pertinent data—learning to think critically; (d) from learning segments of knowledge from separate disciplines without meaning or purpose, to the study and analysis of broad and significant real-life problems, drawing on the various disciplines as needed.

3. *Appropriate instructional processes.* A variety of instructional processes are needed, depending on the situation, but in general the emphasis should be: (a) from single textbook toward multimedia sources of information; (b) from teacher-prescribed toward learner-selected activities; (c) from highly prescribed sequences of "steps" in learning toward nonsequential units of study based on pertinence and timeliness; (d) from teacher-paced instruction, keeping the whole class or ability groups together, toward self-paced activities allowing each learner to proceed at his own rate; (e) from learning from one teacher in grade or subject area toward learning from many human resources (multiple staffing and community resources); and (f) from closely graded to multiage grouping.

4. *Flexible use of time and learning facilities.* So that students can attain optimum use of time and facilities, the time and place scheduling procedures should be changed: (a) from rigid time modules in terms of length of class period, length of day, week, and year, to

flexible scheduling with variable lengths of study periods, with the time of day, week, and year adjusted to individual needs; (b) from the concept that all learning takes place in the classroom to the concept that learning is continuous and takes place in the total environment; and (c) from the school being the isolated place of learning to the appropriate use of the total community as the classroom.

5. *A humane and rational pupil evaluation system.* Each learner needs to have adequate feedback to know realistically how well he is achieving or progressing, but the evaluation system must function in ways that: (a) do not compare students with each other on artificial or prejudiced bases but evaluate each student on the basis of his attainment of specified goals or objectives; and (b) do not provide for "pass or fail" decisions at the end of a unit of study or school year, but provide for continuous progress with variable time limitations, as needed, for attainment of goals and objectives.

The Impact of Year-Round Education on Quality Education with Equality in Educational Opportunity

One of the major reasons given by advocates of year-round education is that it increases the quality of education with equality in educational opportunity. Some of the purported changes are inherent in the change of the time structure itself, while others are part of the broader educational reform effort that logically comes about with the changes in the school calendar.

The educational advantages often attributed to year-round education will be reviewed here, together with an analysis of the relationship between the purported change and the various all-year school plans.

A More Relevant Curriculum

Many of the educational practices in our public schools came about for logical reasons and have served worthwhile purposes, but now need to be changed to be more relevant to the needs of children and youth in a technologically advanced and rapidly changing society.

In order to put any of the all-year school plans into operation it is necessary for a local school district to examine carefully, and in most cases reorganize, the curriculum. There are two basic considerations inherent in the change of time structure: (1) the length of each course (in terms of study time), and (2) the sequences in which the courses are offered.

Most courses now used in the public schools are organized on a semester or full-year basis. To adapt these courses for all-year school use, they must be restructured to correspond with the length of sessions of each particular all-year school plan. The various all-year school plans and the length of sessions for each are listed in table 5-1. The length of sessions listed are the most commonly used, based on a standard school year of 180 days. This may vary slightly from state to state.

Table 5-1. Length of Courses for All-Year School Plans

School plan	Length of session
Regular school year	9 months – 180 days
Semester plan	4½ months – 90 days
Mandated four-quarter plan	3 months – 60 days
Optional four-quarter plan	3 months – 60 days
45-15 plan	9 weeks – 45 days
Quinmester plan	9 weeks – 45 days
Trimester plan	75 days
Eleven-month plan	11 months – 220 days
Flexible all-year school plan	Not organized on session basis*

*No specific length of course is required but numerous courses of varying lengths are needed in each subject area to facilitate scheduling.

As can be seen from table 5-1, most of the all-year school plans are organized with sessions in lengths that are factors of the regular school year. The four-quarter plans simply divide the regular school year into thirds, to comprise three quarters (180 days ÷ 3 = 60 days), then add the fourth quarter in the summer. The quinmester and the 45-15 plans divide the regular school year into four equal parts (180 days ÷ 4 = 45 days), then add one more to equal five sessions a year.

If each section of students were taught as a separate unit, with the time of beginning and ending their school year as a primary difference, little change would be necessary in the courses of study. In, for example, the *mandated* four-quarter plan, the student body is divided into four sections and each section is assigned the quarters they will attend school. Each section, however, is in school for three consecutive quarters or 180 days, as illustrated below, and any regular school year course could be taught to each group in the same way it is now being taught. Group A could begin American literature in session 1 and pursue it for three consecutive sessions (180 days), then be on vacation the following quarter. Group B would study the same American literature course, beginning with session 2, and so on, until each of the sections had completed the course in American literature, and all of the other courses.

Table 5-2. Mandated Four-Quarter Plan

Session	1	2	3	4	5	6
Group A	◄—— American literature ——►			V		
Group B		◄—— American literature ——►			V	
Group C			◄——American literature ——►			V
Group D				V	◄———American literature ——►	

Only the mandated plans can operate in this fashion, i.e., the mandated four-quarter plan and the 45-15 plan. The optional plans, which permit the student to select the session he wishes to be on vacation each year, must offer courses that are designed to begin and be completed in the same session—thus the courses of study must be reorganized.

The consideration of course sequence is also an important factor in developing an all-year school program that is both operational and economically feasible. Sectioning the students into four attendance groups (as in the case of the four-quarter plans) and scheduling them *separately* is, in essence, like operating four separate schools within a school. This creates severe scheduling problems, particularly at the secondary level where instruction is departmentalized and many of the more advanced or specialized courses are offered only if enrollment is sufficient. Maintaining four separate schedules, operating as four separate student bodies, is very undesirable from the class scheduling standpoint. It would be much better if in scheduling classes the sections could be commingled. For example, the course in American literature might include such topics as the modern short story, the novel, essays, biography, and poetry; writings of colonial authors, the periods of the making of the nation and the literature of the advancing frontier; modern poetry, modern drama, writings of the periods of conflict and the postwar era, trends in poetry and prose, and American literature in the modern world. (This is the topical outline of the Armed Forces Institute course in American literature as a one-year, one Carnegie unit, course.) This one-year course might be divided logically into three or four shorter units (or even more) and offered to any student, regardless of the section he is in, *without one course being a prerequisite to another.*

For scheduling purposes this would have the effect of reducing the student body to three-fourths of its regular size rather than to one-fourth, as it would be if the four sections were kept separate (as in the four-quarter plans). It would therefore be desirable, even in the case of the mandated four-quatter plan, to reorganize the courses of study into shorter units.

The only all-year school plan that cannot use this approach of commingling in the scheduling of students regardless of their sections with the use of conventional teaching techniques, is the 45-15 plan. All of the commonly discussed all-year school plans which divide the school year into sessions, except the 45-15 plan, have common starting and stopping dates for each session. All students who attend the fall session, for example, begin that session on the same day and accordingly finish the session at the same time.

In the case of the 45-15 plan, however, each of the four student sections (of each grade level) begins a session at a different time, fifteen school days apart (see table 5-3). The 45-15 plan must operate, for scheduling purposes, as four separate schools within a school, which makes the 45-15 plan very difficult to operate at the

Table 5-3. The 45-15 Plan

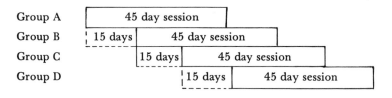

secondary level and in small elementary schools when conventional teaching methods are used. This can be overcome through the use of individualized instruction and multiage grouping, which will be discussed later.

Any local school system planning to initiate an all-year school plan *of any kind* must *first* reorganize the courses of study to be compatible with the all-year school plan being initiated. This fact has two important effects. First of all, a local school system that is planning to develop an all-year program soon learns that it takes time (usually several years) and money to revise the curriculum, so that putting the program into operation must be delayed. (This problem will be overcome as more and more courses designed to meet this need become readily available and as teachers become more skilled in flexible scheduling and individualized instruction.) Secondly, as faculty committees and others working with them begin revising the curriculum, they must face the question of relevance. The more the uniqueness of each student and the complexity of our society are recognized, the more it is apparent that the traditional curriculum is obsolete, and must be expanded from a relatively linear program to an ever-branching one that offers each student many options and opportunities to learn the skills, concepts, and knowledge that are meaningful to him. This is reflected in the proliferation of courses that tend to emerge as the curriculum is revised into shorter courses, and as the curriculum writers attempt to organize the course content into a logical but nonsequential (without prerequisite) order. For example, Dade County, Florida, initiated the optional quinmester plan and has developed a high school curriculum of 1,600 or more courses. Atlanta, Georgia, initiated the optional four-quarter plan at the secondary level and has developed 600 course offerings. Both are still adding new courses to their list of offerings. This same pattern of an expanded, more relevant curriculum tends to accompany the development of all-year school programs, particularly at the secondary level.

Revising and broadening the curriculum does not in itself guarantee that curriculum content will be more relevant to the real needs of the individual or society, but the very fact that the school is undergoing a major revision and is analyzing its needs in relation to the community fosters such changes.

Appropriate Instructional Processes

Adjustment of (1) the courses of study from a full year to the length of the sessions and (2) the structures of the curriculum content into independent, nonsequential courses almost necessitates the use of multiple instructional resources, rather than relying on a single textbook. At the same time, it breaks up by design the long sequences of prerequisites as courses become self-contained units of study. This is most difficult to achieve in the skills areas, particularly mathematics, and some prerequisites will always be necessary, but they are minimized for operational expediency.

Another factor in operating an all-year school program that has impact on instructional processes is dividing the students into attendance groups, as in the mandated four-quarter, the 45-15, and all other mandated plans. It is impractical in a small elementary school, for example, to organize students into four attendance groups and still retain the grade-grouping process. If an elementary school with one teacher and an enrollment of twenty-four to thirty-two students in each grade, were divided into separate operating units and continued to divide students by grade, there would be only six to eight children in each group in each grade. This would necessitate employing four teachers for each grade instead of one, greatly increasing the cost of operating the school, which of course is not feasible. The alternatives are to eliminate the small schools by consolidating them with larger schools (this is a common recommendation by local committees who study the feasibility of year-round education) or to create multiage groups of students by either nongrading or multigrade grouping techniques.

Schools with four teachers or multiples of four teachers per grade (eight, twelve, etc.) are easy to divide into four attendance groups. But what about a school with five or six teachers per grade? Grouping students into four groups also becomes a problem in these cases, unless multiage grouping is used for at least part of the students.

Multiage grouping can be used appropriately at the elementary level as a solution to this problem, but at the departmentalized, secondary level it is more difficult. For example, in the average-sized high school there is likely to be only one teacher to teach an advanced course in foreign language, mathematics, physics, chemistry, and many other subjects. If each of these teachers taught in the traditional way it would be very difficult to schedule such classes without hiring many more teachers and maintaining a very low teacher-pupil ratio. The solution to this problem is individualized instruction, just as in the case of nongrading at the elementary level. A logical outcome, then, of year-round education is the breaking of the lockstepped curriculum and instructional practices, changing to multiage grouping and individualized instruction. At the same time, as staffing problems are dealt with, it is apparent that multiple staffing also becomes expedient. With the expanded curriculum and greater flexibility in scheduling and instructional procedures, a greater utilization of community resources becomes feasible.

So far attention has been given to those all-year school plans that are based on dividing the students into attendance groups and dividing the school year into attendance sessions of specified lengths of time. The flexible all-year school, however, with no beginning or ending of the school year, with students beginning school whenever they are "ready" and taking their vacations whenever needed, must be based on an individually scheduled educational program with a high degree of flexibility in the curriculum content and in the instructional and grouping processes—otherwise the plan cannot operate.

Flexible Use of Time and Learning Facilities

The flexibility generated by multiage grouping, individualized instruction, and multiple staffing makes it much more practical to develop flexible scheduling, moving from rigid time modules to variable class periods. This flexibility also makes it possible to utilize the total environment more effectively. A teacher locked into time modules of fifty-minute periods would find it impossible to take a class of students on an extended field trip without disturbing the other teachers and their classes. The increased flexibility in time structures breaks that lockstep, and facilitates the appropriate use of the total community as the "classroom."

With the school operating all year, or nearly all year, scheduling students for makeup work or extended schoolwork is facilitated. The more individualized and personalized the total instructional program, the more easily the special needs of individual students are accommodated. It should be recognized, however, that as the number of students who use the services of the school beyond the standard school year of 180 days increases, the cost of operating the school also increases. If the prime objective in initiating an all-year school program is to keep taxes down, this may defeat the purpose if the extended time is used for enrichment purposes. However, if a student who has been absent from school for an extended period of time due to illness or other causes, can catch up by attending classes during his vacation periods, he may avoid repeating a whole year's work of a grade or subject area. On the other hand, a factor that should be carefully examined is the probability that the retention rate, or the number of students who "fail," will *increase* in all-year school plans that divide the year into shorter sessions. A student who is ill and out of school for three weeks may find it very difficult to catch up before the end of a forty-five-day quinmester or a sixty-day quarter; and teachers are likely to think that it would be easier for a student to repeat the course, since it is such a short period of time. This could have a damaging impact on the student psychologically, and could build up into an economic burden for the school district as well. This does not apply to the flexible all-year school, since a student could simply return to school and continue from where he left off, and proceed at his own rate in catching up.

A Humane and Rational Pupil Evaluation System

One of the subtle tools our society uses to maintain the status quo is the grading system. Children from the "right side of the track" tend to get better grades, for a variety of socioeconomic and psychological reasons, than children from the "wrong side of the track." As long as instruction is organized on a class basis, with all the students pursuing the same course at the same time, teachers are prone and in fact expected to grade students on a rank order basis. The underlying forces of the power structure come into operation as most teachers tend to grade students on a subjective basis, considering—even though subconsciously—such factors as the student's general behavior (discipline), personal appearance, social status, the teacher's or school's relationship to the parents, and many other factors unrelated to the specific progress in learning the course being taught. The more the school is able to personalize the instructional program, using continuous progress practice, the more likely pupil evaluation is to be based on the individual's own achievement rather than on a comparative ranking basis.

A Humane Learning Environment

The time structure of the school cannot make the school humane. It takes humane people to humanize the learning environment. It takes teachers who love and respect children, teachers who can smile and make a child feel that he belongs even when he has made a mistake. It takes teachers who really understand children who are different, who will help other children to accept and respect them. Such teachers are far too few in number. Teachers are human, too; most teachers who know they might be fired or at least fall in the administration's disfavor or that of the other teachers or the parents for doing so, would hesitate to individualize instruction, change the grading system, or act as ombudsman for the rejected child. Teachers tend to conform to the patterns of expectation, and our society has expected them to conform to the lockstepped system.

The all-year school movement is helping to change those expectations, along with other forces in our society. Restructuring the curriculum content, the instructional processes, and the time and place structures for instruction, which is inherent in the all-year school programs, helps to facilitate personalizing and humanizing the school experience for all children. Much of this can be done without changing to an all-year school, nor is there anything magical about an all-year school that guarantees it will be more humane. The development of an all-year school program by a local community, however, can be the central point about which educators, parents, and civic, social, economic, and ethical groups can rally, to plan an educational program that is appropriate to the needs of the individual students as well as the needs of the community.

Notes

1. James Truslow Adams, *The Epic of America* (Boston: Little, Brown and Co., 1932), p. 40.
2. Ibid., p. 196.
3. William H. Boyer and Paul Walsh, "Are Children Born Unequal," *Saturday Review*, October 19, 1968.

4. René Jules Dubos, "The Potentialities of Man," address delivered at the Third Plenary Session of the Tenth National Conference of the United States National Commission for UNESCO, November 18, 1965 (mimeographed), pp. 4-5.

5. James S. Coleman et al., *Equality in Educational Opportunity* (Washington, D.C.: Government Printing Office, 1966), p. 22.

6. Task Force on Education, *Imperatives for Education So That Man May Survive and Live in Dignity*, Committee on Children and Youth, Governor's Council for Human Services, Pennsylvania, 1970, pp. 17-18.

7. Robert J. Havighurst, "How Education Changes Society," *Confluence: An International Forum* 6, no. 1 (spring 1957): 86.

8. Maurice P. Hunt and Lawrence E. Metcalf, *Teaching High School Social Studies: Problems in Reflective Thinking and Social Understanding* (New York: Harper and Brothers, 1955), p. 230.

9. Franklin Patterson, ed., *Citizenship and a Free Society: Education for the Future*, 30th Yearbook of the National Council for the Social Studies (Washington, D. C.: National Education Association, 1960), pp. 12-13.

10. Ibid.

6 * Taj Mahals of Education

The greatest single force propelling the current all-year school movement is the desire of many taxpayers to save money by reducing the size of a new school, or by avoiding adding to an old one. Before rushing into a plan to delimit the size of a school building, it is prudent to analyze the underlying factors that have caused our society to design the schools as they have been designed in the past.

An important characteristic of the American way of life is the drive to move upward in the socioeconomic strata of our society. A farmer was judged by the size of his farm, so he sought to accumulate larger and more efficient machines to manage more acres of land, raising more livestock and larger crops, until now farming is less and less carried on by individual farmers and their families but is instead agri-industry, managed by corporate bodies.

The entrepreneur was judged by the size of his store or factory, so he sought to accumulate larger and more efficient machines in order to produce and market greater quantities and varieties of goods; and the entrepreneural system, under the personal leadership of the owner, has given way to corporations and conglomerates of corporations.

Workers in factories organized to gain improved working conditions and higher wages; they elected leaders as spokesmen to bargain on the issues they felt were important. The labor leaders sought to represent larger bodies of workers to gain greater bargaining strength, so that the unions, too, have become impersonal corporate bodies far removed from the workers themselves.

Town halls, where the local citizen came to share in the shaping of laws and decision making about community needs, grew in size to match the ever-expanding bodies of vested interest groups that needed to be regulated in the interest of society. City, state, and national governments have become less a function of people making decisions for themselves and more the vying of front groups for control of power for vested interests.

It may be argued that city hall has become a monument to political power just as the union hall may be to bargaining power and the skyscrapers may be to industrial power. Men with power tend to build Taj Mahals to sanctify and memorialize their own efforts. However, the forces behind the movement toward increasing bigness are complex and cannot simply be described as the drive for greater wealth, power over other people, or to commemorate oneself. Even though it may have been poorly defined, there was also a struggle for increased *quality*—quality of product, quality of service, quality of life.

If we don't clearly define our personal or societal goals in advance, or the procedures to be followed to reach those goals, it sometimes becomes difficult to know when the goals have been met or when the effort being expended ceases to move us toward their attainment. In terms of bigness, we may have overshot the target in many ways, so we look back to the "good old days" with a feeling that the quality of life we are seeking somehow lies behind us rather than ahead. Such may be the case with the Taj Mahals of education today. The one-room school, so long a part of American life, gave way to the consolidated school large enough to be graded. Many rural schools, however, did not include high school, so those who aspired to go to college and had enough money to move into town left the farm and went to the town high school. To make a high school education available to all American youth, the consolidated schools were reorganized into unified systems, each with its own high schools. As this process of reorganization continues, uniting small high schools into new secondary units, the size of the buildings gets commensurately larger.

Few would choose to go back to the one-room school of the agricultural era and the way of life it represented. In 1917 Kirkpatrick described the rural school:

The teacher is janitor, parent, and nurse. He (or she) must be on hand early on cold mornings to start the fire, sweep the drifts of snow from the porch, shovel walks to woodpile or coal house, pump (if there be one) and to the outhouses which upon such mornings are likely to be drifted full of snow. It is the duty of the teacher not to make everything comfortable, but to make, so far as possible, things less miserable.[1]

In discussing the pros and cons of consolidation of the rural schools with the town schools, Kirkpatrick stated:

(a) If rural schools are poorly graded, and it is almost impossible properly to classify the pupils, and these defects can be remedied through consolidation, two very good reasons may be offered for consideration: better grading and classification will permit both teacher and pupil to work more effectively; more time can be given to recitation and greater opportunity for much needed correlation.

(b) If such cultural subjects as nature study, drawing and music, and vocational subjects such as manual training, mechanical drawing, agriculture, domestic science and domestic art, are, while very valuable subjects, an impossibility in the one-room school, but entirely possible in a consolidated school, two additional reasons may be given for consolidation.

(c) If nine months is a better length of school term than seven months, the consolidated school is better, because it is more likely to give the nine months' term.

(d) If it is true, as charged, that rural teachers are young, immature, untrained and inefficient, and the ablest of these find better positions in the town schools; and if it is true, as teachers themselves testify, that pupils in the small rural schools do not feel the inspiration of the highly competitive life, then the consolidated school is better because it insures better teachers, and more contented teachers, and the retention of teachers, and . . . the stimuli of large classes, creating enthusiasm and intellectual rivalry and a confidence which comes only from contact with numbers.

(e) If, as claimed by those who have tried consolidation, the consolidated school results in more regular attendance, affords a broader companionship and culture and quickens the public interest, is there not abundant evidence that the consolidated schools can serve a real need in country life?

. . . It is practically safe to predict that the school is to become a school for the people. Up till recent years, the public has been slow to act in matters pertaining to education; but now the nation has awakened, and . . . it is demanding an education that will function with life that is to be lived in a practical world. It is demanding an education that will work.[2]

The nation's demand for an education that would "function with life that is to be lived in a practical world" reflected the basic changes society was undergoing as it progressed in the machine age. The United States had been making war goods for the Allies in Europe for several years. This had triggered the technological development of vehicles and other machines and the processing and preserving of foods, which had application to our own society. The entry of the United States into the war in 1917 created a shortage of labor in American factories and farms. The first major attempt by the federal government to affect the curriculum of the basic public school, through the 1917 Smith-Hughes Act, reflected these needs of society. It provided funds to train and employ high school teachers, develop courses of study, and obtain necessary equipment for programs in trades, industry, agriculture, and home economics. The youth, through the new high schools, had to help America adapt to a way of life the parents had never known. They had to learn to make tractors and to use them on the farm. They had to learn to make and use sewing machines, fruit jars, and other domestic equipment. As they used labor-saving devices to their own advantage, these things became a part of their way of life.

The school districts consolidated and unified. They built larger schools and transported students, not to save money but to provide the educational experiences our society needed. The school became the rallying point as communities made the transition to industrialization.

During the past decade our society has been undergoing a similar but more massive change. When Russia launched Sputnik in 1957, it shocked the world and triggered the United States into a technological speedup to "out-science Russia." The first impact, of course, was in the application to space exploration and the military. By the early 1960s, the effects of automation, even cybernation, and other technological breakthroughs permeated the production systems of our society. Machines were displacing workers at the rate of 20,000 per week. (The rate is now over 40,000 per week.) The new jobs being created required skills and competencies not usually attained by the high school dropout. The jobs high school dropouts had previously obtained were rapidly disappearing, so the unemployment rate grew. In the summer of 1964, the National Education Association, the mass media, and others launched a campaign to keep the youth in school: "If you know a high school student who plans to drop out of school, talk to him. Tell him how important it is to him to graduate from high school."

In September of that year the newspapers carried stories, cheerfully announcing that many millions of youths had been "saved" by the campaign. In October, the cheer began to wane; and in November, the realization was growing that our schools were not designed to educate all American youth. Those who had been talked into staying in school were rapidly becoming discouraged again and leaving; the school did not have the holding power to keep them. By December 1964 the Congress was hard at work on the Elementary and Secondary Education Act, which was passed and became law in May 1965.

Like the Smith-Hughes Act, the ESEA was designed to help our society adapt to the rapid technological changes it was undergoing, but the needs for change in a society entering the cybernation era are more complex and more pervasive than learning, in 1917, to use what we now consider rather simple machines. Educators had no ready answers for this dilemma in the 1960s. The public, including most educators, decried the *failures* of our public school system. In reality, the dropout problem was a product of the *success* of our American school system. It had responded to the need and educated society to such a level of competence that our enterprise system was able to spawn the cybernetic revolution. The fact that jobs previously held by high school dropouts were disappearing could not mean that the schools had failed, but it did mean the schools had to undertake the mammoth job of meeting the demand for new educational competencies. (In 1900, less than five percent of American youth were graduating from high school. The rate graduating grew rapidly, with the consolidated high school movement and the Smith-Hughes Act, and reached 42 percent in the late 1930s under pressure to get the youth off the labor market. This dropped to 38 percent in the early 1940s as the shortage of labor attracted the youth into the war goods factories of World War II. In 1950, for the first time half of our American youth were graduating from high school. It has increased about 1.5 percent per year since then and is now about 80 percent.)

The American penchant for bigness, which has prevailed so long in our society, is based on the idea that the way to make things better is to make them bigger. The bandwagon began to move with force in education as James B. Conant and many others advocated new standards to increase the size of the school to overcome the "failures of the past." In response, the schools became larger and larger.

Homage to bigness was recently illustrated by the actions of a city school system in Pennsylvania. The retiring superintendent was honored with much affection by the teachers and school board members with whom he had worked for twenty-four years as chief school administrator. His accomplishments were reported in the local paper as follows:

"A new senior high school and four new elementary buildings were built and other buildings renovated, the school district was formed by joining [three other] school districts with the city system, and several new programs were initiated.

"During his years as superintendent, the school system grew in enrollment from 2,500 to 4,500; and the budget increased from barely $500,000 to almost $4 million."

No mention was made, in the local paper at least, of his pioneer efforts to make teaching an all-year profession and to make the school a community cultural center, nor his lifelong efforts to revise the curriculum and upgrade the learning experiences of the children and youth of the community.

(One subtle, but significant, reason why many alumni have supported the increase in size of a high school is to have a wider selection of good athletes in order to win more games, even though this limits the number of students who have an opportunity to represent their school in athletics.)

As Kirkpatrick said when analyzing the need for consolidation, "In making a business venture, it is fully proper to estimate the gains and the probability of gains as it is to estimate the losses and the probability of losses."[3] What, specifically, are the estimated gains or probability of gains in the construction of larger schools at this time? What are the estimated losses or probability of losses that might result from larger schools?

The basic reason for increasing the size of the school is to increase the quality of education; this occurs in several ways:

1. As presently keyed to the lockstepped, graded, and departmentalized system, it is necessary to have a student body large enough to have at least one class of students in each of the specialized courses, such as advanced physics, chemistry, mathematics, foreign language (third and fourth years), and many other activities. As long as the school is attuned to the lockstepped system, and the more diversified and specialized the courses of study become, *the larger the school must be.*

2. To the extent that specialized courses require classroom teachers with specialized talents, skills, or knowledge, the school must also be large enough to provide full-time employment for these teachers.

3. To the extent that specialized courses require specialized and expensive equipment, the school must be large enough to justify the acquisition of such equipment through frequent use.

These factors represent sincere efforts to deal with the dilemma of the public school system as it attempts to achieve its academic goals in the face of increased available knowledge, increased complexity of the tasks to be performed, increased diversity in future occupations of students, and increased demands by society for higher levels of performance.

Kirkpatrick argued that the school should bring urban and rural cultures together, to integrate the society that had been sharply dichotomized by technological developments that had taken place in the city but had not yet reached the farm. This is not unlike busing students or building educational parks to bring together the cultures of a city fragmented by social and economic forces.

The ever-increasing size of the school, then, is an attempt to increase the quality of education or otherwise meet the educational needs of our society, not only in terms of academic achievement but in social and cultural development as well. The fact that these are basic needs does not necessarily mean that the best approach is to build bigger schools. The objectives must be examined to make sure they are based on the real needs or expectations of the community and how the construction of the school will contribute to the attainment of these objectives. Are there alternative ways by which the objectives can be met? If so, which way is most appropriate in terms of meeting societal needs and community expectations?

1. If a major objective for increasing the size of the school is to add diversity to the curriculum, are there ways to add diversity to the curriculum without the increase in size?

It is rapidly becoming accepted that it is imperative for the schools to *individualize and personalize instruction* so that each learner may have opportunities to select learning experiences of his own interest and to pursue them at his own rate of learning. This eliminates the necessity of having a class of thirty students (or whatever a traditional class must be) for each subject or specialized course that is taught. Thus, one factor behind the need for a larger building will be eliminated.

2. If a major objective for increasing the size of the school is to provide competent teachers in specialized areas, are there alternative ways to provide specialized instruction?

As teachers learn how to individualize and personalize instruction, the role of the teacher changes. The teacher becomes more of a manager of the learning environment for students, and less an imparter of knowledge *at* students. He is responsible for his students' well-being and educational progress, helping them to seek and find answers to their questions rather than giving them answers. They learn to use a variety of resources, both material and human, within and outside the school. This process eliminates the need for continually increasing the size of the school to attract highly specialized teachers as the only way to expand the curriculum.

3. If a major objective for increasing the size of the school is to afford expensive instructional equipment, are there alternative ways of doing this?

Educational technology is rapidly changing. Hardware is being deemphasized (compared to recent years) as too impersonal and too expensive. Although the use of equipment like television and computer and other systems is likely to increase in the future, the use of terminals and other decentralizing devices greatly reduces the need to plan larger schools, simply to make their use economical. From the academic goals standpoint, the need for Taj Mahals in education is disappearing.

In a well-planned individualized program, the teacher-manager also serves as teacher-counselor. The teacher needs to know the personal growth and unmet needs of his students, and to be able to draw on resources (social, psychological, health, cultural, etc.) as needed. An established plan by which such resources are available on request, of course, must be provided.

The need for continued growth in the size of school is being made obsolete by increase in *flexibility*—in the curriculum, in staff utilization, and in utilization of resource materials. A school building, as used in the past, has little elasticity in its structure and use; it is a self-contained unit within which all learning under the jurisdiction of the school takes place. Elaboration in the curriculum necessitates increase in size of the building. The size and shape of the school correspond to the number of students and the contemporary curriculum and grouping practices.

If the teacher becomes a teacher-manager, helping students to learn whatever they need to know and to draw on the requisite human and material resources in the school or elsewhere in the community, and if the needs and interests of the students focus on the "real world," how much of the student's time will be spent sitting at his desk? If each student will be away from his desk a good deal of the time, how many desks will be needed? Will one desk serve more than one student?

What are the losses or probability of losses by the continued use of the approach of "continually adding on"? There is a growing feeling that the larger the school becomes the farther removed it is from the people, and the less sensitive it becomes to the "real world." Perhaps schools can get so large that the student and teacher become "lost" in the vastness of numbers.

There is also a feeling that larger schools are too costly, that they tend to include more "frills" and "gingerbread." At one time, a water pump was considered a "frill" that a school could not afford; the teacher could bring water in the "drinking bucket." We have long since considered readily available drinking water as essential. We expect schools to have lights and inside toilets. Some people still consider gymnasiums as extras; even more consider a swimming pool to be a frill. Some people are willing to sacrifice appearance, facilities, sometimes even safety, to save money, even though in their own homes and business establishments they want the environment to be comfortable and pleasant.

If the large school becomes too impersonal and too far removed from the people, as it seems to be, and with the teaching technologies making more individualized and personalized instruction feasible, perhaps schools in the future will be less centralized, more problem-focused, and more a part of all of life. Perhaps if schools cost too much, the architects and other school planners will carefully analyze the real building needs in terms of modern technologies of personalized instruction and design schools that are economical, practical, and still comfortable and pleasant, thus helping to carry out the inevitable function proclaimed by Winston Churchill, "First we shape our buildings, then our buildings shape us."

Notes

1. M. G. Kirkpatrick, *The Rural School from Within* (Philadelphia: J. B. Lippincott Co., 1917), p. 153.
    2. Ibid., p. 262.
    3. Ibid.

7 * The School of Tomorrow in Design

The American school is in a state of flux. This is an era of innovative ideas, pilot projects, experimental programs, and demonstration activities designed to individualize, nongrade, and team teach, using multimedia technology and differentiated staffing in efforts to educate the disadvantaged, to provide equality in educational opportunity, and to make the curriculum more relevant to the needs of the learner and society. Teachers are becoming familiar with such terms as behavioral objectives, competency-based instruction, systems analysis, and accountability. The general public is also being exposed to such ideas as performance contracting, the British infant school, the open space school, the open school, the free school, the storefront school, and schools within a school.

This search for new ways to operate the schools has been conducted with great hopes and aspirations by some, with pangs of anxiety and frustration by many, and with considerable disappointment and even anger by others. Probably most educators have experienced all these feelings as they strive to provide the kind of education our children and youth need.

In the 1971 annual report to Congress on the condition of

education in the nation, U.S. Commissioner of Education Sidney P. Marland described this ferment:

Change is in the air at all levels of schooling, and there seems to be less resistance to reform than was true even two or three years ago. For where circumstances are right and money available, school systems and universities have been willing to abandon routine in favor of novel, promising but untested techniques. . . . We find ourselves involved in an educational renaissance that has no ending, a ferment of advances that can only produce greater public expectation for further progress.[1]

There is a great deal of evidence, however, that not all innovations lead in the same direction. For example, there are individualized programs that provide opportunities for the learner to pursue the activities important to him, as well as individualized programs that prescribe and greatly limit his choices. There are programs designed to humanize the learning experience and others designed to mechanize it. There are team teaching programs designed to enrich the experiences of the learner and team teaching programs designed to lessen the responsibilities of the teachers by departmentalizing the elementary grades. In the past ten years many new courses have been designed with many millions of dollars of funds supplied by the National Science Foundation and the U.S. Office of Education to generate the skills and competencies our society needs, while some educators contend that education should be an end in itself and the learner should live for today. There are those who say the public schools have served our society well but need to change with the changing needs, while a growing number of others contend that the schools have failed and that the responsibility for educating our society should be turned over to private enterprises—the industrialists who have already demonstrated their ability to succeed.

Confronted with change, most of us have neither remained loyal to our traditional goals nor claimed a new role as ministers of change. We are drifting along between the past and the present. Our thoughts about school and education have been altered by forces we do not even recognize and are not involved in shaping. As Dr. Marland implied, if the money is there for almost any kind of an educational innovation, most of us are willing to jump on the bandwagon, grab a federal grant, and undertake a project to change—even though we do not have a clear understanding of what we are doing or why.

Redefining Our Basic Goals

We are in a crisis-oriented era, caught in the tensions between the "no longer" and the "not yet." We realize our schools are no longer adequate for the needs of today and tomorrow, but we do not yet know what needs to be done or how to do it. As a society, we need to clarify our basic goals or purposes and make a commitment to work toward those ends.

Speaking to that point, John Gardner, founder of Common Cause and former Secretary of Health, Education, and Welfare, in his continued effort to restore our vision and perspective and to steer us toward the basic goal of the American dream, stated:

The basic American commitment is not to affluence, not to power, not to all the marvelously cushioned comforts of a well-fed nation, but to the liberation of the human spirit, the release of human potential, the enhancement of individual dignity.[2]

Human dignity cannot be achieved for one man alone, however. As Adlai Stevenson so eloquently put it in his last speech to the United Nations Economic and Social Council in Geneva in 1965, stressing the interdependence of men, "We travel together, passengers on a fragile spaceship, dependent upon its vulnerable reserves of air and soil; all committed for our safety to its security and peace; preserved from annihilation only by the care, the work, and I will say, the love we give our fragile craft."[3]

If these statements by Gardner and Stevenson are right, as most of us would agree, then we must be concerned with not only the individual person but also the dignity of man, collectively, and the related integrity of nature.

Our nation and our world, today, are faced with three great crises: the environmental crisis, the human rights revolution, and the participatory crisis. The environmental crisis is comprised of the unsolved problems arising from the population explosion, the depletion of mineral and energy resources, and the pollution of life-sustaining resources. The human rights revolution is arising from the restless millions of people who are hungry, sick, ill-clothed, inadequately housed—without an adequate way to live or make a living—in a nation and a world that have the technological know-how but not the will to change these conditions. The participatory crisis arises from the growing demand of the young, the minorities, the poor, the women, and other special interest groups to participate in the decision-making processes that affect their lives and in the operation of our society.

As professional educators and concerned citizens, we should be addressing our attention to seeking solutions to the three great crises if we are to achieve human "ecolibrium" in a free society—a state of balance within and between the natural ecosystems and the social ecosystems through democratic processes. We should be asking ourselves these questions: How can we direct our efforts toward devising schools and educational programs designed to respond effectively to the basic human needs of individuals and to the urgent problems of society? What are the tasks that need to be done? How can we do them?

In our state of flux, we must ferret out and define the main issues that relate to educational change. We must be able to recognize which innovations take us away from our goals and which lead us toward them, and to choose accordingly.

Some of the key issues that must be resolved, as our society designs the school of tomorrow, are the following: Is public school education an end in itself or a means to an end? What is the appropriate use of technology in the educational process? What is the appropriate role of private enterprise in public education? How can we use most effectively the human and other community resources that will enrich the learning experiences of children and youth? How should our society provide for needed learning experiences on a continuous life-span basis?

Education—Means or End?

There are numerous approaches to the fundamental questions of education. One such question is: How do we provide quality education with equality in education? One of the responses has been individualization of instruction within the framework of the traditional school. Another response has been a more radical departure—the British infant school's informal method of education and similar programs: the "open corridor," the "integrated day," and the "open school." Central to all these is the commitment to meeting the educational needs of children through their self-fulfillment. The Wave Hill Open Classroom Program, operating in six elementary schools in New York City, is such a program. Its salient features are described by Wave Hill Director Joseph D. Hasset:

1. It capitalizes on each child's natural curiosity and desire to learn about the things that interest him by providing, or allowing the children to provide, or by a combination of both, a multitude of materials and learning experiences. In this way, each child can find, whether alone or in a group activity, what interests or challenges him at his present stage of development. By "materials" we do not mean manufactured educational materials, although some of them may be useful; rather, "materials" here means things found frequently in the child's environment that he wants to learn more about, or things deliberately introduced into his environment as "turn on" agents—that is, resources of motivation with many possibilities for educative projects.

2. It encourages the child toward inventive activity with whatever interests him at his own level of development. Reading, spelling, arithmetic, science, and art are not taught as distinct disciplines; instead they are learned as instruments that enable one to attain an objective or goal. The teacher must exercise his ingenuity in setting up these situations and in preparing the various materials to be integrated.

3. It is, therefore, an interdisciplinary approach. The student, generally speaking, learns not by subject matter, but by working on projects that bring into play a number of different "school subjects." The teacher's judgment determines which approach is called for at a given time with a given class.

4. The teacher ordinarily does not teach the whole class as a group, although he may do so if he considers it helpful. Instead, the teacher has the children work on projects either as interested groups or as individuals.

5. The teacher introduces a number of materials from nature, such as animals (gerbils, hamsters, turtles, goldfish, toads) and various types of plants to show the relationship among the things of nature, both "natural" and man-contrived. Here again, the principle is to present things in their context and to have the pupil come to an understanding of relationships among things and subjects in school.

6. It brings home the importance of environment to the child by emphasizing the effect of the environment on human living and by demonstrating that we can do a great deal about making our environment better for human beings.[4]

In a recent book, *Inequality: A Reassessment of the Effect of Family and Schooling in America,* by Christopher Jencks and others (New York: Basic Books, 1972), Jencks advocates that school life should be an end in itself. In reviewing this book in the NEA journal *Today's Education,* Becker and Darland state:

Jencks says, "If we think of school life as an end in itself rather than a means to some other end, such differences (as to whether schools are dull, depressing, even terrifying or lively, comfortable and reassuring) are enormously important." This observation may be the most important statement in the book. Kant held that every person was an end in himself and should be treated as such. Oh, that we could wave a wand and have an opportunity to function this way!

We'd add that "thinking of school life as an end in itself" is a means for each person to create a viable future for himself because he has learned the art of becoming. . . .

For teachers, a new struggle will begin. Currently, the public emphasis appears to be 180 degrees away from what Jencks perceives in speaking of "school life as an end in itself." Rather, we have a drive for a narrowly conceived concept of accountability based on the 3Rs. Is the public ready to create policy enabling the schools to carry out those functions for which it is best prepared? Is the public willing to make a long-term investment in both the preparation and beginnings of sustained reform? If the answer is yes, then the public must be prepared to work closely with teachers in shaping new alternatives within the context of the public schools.[5]

Becker and Darland further express the opinion that "such an approach is bound to be more expensive."[6] Perhaps the cost will depend more on the materials and equipment bought to carry out such a program. Probably the approach described by Hasset at Wave Hill, which capitalizes on "things found frequently in a child's environment," would even cost less. Furthermore, society is already making a huge long-term investment in the sustained reform of public education, and it expects reform to take place.

The most significant question may be whether an educational experience that is designed to be self-fulfilling for the learner (whether it is "education as an end in itself" or "education as a means to meeting the learner's immediate needs" is a semantic question) can also prepare him with the skills, knowledge, and concepts he will need to function as a member of society and to deal with society's urgent problems.

Limited evidence indicates that this not only is possible but may also be the most productive way to achieve the dual goals of meeting the basic needs of the individual and the society. This does not mean that a student can be merely turned loose to do as he pleases and still achieve these goals. It will require the skillful leadership of teachers to structure the environment so that the goals *will* be achieved.

In conclusion, it might be said that our schools need to design programs that will help each learner live for today but plan for tomorrow in order to achieve an enriched yesterday.

Use of Technology in Education

The second key issue, the appropriate use of technology in the educational process, will become a vital concern in designing the school of tomorrow. Technology, in its strictest (broadest) sense, includes the textbook and all other man-made devices commonly used in the classroom. Generally we think only of the audiovisual media as technology—motion pictures, filmstrips, slides, overhead transparencies, recordings, audiotapes, and more recently educational television (since its advent in the Hagerstown, Maryland, school system in 1956) and computer-assisted instruction (since its advent at Pennsylvania State University in 1958).

Use of all these devices has developed rather slowly in most public schools for several reasons. The machines used to present the programs are expensive, operation of the machines places a burden on the classroom teacher that he is reluctant to accept, the burden of scheduling both the equipment and the software (film, filmstrip, tape, etc.) is time consuming, the arrival of both equipment and software at the place and time needed is uncertain, and the quality of the programs available in general is mediocre.

Several trends in software development and equipment design herald a new era in education. In response to the emphasis on individualized instruction, many materials are being designed for individual use rather than class group presentation; instructional materials are becoming more accessible for classroom use through such devices as cartridge-loading tapes and projectors, low-cost prints and duplication, microfilming, and dial access; more self-contained multimedia packages of materials, often organized to accompany a particular textbook, with the order of presentation, teacher use, and evaluation activities built in, are becoming available; there is an increase in the number of eight-millimeter single-concept films available, and the general quality of many of these materials is improving.

Although all these trends will have an impact on the total instructional program, it is very small compared to the technology in the offing for the near future. This potential and its impact on the school of tomorrow are aptly described by Wall and Williams:

By the turn of the century (2000 A.D.), we speculate that schools will have undergone a fundamental change. Advanced communications technology, coupled with competency-based instruction, will provide two of the basic features traditionally provided by schools: (1) providing information and training, and (2) certifying the quality of student performance. It will generally become more convenient and economical to provide these features outside of what we have known as a traditional school building.

Information and training, heretofore provided by teachers to pupils in a classroom, will be offered by a vast array of communication devices that will make it possible for the learner to receive instruction in a variety of settings, and the learner can pick out that which is most important for him. A variety of tools will break our dependence on the classroom teaching setting. Some such devices are: audio and video cassettes that can be played through a television receiver, and miniature computer terminals in each home attached by satellites to information banks throughout the world that will expand the speed and accuracy of learning. Holography, a concept that just a few years ago was thought to be wild speculation but today is reality, will allow free-standing, three-dimensional images to outdate the television set. Three-dimensional films are already in the laboratory production stage of development.

Through technology, students will have access to the best teachers and the most carefully thought out and executed learning experiences. The numerous traditional school buildings that are found in cities today will be replaced by a few Community Learning Centers, conveniently located for all to use.[7]

John G. Kemeny, President of Dartmouth College and a renowned expert in computer technology, spoke in similar terms (except for the holograph) in 1965, on the occasion of dedication of the Kiewit Computer Center at Dartmouth. He painted a vision of home-centered learning services in twenty-five years (1990). Reflecting on his 1965 prediction, Kemeny commented in 1972:

I still feel that the date 1990, which I chose at that time, was a fortunate one. Although everything I describe here and elsewhere about computer terminals in the home could be in effect by 1980, it is more likely that this will not become a reality until a decade later. This is not because there are any technological difficulties but because people have demonstrated discouragingly during the past decade that they are extremely slow in taking advantage of the potential of new technology.[8]

These developing technologies will no doubt provide, as never before, alternatives to consider. As pointed out in chapter 3, the public school emerged as a system to teach members of society what they needed to know but would not learn adequately or conveniently without a formal transmitting structure. It appears at this time that modern computer and television technologies have the potential of providing a convenient and flexible formal instructional structure in the home, or wherever we desire to locate it, to transmit knowledge. It seems likely that these devices, coupled and used wisely, can not only perform many, if not most, of the services provided by the traditional teacher in a lockstepped program, but also do them more effectively.

One of the great needs of our society today is more humane schools—schools where human beings interact with each other, sharing ideas and challenging each other's thoughts. A very significant, though perhaps unrecognized, part of the curriculum is developing social behavior. It is not likely that machines will displace teachers, but the role of the teacher in the instructional process is likely to change significantly.

The Role of Private Enterprise

Closely related to the issue of technology is the relationship between the public school and private enterprise. The idea that such a relationship exists is, of course, not new. Virtually all educational supplies, materials, and equipment are produced by private enterprise; and, in order for companies to produce the supplies and equipment the schools need and want, there has to be a close relationship between the two. That relationship, however, is changing in several ways.

Historically, textbook publishing firms were primarily family-owned enterprises, and usually the families had come from the field of education. After World War II, with the baby boom and increased enrollments in schools, the demand for textbooks grew rapidly. This demand called for the use of new printing presses and other equipment being developed in the printing industry, which were expensive. The result was that textbook companies were acquired by larger industrial firms. This change was accompanied by a rapid expansion of the educational technology industry producing hardware to be sold to schools. During World War II, the military services successfully used multimedia techniques for rapidly training large numbers of servicemen. They paved the way for introduction of these techniques in the public schools.

The Department of Defense still operates a worldwide network of training centers, schools, colleges, and universities for the military services and is, of course, concerned about the effectiveness of this massive school system. In order to stimulate thought about improved application of technology in the educational process, particularly within the industrial and educational communities, Assistant Secretary of Defense (Manpower) Thomas D. Morris, in January 1966, invited the National Security Industrial Association to assist the Department of Defense in sponsoring a conference on "The Systematic Application of Technology to Education and Training." The

Office of Education and the Department of Labor were also invited to cosponsor the conference, which was held in Washington, D.C., on June 14 and 15, 1966. The outgrowth of this conference was Project ARISTOTLE (Annual Review and Information Symposium on the Technology of Training, Learning, and Education). The first ARISTOTLE symposium was conducted in Washington in December 1967 and was attended by many notable and distinguished individuals, particularly from the military, the industrial establishment, and the government. Few educators from the public sector attended. The opening address was presented by Leonard A. Muller, Director of Education Systems, International Business Machines. The tone of the conference is reflected in his opening remarks:

> As a point of departure, I would like to quote from three sources.
>
> In a recent issue of *Harper's Magazine,* Michael Harrington began an article with the lead sentence: "American business has long scrambled over the common good in its haste to pursue for profit." He then added with a touch of irony: "Now the corporation proudly threatens a new, distinctive, and paradoxical danger. Instead of creating social problems, they are going to solve them."
>
> In another magazine article this year, a professor of education, Richard Wynn, wrote: "Although schools should use the new technology that holds promise for better instruction, the potential danger of industry and government controlling education is formidable. . . ." To underline his point: "These mighty industrial combines are well-staffed, well-financed, well-organized, and unencumbered by inarticulate or modest salesmen."
>
> My last quote comes from one of our Federal Trade Commissioners, Mary Gardner Jones, who warns against becoming so fascinated by technology that, ". . . we concentrate our efforts on computerizing ever-widening areas of our educational processes and permit the new technology to turn our education into an assembly line dispenser of information. . . ."
>
> These, we are told, are the perils of business in education: its preoccupation with profits, its reach for control, and its insensitivity to humane goals.
>
> Admittedly, I have taken these quotes from a larger context; and they do not completely reflect each author's total view. Nevertheless, I suggest they are early warning signals. They reflect the concerns, the legitimate concerns, of highly responsible and intelligent people. They represent problems; real problems that we cannot dismiss. . . .
>
> We have to make certain that the profit-making machinery of business can properly serve the noncommercial ends of education, that the benefit of technology can be secured without compromising our humanistic values and historic heritage.[9]

The next speaker at this symposium was Robert W. Locke, Senior Vice-President, McGraw-Hill Book Company. He pointed out that much of an individual's education is acquired outside the formal institution called school; for example, children learn many things at home, even before they enter school, and more vocational education takes place in industry than in schools. "Thus, we *see* the world of education in much broader perspective than before; education does not begin and end at the schoolhouse door. This is the first new assumption we have got to accept."[10]

Locke pointed out that the armed forces are the largest educational system in the nation; that for many young men the education supplied by the Department of Defense is more significant than that provided by the local school systems; and that many of the educational innovations of the past generation had their first tryouts in the armed forces. He continued:

> A more startling development is the delegation to industry of responsibility for running Job Corps centers because this puts profit-making firms in charge of important bellwether educational institutions that are paid for with public funds. This is in sharp conflict with the concept that educational institutions should be run by public boards, either elected by the public they represent or appointed by their peers; and its *educational* results have been better than many people expected. Its success has even led to the suggestion that profit-making firms might be invited to share in the management of more conventional schools or colleges, perhaps through the device of public corporations. . . .
>
> Therefore, if we are going to develop a perspective about education that is broader than formal school and college education, we must assume that much of education will be controlled by groups other than public bodies, and that some of them will be interested in getting a return on their investment.[11]

This, of course, has been followed by the movement advocating performance contracting and voucher systems, led primarily by the Office of Economic Opportunity, and by the broader movement for alternative schools financed by public funds.

In an address to the San Francisco Chamber of Commerce, Donald Rumsfeld, Director of the Office of Economic Opportunity, explained these two experiments:

> Under performance contracting, a school district contracts with a specific group—a private firm or its teachers' association, for example—to provide instruction to children in the school district who are not achieving at grade level norms. Contractors are paid only to the extent that they are successful in improving the educational skills of the children they instruct. In the experiment, the contractors will be paid only if they increase skills by more than one grade level. They will make a profit only if skills increase by 1.6 grade levels, nearly four times the average now attained in schools serving poor neighborhoods.
>
> Within broad policy guidelines established by the school board, the contractors are free to use a variety of approaches to achieve their results. Some are

using computers and teaching machines. Others are using special instructional materials. Some are offering incentives to teachers and even to the students themselves. But from the standpoint of potential educational reform, the more significant feature of this concept is accountability: no success, no pay.

The experiment is under way in eighteen school districts and will be expanded to twenty-one districts. In each of the eighteen districts, one of six firms is under a performance-based contract to teach math and reading to a sample of youngsters in grades 1, 2, and 3 and 7, 8, and 9. In the additional three districts, the teachers' organization or the school district itself will be the contractor. Nearly 30,000 students will be a part of this experiment with approximately 12,000 receiving the experimental services. An independent, third party organization is carrying out the evaluation of the performance of the private firms; and a follow-up study of the students will enable us to determine the impact of improvements of basic skills on subsequent school performance.

The second experiment, now in the planning stage, will deal with ways of increasing the students' and parents' role in choosing the type of education they receive. There are many ways of doing this.

In one aspect of this test, poor parents would be provided with vouchers roughly equal to the current per-pupil expenditures of the public schools in their community. The parents will then be free to use the vouchers as tuition in the school of their choice; public, private, or parochial. Safeguards would prohibit use of the vouchers to finance religious instruction or to encourage or permit segregation. As a result, for the first time, poor parents would be able to exercise some opportunity to choose, similar to that now enjoyed by wealthier parents, who can move to a "better" public school district or send their children to private schools. [12]

These inroads in public education pose a threat to the future of the American public school system. In the process, our society may "throw the baby out with the bathwater." School is much more complex than reading, writing, and arithmetic. The public school has served our society in many subtle ways, adapting to the changing needs of our society and helping to develop American character. We could lose these benefits and responses to the needs of our society if we reduce formal education to those skills and competencies that are easy to measure, and then contract the responsibility of teaching them to vested interests.

The support for alternative schools comes from several sources. First, and perhaps foremost, the private enterprise sector recognizes that public education has become big business, ranking second only to national defense, and that there is a profit to be made if it can be opened up. Secondly, the parochial schools are in financial difficulties and would welcome some form of financial aid from public funds, as President Nixon promised in his 1972 campaign. Thirdly, some parents, teachers, and others are extremely discontented with the public school as it exists and believe the best way to achieve the changes they desire is through a system of alternative schools.

There is an old saying: "The best defense is a good offense." The major force promoting alternative schools is the purported failure of the public school system. The best way to safeguard the public school as a viable system of a free society, then, is to define carefully what kinds of public schools we really need and to develop them.

Use of Community Resources

A fourth basic issue is how we can use most effectively the human and other community resources that will enrich the learning experiences of children and youth. The issues that our schools must face here concern liability, accountability, and credibility. As schools begin to open up and become more a part of the "real world," the students will become more active instead of sitting in their seats all day. It may be expected that accidents will occur, and the question of legal liability will arise. As the students are encouraged to become more self-directed and to pursue those aspects of learning most important to them, they will be less under the direct and immediate supervision of the teacher. To what extent will our society support this new freedom, and to what extent will it hold the teacher accountable for the whereabouts and conduct of the children at all times? If we use human resources in the community as a source of enriched learning, we will be using the skills and talents of people who are not trained in teacher education. For example, a high school student may serve an internship in court with a judge for a week as a part of an investigation of social problems in a community. To what extent will the use of nonteachers create a teacher certification problem? What procedures will be used to give students credit for the study they undertake at places other than the school building and other than under the direct supervision of the teacher? These problems must be resolved if our schools are going to have the necessary flexibility to meet the needs and expectations of society.

Life-span Education

Finally, the need for continuous, lifespan education will raise the issue of the domain of the free public school system at the local community level. Traditionally this has included grades one through twelve and, in some states, kindergarten, but there are social pressures to expand it at both ends.

The Education Policies Commission, in 1965, called for an extension of public educational experiences downward to children in infancy:

Lack of love or care in the home can have disastrous impact on the child's self-concept, attitude toward the world, speech development, and general ability to learn. Some parents, whether (economically) disadvantaged or not, deprive their children of love and care. The reason may include personality problems of the parents, marital problems, over-crowding in the home, or the need for parents to work outside of the home during the child's waking hours. Such situations are particularly common among the (economically) disadvantaged. In these cases, it is hard to believe that there is an age too young for nursery school experience; therefore, the public should make provision for this experience beginning in infancy.[13]

In considering this as one of the imperatives in education, the Pennsylvania Governor's Committee on Children and Youth, Task Force on Education, added:

This should not be an attempt, nor looked upon as an attempt, to take a child away from his mother at an ever-earlier age with the school usurping more and more of the responsibilities of the home. To the contrary, early childhood education is inevitably and basically a parental undertaking. The role of the school is to provide opportunities for those learning experiences an individual needs but does not acquire in his informal learning situation. It should be the basic right of every individual to attain the kinds of experiences in his early childhood that will permit him to mature as a healthy, well-functioning individual. Early childhood education does and must take place in the home, and appropriate training of parents (or substitute parents) should be provided as needed *to help make the home an enriched environment with a wealth of growth-stimulating experiences.* Home situations vary greatly; and for many children, the best hope to experience many of these needed opportunities is a parent-child center or a nursery school, even though there is no adequate substitute for home and mother love. Furthermore, the development of certain skills of socialization such as playing and working with other children, following directions and learning to be self-directed in a peer situation, can best be achieved by all children in group settings not normally available in the home.[14]

Another area of expansion that the school may be called on to make is the transition from school to work. At a time when the primary prerequisites for employment were physical strength and the appropriate age, the school was little concerned about teaching occupational education. Now it is becoming a part of the curriculum, beginning at the primary level. As the schools become more flexible and more closely related to the world of work, it may be that they will become more concerned about, and even responsible for, assisting the individual in his efforts to attain gainful employment.

Also of public concern is the transition from one job to another, the transition from one way of life to another, the use of leisure time by the adult population, as well as by children and youth, and the transition from work to retirement. Our society may decide that a community learning center for all people in the community is the most appropriate vehicle to help them adapt to many of the changes our society is undergoing.

As our schools explore the various changes in educational programs, and as our society toils with the issues before it, they are giving shape to the school of tomorrow. Out of the present state of flux will emerge the patterns that seem to provide the most appropriate solutions in terms of how our society perceives the problems. How accurately we perceive the issues and how wisely we select the alternatives depends on how well informed we are about the human situation. This, in itself, is a formidable educational need.

Professional educators, citizens' committees, and others who undertake study of the structure of the school should consider these matters carefully and accept responsibility for informing the public in such ways that intelligent decisions can and will be made.

Notes

1. Sidney P. Marland, *The Endless Renaissance: The Commissioner of Education Makes His Annual Report*, U.S. Department of Health, Education, and Welfare, Office of Education, Publication no. (OE) 72-101 (Washington, D.C.: Government Printing Office, 1972), p. 2.

2. John Gardner, *Time*, January 20, 1966, p. 18.

3. Adlai E. Stevenson, speech given before the United Nations Economic and Social Council, at Geneva, Switzerland, July 9, 1965.

4. Joseph D. Hasset and Arline Weisberg, *Open Education: Alternatives within Our Tradition* (Englewood Cliffs, N.J.: Prentice-Hall, 1972), p. 6.

5. James W. Becker and Dave Darland, "About Christopher Jencks' New Book—Inequality," *Today's Education*, December 1972, p. 33.

6. Ibid.

7. Charles C. Wall and Richard C. Williams, "Relating Communications Technology to Competency-based Education," *Educational Technology* 12, no. 11 (November 1972): 50-51.

8. John G. Kemeny, *Man and the Computer* (New York: Charles Scribner's Sons, 1972), p. 82.

9. Leonard A. Muller, "Proposed Guidelines for Industry in Education," in *Education, Government, Industry,* Proceedings of Project ARISTOTLE Symposium, December 6-7, 1967 (Washington, D.C.: National Security Industrial Association, 1967), p. 5.

10. Robert W. Locke, "Proposed Guidelines for Industry in Education," p. 10.

11. Ibid.

12. Donald Rumsfeld, "Experiments In Education," speech delivered to San Francisco Chamber of Commerce, September 23, 1970 (Washington, D.C.: Office of Economic Opportunity, 1970), pp. 5-6.

13. Educational Policies Commission, *American Education and the Search for Equal Opportunity* (Washington, D.C.: National Education Association, 1965), p. 9.

14. Task Force on Education, *Imperatives in Education that Man May Survive and Live in Dignity* (Harrisburg, Pa.: Committee on Children and Youth, Governor's Council on Human Services, 1970), p. 3.

8 * Transition to Flexible All-Year Schools

Most educators who have carefully analyzed the issue of all-year schools agree that in the long run our schools must be flexible in terms of curriculum content, instructional processes, time structures, and the place of learning, at the same time retaining credibility, accountability, and economic efficiency. Most educators also agree that it would not be practical to attempt to implement an all-year program in their own schools at this time. The problems of redesigning the curriculum, retraining the entire staff, educating the public, and working out all the other details are too complex, too time consuming, and too expensive.

A practical plan that will make it possible for any local school district to begin the transition without delay has been undertaken by the Pennsylvania Department of Education, in conjunction with Clarion State College.

The first step was to establish the legal base on which the program could operate. The second was to establish a research-demonstration model of the flexible all-year school. The third step was to establish a state service center to work with those schools interested in any aspect of the program. The fourth step was to provide financial assistance to local school systems desiring to initiate plans for an all-year school program.

To establish the legal base, the state legislature enacted a law providing for maximum flexibility in the time structure of the school. The law provided that:

Upon request of a board of school directors for an exception to the aforesaid daily schedule, the Superintendent of Public Instruction[1] may, when in his opinion a meritorious educational program warrants, approve a school week containing a minimum of twenty-seven and one-half hours of instruction as the equivalent of five (5) days, or a school year containing a minimum of nine hundred ninety hours of instruction as the equivalent of one hundred eighty (180) school days.[2]

The Pennsylvania State Board of Education adopted new General Curriculum Regulations (see Appendix B) to help achieve the goal of increased flexibility:

It shall be the policy of the State Board of Education through the Superintendent of Public Instruction to delegate to a Board of School Directors the greatest possible flexibility in curriculum planning consistent with a high quality of education for every pupil in the Commonwealth.[3]

These regulations provide for flexibility in terms of *what* a person studies, *when* he studies, *where* he studies, *how* he studies, *with whom* he studies, and the *rate* at which he proceeds, all through an orderly structure.

State and federal funds were appropriated to Clarion State College to construct a research-learning center, which will include a 300-pupil, nursery through high school, research-demonstration model of the flexible all-year school. Construction of the building has been completed, and the Center is expected to open in mid-1973.

The State Department of Education established the Pennsylvania Center for Year-Round Education as a component of the Research-Learning Center at Clarion State College. This component is now operational and has the following assigned program activities:

Develop interpretative materials to explain basic assumptions and operation of various all-year school plans and research related to their application.

Develop techniques and procedures for analyzing community needs and the impact of various all-year school plans for those needs.

Develop guidelines for use of such techniques and procedures by local schools.

Conduct general information conferences and workshops about year-round education and/or related programs increasing options and flexibility in curriculum, educational process and time schedules.

Provide inservice and technical assistance to local schools considering the feasibility and/or the implementation of such programs.
Disseminate information about applicable research and innovative programs through reports, guidelines, and newsletters.[4]

Financial incentive for local school systems was provided for by a program revision of the Department of Education budget, which established an item in the budget for experimental or exploratory programs on year-round education. In accordance with the Statement on Year-Round Education adopted by the National Seminar on Year-Round Education (see chapter 2), no particular plan was selected by the state but the matter was left open for local consideration. For the first year of operation under this program (1972-73), a sum of $500,000 was appropriated by the state legislature. A similar amount is anticipated in subsequent years. Seven pilot studies were approved and are under study in the program's initial action.

This chapter provides some detail on: (1) how the law and curriculum regulations, which were designed to provide maximum flexibility consistent with a high quality of education, are being applied in the development of the flexible all-year school program at the Research-Learning Center of Clarion State College; and (2) the services being provided by the Pennsylvania Center for Year-Round Education to help local schools implement flexible instructional programs.

Any program must be based on assumptions that are held to be true, and must be acceptable to those who would accept the model as a valid approach to attaining the goal. As a point of departure, the Research-Learning Center established the following basic assumptions on which the research-demonstration model would be developed (in essence, these assumptions are based on the concepts and data presented in earlier chapters of this book). It is assumed that:

1. The basic role of the public school system of our society is to provide the learning experiences *all* members of society need and would not otherwise acquire or could acquire most appropriately in school. This implies that: (a) school experiences are designed to augment the students' total learning experiences, which take place not just in school but in their total environment and throughout their lifetimes; (b) if quality education is to be achieved by the school, the educational experiences provided by the school must be relevant and applicable to the real needs of the individual as he

functions in society; and (c) appropriateness is achieved when the school experiences are compatible with the life-styles and living patterns of the members of society.

2. All members of our society have in common many experiences, needs, and goals, and therefore do have and need *common educational experiences*. One's self-concept is an important factor in how well he learns, and a need common to all is to have a learning environment that provides opportunity for the individual to explore new ideas and live new experiences in a situation where he (a) feels accepted (wanted, loved) by his family, his peers, and others with whom he interacts, (b) succeeds in the activities that he is expected to do to the extent that he expects to be successful as a person, and (c) succeeds in the activities that are important to him and to the people who are important to him. It is recognized that each individual is unique in terms of specific needs, experiences, competencies, capacities, and aspirations. *Equality in educational opportunity* does not mean that all students of a given age or grade are taught the same things in the same way at the same time. Rather, it means that all individuals have an equal chance to learn what they need to know, when they need to learn it, in ways and in an environment that are most conducive to them to learn it.

3. Our society is undergoing continuous change, and educational needs change as our society changes. The school must have built-in processes by which it is able to assess needs so that it may (a) retain what is useful and effective, (b) eliminate what is obsolete or nonproductive, and (c) add what is missing but needed. Further, if an individual is to see order and direction in change and adapt to it, he must acquire the basic skills and knowledge that are essential to understanding basic principles and their interrelationships, and be able to make broad generalizations as a basis for drawing conclusions and making decisions in solving his own problems.

4. In a free society it is always the citizens who are ultimately responsible for the choices made and the actions taken that shape the future. The public school is a key social institution and, as such, must be responsible to the citizens. If the school is to maintain credibility, it must provide opportunities (a) for the citizens to let their needs and concerns be known and (b) for professional educators to translate this into programs of action designed to meet the needs in ways consistent with the commitments of our society and

our knowledge about human needs and the learning processes. If the school is to maintain accountability, it must provide ways for the citizens to understand the goals of the school, how they may be achieved, and how successful the school is in achieving them.

5. Finally, *optimum economic efficiency* in the operation of a school is attained when: (a) the unmet educational needs that are to be dealt with by the school are clearly defined; (b) the resources that are available to meet educational needs are identified (these include the human and material resources of the community as well as those commonly thought of as "belonging to the school"); (c) the alternative ways in which the resources may be used to meet the needs are carefully considered; and (d) the most appropriate alternatives are selected, in terms of how the job can be done effectively and how the resources can be used most efficiently.

Flexible Schedules

The flexible all-year school is designed to operate all year except for holidays or at other times when there is no "demand" for its use. With continuous operation there is no "beginning" or "ending" of a school year. (For budgetary purposes the fiscal year, July 1 to June 30, is used.) There is no time when all or groups of students are scheduled to be on vacation for an extended period. It is the responsibility of each student, with written approval of his parents, to establish and maintain a study schedule, indicating when he plans to be enrolled in school and when he plans to be on vacation. In general practice a student will be enrolled in school regularly five days a week unless other time schedules are arranged. There is no definite time limit as to how far in advance he must file for vacation. Except in cases of emergency, however, a student should plan ahead, to provide for an orderly termination of his study before he goes on vacation.

A student may take one or more vacations each year, however long desired, provided that he is enrolled in school a minimum of 990 hours (900 for elementary) during a fiscal year beginning July 1 and ending June 30. He may exceed the minimum, however, as he and his parents choose, within the operational time structure of the school.

The standard school day and the standard school week are the same as are scheduled by the local school district in which the Center is located (Clarion Area School District), except as may be scheduled otherwise by the school faculty or arranged by a teacher and students with whom he is working. In accordance with the state school codes, a teaching member of the staff may arrange for a student or group of students to be in school attendance before or after regular school hours and for a longer or shorter period of time than the standard school day or school week.

A student may enter school any time of the year provided that he has met the age requirement. Initially, the age requirements established by the local school district will be used by the Center. This matter is under study, however, and it is anticipated that a policy will be established to allow a student to begin kindergarten or primary school whenever he is "ready." Chronological age may be used as the major criterion. For example, a child may be allowed to enter kindergarten when he attains the age of five years, or to enter primary school when he attains the age of six, no matter what time of the year this occurs. This would solve the problem of a child being only a few days too young to enter school in September and having to wait another year. He could enter in October, or December, or March, or whenever he *is* old enough. The major concern in this procedure is not how the flexible all-year school would manage to accept the child any time of the year, but what would happen to him if he transferred to another school where the graded system was used with September as the starting date. It is likely that this open-entry-date policy will be established, and any parent entering a child other than during early fall will be counseled as to the possible implications in case the family should move to another community.

Individualization of Instruction

It is obvious that such a flexible time schedule cannot be followed unless the instructional program is also flexible. (This is an important point to remember. A school district cannot initiate a flexible all-year school program unless and until the instructional program is flexible enough to adapt to the flexible time structures.)

In accordance with the basic assumptions and the recommendations of the Educational Policies Commission of the National Education Association, instruction will be individualized. The commission report, which was officially adopted by the NEA, states:

The school should be so arranged that each child moves ahead at his own best rate, without fixed standards holding him back in learning or convincing him that he is retarded. Educators realize full well that no two children can be expected to learn the same thing in equal time, but few schools have been structured to correspond with this fact. This failure has worked to the detriment of the disadvantaged children in particular, in part because of the invidious comparisons made, in part because of the stiffness and formality of the typical school structure and expectations. Many children who learn slowly can learn well and in considerable quantity; the lock-step may deprive them of the time they need, and their failure to progress at a standard speed may deprive them of the will to try any more. Their learning may be reduced, rather than stimulated, by the insistence on grade standards.

. . . .

True individualization of programs provides an excellent opportunity for demonstration of the teacher's professional competence. Execution of a centrally determined syllabus, with all children more or less in the same mold, is stultifying for the teacher and, in particular for disadvantaged children, often fruitless.

Another important step in the direction of individualized instruction would be elimination of excessive emphasis on the remedial concept. The argument here is not semantic: all education is in a sense remediation, in that it is an attempt to fill in gaps. But education should rather be viewed as a permanent state of progress, the duty of the school being to provide the proper stimulation for any child, wherever he is intellectually and whatever his interest may be. Concepts that force teachers to see all children solely in relation to an artificial standard militate against this view.[5]

At the Center, individualization of instruction does not mean each child works alone all day at some machine or with programmed materials in independent study. Rather, it means that the curriculum is adapted to the needs of the individual student. He will work with machines and programmed materials at times. He also needs to do things with people—to share experiences, to challenge and be challenged, to work with others for common goals as part of a team.

The major characteristics of the individualized and personalized program include: (1) opportunities for self-direction and self-selection of learning experiences in terms of one's own recognized needs and interests; (2) self-pacing so that each learner may progress in any area of learning at his own best rate; and (3) diagnosis of individual needs, to prescribe individual learning experiences to the extent necessary to overcome serious individual problems or to guarantee acquisition of essential skills, concepts, and knowledge.

Anyone living in a society must function within certain limitations and constraints; one person does not have a right to infringe upon the rights of others. For example, we drive on the right side of the highway not only because it is the commonly agreed on and legal custom, but because it facilitates social order. A student who pursues learning experiences of his own choice must also use prudence in making his selections, and to do this he must be aware of the limitations and constraints as well as the opportunities that are available to him.

The Pennsylvania General Curriculum Regulations establish standards in terms of courses that must be offered and completed for a student to graduate. A student must accumulate a total of thirteen course credits to graduate from high school. Logically, within this framework a high school student would select activities that would help him graduate if they were available and of interest to him.

A teacher-counselor is available to all students to assist them in choosing their goals, taking the steps necessary to achieve these goals, and selecting the appropriate activities. It should be emphasized that the goals are those of the student, not the teacher, the school, or the state, but they exist within the framework of the expectations of the school and the state.

Progressing at one's own best rate also has limitations and constraints. A student should not be subjected to undue pressure or harassment to keep up with the group when he is unable to cope with the situation, but if a group of students agrees to meet at a certain place at a certain time to go on a field trip, each student should be there on time. The commitment to work with a group, if made voluntarily, carries with it the obligation to do one's share in the group activity.

Diagnosis of individual needs and prescription of learning experiences to the extent necessary are an important teacher-counselor function, just as obtaining medical advice from a physician is sometimes an important function to help a sick person regain his health. Except in extreme cases, however, a highly prescribed program should not be the "main course" of a student's curriculum.

Course Requirements

Pennsylvania's General Curriculum Regulations specify by subject area a minimum course of study for elementary and secondary schools.

Elementary. The course of study at the elementary level *shall* include a planned course in each year in the following: fine arts (art and music), health, language arts, mathematics, physical education, science, and social studies. Modern foreign language and practical arts *may* be included in the elementary curriculum.

Junior high. The course of study at the junior high level *shall* include, as a minimum, two planned courses (during the three years of grades seven through nine or their equivalent) in each of the following: English, laboratory science, mathematics, and social studies, including United States and world cultures. In addition, it *shall* include one planned course in developmental reading, fine arts (art and music), industrial arts, and homemaking. Physical education *shall* be provided twice weekly. Modern foreign language *may* be offered.

Senior high. The senior high school curriculum *shall* include three planned courses in English, two in social studies, including United States and world cultures, and one each in mathematics and science. In addition to the required courses, elective courses, as a minimum, *shall* include adaptive physical education, business education, conservation and outdoor education, consumer education, fine arts, at least two foreign languages, one of which shall be modern foreign language given in a minimum four-year sequence, home economics and family studies, industrial arts, laboratory sciences (including biology, physics, and chemistry), at least three years of mathematics acceptable for college admission, and personal and family survival.

Additional elective courses at all levels. In addition to the courses mentioned above, a school *may* offer additional planned courses at any of the levels (elementary, junior high, and senior high) in general areas of mathematics, social studies, foreign language, humanities, English, fine arts, vocational-technical education, home economics, science, industrial arts, family studies, driver education, and aviation education.

Multidisciplinary courses. Any planned course may be integrated with other courses or may be taught separately.

Flexibility in Course Offerings

The curriculum regulations offer flexibility in course placement and manner of study as may be appropriate for all learners, including slow learners and advanced students.

Subject placement. At the discretion of the school district, courses offered below senior high school level may be used to meet graduation requirements if the standards for awarding credit are equivalent to those used in the equivalent senior high school course.

Preparing for occupational skills. Any pupil fourteen years of age or older who is not benefiting from the regular program (as determined by his teacher) may, with the permission of his parents and the school principal, have an individualized schedule that contains subjects from which he can profit, to prepare him for an occupational skill. All such programs shall include appropriate instruction in citizenship and communication skills.

Method of study. Students may earn credit through correspondence study, attendance at summer school, Saturday classes, evening classes, study at summer camps, independent study courses, or in any other manner considered appropriate by the principal and approved by the superintendent of public instruction.

College advanced placement. College-level advanced placement courses may be offered as part of the senior high school program of studies.

Part-time college enrollment. High school students may enroll part-time in college with the approval of the high school principal.

Full-time college enrollment. Exceptionally able students may leave high school before the senior year to attend approved colleges full-time at the discretion of the school district. The high school diploma will be awarded to these students on successful completion of the freshman year in college.

Awarding Credit

One of the difficult problems most schools have in scheduling classes is the Carnegie unit of credit. While retaining the basic structure of the Carnegie unit, the curriculum regulations provide flexibility in awarding credits.

Unit of credit. For general course planning purposes only, a unit of credit shall be defined as a planned course of 120 clock hours.

Fractional units of credit. Courses may be planned on the basis of fractional credit at the discretion of the principal in consultation with the teacher.

Laboratory work. Laboratory hours in art, English, social studies, mathematics, science, business education, and modern foreign languages may be equated with classroom hours.

Exceptions to hours of instruction. In accordance with the policies established by the Board of School Directors, and at the discretion of the principal in consultation with the teacher, credit may be awarded (1) for satisfactory completion of a planned course regardless of the time actually spent in class, and (2) to regularly enrolled students who pass an examination that assesses mastery of a planned course, regardless of the time spent receiving formal instruction in the course.

Planned Courses

A planned course shall consist of at least (1) a written statement of *objectives* to be achieved by students, (2) *content* to be used to reach objectives for which credit is awarded at the junior and senior high levels, (3) *expected* levels of *achievement,* and (4) procedures for *evaluation.*

Thirteen planned courses for credit in grades ten, eleven, and twelve shall be required of all students for graduation from senior high school. Thirteen planned courses are not necessarily equivalent to thirteen units of credit. Planned courses may be offered as a unit of credit or any fraction thereof.

Library of Planned Courses

At one time the student's major source of information was the teacher or tutor, when books were scarce and the primary teaching tool was a slate. As the printing technology advanced, textbooks became (and perhaps still are) the heart of the curriculum. In recent years, again with the advance of the printing technology and other technologies of communication, the school library is becoming the hub of the planned curriculum experiences provided by the school. Perhaps by the year 1990 or 2000 the computer, with television and/or the holograph, will replace the library as a ready source of references and instructional material, but the school will probably retain an important function in our society, because it provides the human touch—the interaction of people as they pursue common goals, as they challenge each other's thinking, as they share common experiences.

As an organizing force for cohesiveness and direction, not replacing the library but to be used in conjunction with it, the computer center and the communications center comprise the library of planned courses. This is the foundation of the self-renewing curriculum of the flexible all-year school at the Research-Learning Center.

Included in the library of planned courses will be all the planned courses that are collected or developed as courses of study for use by the students in the Center. Although this will include elementary curriculum, outlines at that level will be less formal since academic units of credit for graduation are not involved. The major focus will be on the secondary level courses.

Authorized course defined. An authorized course, as defined by the curriculum regulations, is a planned course approved for inclusion in the secondary curriculum. In addition to the four requirements specified above (objectives, content, expected achievement, evaluation), to be accepted for inclusion in the Center's library of planned courses, an authorized course must include: (1) an outline or list of materials or equipment needed (if any) and/or a bibliography of study materials; (2) the estimated number of clock hours normally required to complete the course; (3) specifications as to prerequisites (if any), subject area (whether it satisfies a state requirement or is offered as an elective), and other pertinent data; and (4) any special conditions, such as time or place, under which the course may be offered. The course must also be approved by the school course-of-study committee.

Length of planned courses. A unit of credit is defined as a course normally completed in 120 clock hours, which is equivalent to one forty-minute class period of study each day of the 180-day (thirty-six-week) school year (180 x 40 minutes = 120 hours). A school year is commonly divided into semesters of ninety days (eighteen weeks), and one-half unit of credit is awarded for the standard one-period-a-day courses. The various all-year school plans divide the school year into whatever units of time fit the plan, and give fractional credits on a prorated basis. The four-quarter plan divides the standard school year into three sixty-day (twelve-week) periods, and gives one-third credit for a standard course. Atlanta, Georgia, has developed 850 such courses for its high schools' optional four-quarter plan. The quinmester and the 45-15 plans divide the standard school year into four units of forty-five days (nine weeks) and give one-fourth credit for a standard course that meets one period a day, each school day of the week. Dade County School District, Florida, has developed approximately 1,600 courses to be used in its high schools under the quinmester plan. (The leaders of both the Atlanta and Dade County programs see this wide range of optional courses as one of the most significant aspects of their all-year school programs for improving the quality of education.) Various schools throughout the country have developed mini-courses that are six weeks in length as a way to give students a greater option in course offerings. The Research-Learning Center is developing mini-mini-courses of fifteen days (three weeks) in length, with emphasis in utilization of community resources. All these courses can be equated in units of credit and are measured in fractions of a year. They can easily be converted into clock hours, as indicated below:

Unit of study	Weeks	Days	Clock hours	Units of credit
School year	36	180	120	1
Semester	18	90	60	1/2
Quarter	12	60	40	1/3
Quinmester	9	45	30	1/4
Mini-course	6	30	20	1/6
Mini-mini-courses	3	15	10	1/12

Types of planned courses. The library is a collection of planned courses covering as many aspects as possible of all subject areas that may be offered for credit in high school. As the library matures it will be able to offer a wide range of courses of varying lengths of time and, accordingly, varying amounts of credit, covering almost any subject area that may be of interest to the student. This includes courses designed for independent self-study; small-group and large-group instruction; courses designed for use at school, in the community, at camp, or other appropriate places; courses that capitalize on the human resources of our society as well as public and private institutions, organizations, and other resources. These can be student or teacher initiated, or courses otherwise available to the library.

Using the library of planned courses. The library is designed to be used much as a library of books is used; teachers and students select from the library the courses a student or group of students wishes to pursue for credit. In Dade County, for example, a team of educators from each high school reviews the list of courses available (all in quinmester length) that could be offered by the high school in terms of staff competencies, facilities, etc. The list of possible course offerings is then submitted to the students, who indicate the courses they would be interested in taking, and this becomes the course offering for the following year. The operation of the library of planned courses at the all-year school is more flexible. Courses may be selected at any time by the teacher, who will be working with a group of students; together they decide which course they wish to pursue as a group, or by a student or small group of students who wish to pursue a course more or less independently. When a student selects his own course he must receive the approval of a teacher certified to teach in that field who will serve as his adviser for the course.

A Self-renewing Curriculum

The library of planned courses will serve as the base for a self-renewing curriculum. The schools have been widely censured for their failure to keep abreast of the changing needs of society and students' interests. Criticism has been made of the narrowness of the curriculum, the obsolescence of curriculum content and instructional procedures, and the effort and time required to bring about changes in the curriculum.

The self-renewing curriculum will be continuously open to new input and adaptation to relevant needs and interests. Figure 8-1 illustrates the processes by which the system operates. (The numbers used in explaining the system correspond with the numbers used on the flow chart.)

1. *Input of planned courses for the library.* Any person, committee, organization, public or commercial agency is invited to submit a planned course at any time for consideration to be included in the library of planned courses. An individual student or committee of students wishing to pursue study in any area of interest or concern may submit a plan for such a course in accordance with the established criteria for planned courses. When students want to pursue the course as soon as possible, the process will be expedited.

2. *Planned courses screening committee.* A screening committee composed of selected students, teachers, college students in teacher

Figure 8-1. Library of Planned Courses for a Self-renewing Curriculum

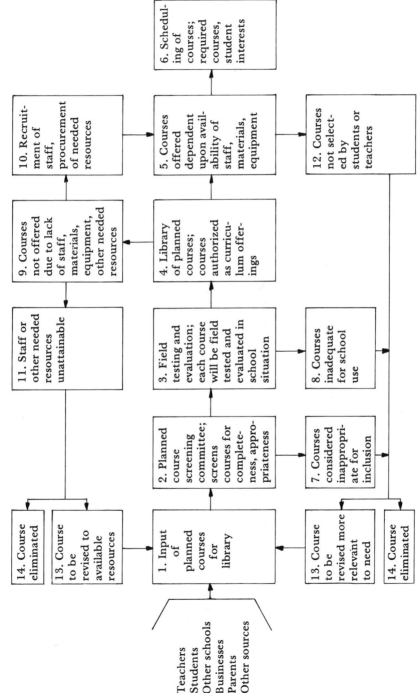

education, parents, and specialists in the various areas of study, will be responsible for examining each planned course in terms of: (a) completeness, in accordance with the established criteria for planned courses; (b) accuracy and authenticity of content; (c) reasonableness, in terms of time allocation and procedures to be used; and (d) appropriateness, in terms of cultural mores and value systems.

3. *Field testing and evaluation.* Each course will be field tested and evaluated before it is included in the library of planned courses for general use. The Center will not field test all courses; courses already in use and obtained from other school systems or commercial agencies may be included without further testing. Courses initiated locally, however, will be field tested. A course initiated by students or teachers at the Research-Learning Center may be field tested by them. Courses initiated by college students as part of their teacher education program or by teachers in other school systems as part of in-service programs may be field tested in other public or private schools and accepted by the library.

4. *Library of planned courses.* Courses that have been field tested and considered adequate will be approved as authorized courses and made available for use not only by the Research-Learning Center but by other interested schools as well.

5. *Courses offered.* The courses offered to the students at the flexible all-year school of the Research-Learning Center will depend upon availability of staff, materials, equipment, and/or other resources needed to conduct the class or to pursue the study. This, of course, is a judgment each school using the library of planned courses will have to make.

6. *Scheduling of courses.* Students and teachers may schedule any course from the approved list at any appropriate time, provided that any special conditions the course itself specifies are met. It is the teacher's responsibility to make sure that the courses selected meet state requirements for graduation from high school. In addition, students may request courses of interest to them, electives that will help accumulate the total number of credits for graduation but that may not satisfy specific subject area requirements.

7 and 8. *Courses considered inappropriate or inadequate.* It is the responsibility of the planned courses screening committee to make a value judgment in deciding whether or not unsatisfactory courses should be rejected completely and thereby eliminated, or revised. In

either case the planned course is returned with an explanation to the person who submitted it.

9. *Courses not offered due to lack of resources.* A course cannot be offered if the appropriate resources are not available. Certain courses in oceanography cannot be offered appropriately in the mountains of Appalachia, for example, nor can a course in gemstone cutting be offered unless a lapidary and the necessary tools are available.

10. *Recruitment of staff and procurement of needed resources.* If the school can arrange to obtain the services of qualified personnel and/or the necessary equipment, the course could then be offered. For example, the school may be able to arrange with an institute of oceanography on the coast to offer the course to students who are able to go there, or a local lapidary may agree to teach a planned course in gemstone cutting under the supervision of the certified art teacher.

11. *Staff or other needed resources unattainable.* If it appears probable that the qualified staff and/or the needed resources will never be attainable, the course must be revised or dropped. For example, a planned course to analyze microscopically the characteristics of rocks from the moon may not be realistic; it is not likely that the government will make moon rocks available for analysis by high school students. The course might be revised to study reports by scientists who *have* analyzed the rocks from the moon, and to do microscopic analysis of tektites, considered by many scientists to be pieces of the moon that came to earth as a shower of meteorites, and which are readily available.

12. *Courses not selected by students or teachers.* Courses that have been offered over a period of years but were not used will either be eliminated or resubmitted for revision.

13. *Courses to be revised.* Courses considered to be of promise for future use but that were rejected because they were inappropriate, inadequate, unattainable, or unattractive, will be returned to the appropriate person or agency together with an explanation of what revisions are expected.

14. *Courses eliminated.* Courses that appear to be of no further value will be eliminated.

With the input of planned courses continuously open to those who wish to affect curriculum change, the use of the courses based on need and interest, and a process for eliminating the obsolete, the end result is a self-renewing curriculum.

The Teacher-Counselor-Ombudsman in the Program

In the flexible all-year school, where a great deal of emphasis is placed on human development, self-directed learning, and the democratic process, the role of the teacher can be described more as that of a teacher-counselor-ombudsman than as the traditional disciplinarian and imparter of knowledge. He still has teaching responsibilities but the way he manages the situation is different.

For example, if an English teacher has thirty students, all pursuing a programmed or other independent study course, her function would be simply to assist each student with any aspect of the program the student could not understand adequately by himself. It should make little difference where each student is in the course. Each would be on his own, continuing from where he previously left off and pacing himself as he chooses or is able. In fact, it would not make any difference in the function of the teacher if each student were pursuing a different course, provided all the courses were within the range of the teacher's competencies.

It is not likely that all the students would choose independent study courses at the same time. This could of course be arranged, but given a free choice of several other options along with independent study, it is not very likely to happen. It is more probable that an average group would be involved in several approaches. Some students may follow independent study courses, while there may be several small groups each pursuing a different course in English, with ten to twenty students in a teacher-led program. As this major core of students works together, interacting with the teacher more or less continuously, the teacher also supervises and assists the individual and small group activities as needed. This may seem an unmanageable situation to the traditional teacher or administrator who is unfamiliar with the open school or individualized programs in which students have an opportunity to select their own pursuits. Those who have actually experienced this situation, however, realize that it is not only manageable but the discipline problems decline and student activity becomes more purposeful. In our example, the English teacher may be responsible for some students who are not even present. With parental approval, one or more students may be at the local newspaper office serving an apprenticeship in journalism for credit. The teacher, in cooperation with the supervising journalist at the newspaper office, would be responsible for determining that the student had attained the expected outcomes of the course in order to receive credit.

The counselor role of the English teacher is to assist all students assigned to her for English activities, in selecting appropriate planned courses. It is her responsibility to make sure that each student (1) is aware of his own strengths and weaknesses in English, (2) is aware of the options he has in selecting courses that will help him overcome his weaknesses, (3) knows the state requirements in English for graduation and where he stands in that regard, and (4) continues at a reasonable rate in selecting and completing courses that will help him achieve his goals in English. Course selection, it should be remembered, is a continuous process, since the courses vary from 10 to 120 clock hours, and each course may be completed in more or less than the estimated average time. A student may choose to spend more time than the traditional class period on a particular course; for example, a student may complete a ten-hour planned course in one, two, or three days.

The ombudsman role of the teacher is to advise her students about any academic problems they may have. She may, for example, resolve scheduling difficulties, or arrange for tutorial assistance from another high school student in a "buddy system" or from a college student under a teacher education program. Guidance with personal problems also enters into this function, in cooperation with the certified guidance counselor on the staff.

The Student in the Program

The program of the flexible all-year school is designed to provide maximum opportunity for the student to seek those activities most meaningful to him and to adjust his schedule to his own felt needs. It is also designed to provide him with sufficient guidance and counseling to give him personal support when he needs it and to assist him in making prudent selections in his curricular activities.

A new factor is each student's responsibility, in cooperation with his parents, to schedule his own vacations when and for how long he chooses. Along with this, he has the responsibility of making sure he is enrolled in educational activities a minimum of 990 hours during each fiscal year (July 1 to June 30). A student who attends classes five days a week during regular school hours has little difficulty keeping track of his own time and knowing how many days of vacation he can schedule during the year. However, if he deviates from the standard schedule, it is his responsibility to make sure that his time sheet reflects his "overtime" so he can take compensatory time off if he wishes. He may get this extra time in school in a variety of ways. In our example, a student, with his parents' approval, may study at the local newspaper as a learning experience in journalism (or printing or several other courses). He may work a regular eight-hour shift for three weeks, carrying out the responsibilities outlined in the planned course and completing it for one full credit toward graduation. (Eight hours per day, five days a week, for three weeks is 120 clock hours.) Certification of completion of the course for credit is the responsibility of the English teacher, but the student himself must arrange with the teacher for the competency test or evaluation at the end of the course, and make sure his time sheet reflects his overtime. In this case, he would have worked two and one-half hours per day longer than the regular school day of five and one-half hours. In the fifteen days, then, he would have accumulated credit for thirty-seven and one-half hours compensatory time.

·A student may sign up at any time for a course that extends beyond the regular school day, but he must make prior arrangements with the teacher who will evaluate his achievement and the resource person with whom he will be working (who must also be approved in advance by the school principal as a resource person for that particular course). He may, for example, select a ten-clock-hour planned course in bird migration (under the supervision of the biology teacher) that includes two Saturday morning bird-watching hikes with an ornithologist, trapping and banding birds, and learning from the ornithologist about bird migration patterns, in accordance with the planned course outline. He would earn one-twelfth of a credit and ten hours compensatory time off. He may also schedule evening classes, such as ceramics at a local pottery shop for art credit, or working at the public library to learn about library science. In planning such activities before and after school, evenings, and weekends, the only limitation is that a planned course must be prepared in advance to outline the learning experiences to be achieved and arrangements made with competent personnel to provide the necessary instruction or internship, in cooperation with the appropriate certified teacher.

The student should plan his vacations in advance and, in cooperation with the teachers, plan his courses so that all courses that involve group activity end before he leaves. Independent study courses can be held in abeyance while he is gone, since he can begin where he left off when he returns.

Transition from the Traditional to the Flexible All-Year School

To change from the standard school year to an all-year school program requires (1) a general revision of the total curriculum, (2) the cooperation of the total staff, and (3) public acceptance of the program. Trying to meet all three conditions can be frustrating to the school administrator, but when they are met the change in the school year takes place on a total school basis.

The transition from the traditional to the flexible all-year school, however, can be gradual and orderly. The change toward greater flexibility can begin now in any school, with just one teacher in just one class if necessary. Any teacher who has access to the library of planned courses can begin to introduce flexibility into the curriculum by selecting a variety of planned courses that would make the semester or year of work more vital to the students.

Suppose, for example, a social studies teacher decides to submit a list of planned courses to his students that they may study instead of the traditional course in world cultures. He may feel the need to keep them all in the same course at first, and may select a short course as an initial tryout. As the students see the possibility of the options, the teacher may decide to allow some to study independently or in small groups, using planned courses designed for use in that way, thus giving the students a wider range of choices in curriculum content and instructional process. One teacher, then, can begin introducing a variety of options in one course, scheduled during the regular class period.

The teacher may decide to expand this practice to all the classes he teaches. He may do this as long as he does not violate the schedules of other teachers. He cannot hold his students over for a time longer than the regular period, for example, and he must be sure that his students complete all courses by the end of the semester, if the school reschedules the students at this time, and by the end of the school year. Within these constraints, however, he may schedule a different combination of planned courses in each of his classes, as illustrated in table 8-1. He can do the same thing with individuals or small groups of students in any of his classes.

Table 8—1

	First semester (18 weeks)			Second semester (18 weeks)		
Class 1	Quarter (12 weeks)		Mini (6 weeks)	Mini-mini (3 weeks)	Quarter (12 weeks)	Mini-mini (3 weeks)
Class 2	Quinmester (9 weeks)	Mini (6 weeks)	Mini-mini (3 weeks)	Quarter (12 weeks)		Mini (6 weeks)
Class 3	Mini (6 weeks)	Mini (6 weeks)	Mini (6 weeks)	Mini-mini (3 weeks)	Quinmester (9 weeks)	Mini (6 weeks)
Class 4	Quinmester (9 weeks)	Quinmester (9 weeks)		Quinmester (9 weeks)	Quinmester (9 weeks)	

Subject to administrative and parental approval, this teacher would also be able to schedule students for planned courses that involve evening or weekend activities, or any other time not in conflict with the school's regular schedule.

If one teacher in each of the basic subjects agrees to work as part of a team, the school could form a school-within-a-school for about one hundred students and give them much greater flexibility. Working as a team, these teachers could allow the students to study any combination of courses, scheduling their time in any way that was appropriate. (The flexible all-year school at the Research-Learning

Center is small, with one group of 100-125 students and a team of teachers at the secondary level.)

This concept of scheduling opens the way for any school district to use the courses of varying lengths of time now being developed by the "pioneer" schools that are moving toward year-round education. It also facilitates the development of what most educational leaders in the all-year school movement recognize as the ultimate goal: the flexible all-year school. Beginning with one teacher or a team of teachers, a school could expand the program until it was operating a flexible school program within the standard school year. Once this is achieved, it would be simple to initiate the flexible all-year school program, providing a wider range of flexibility in scheduling and continuous progress.

A school district can actually begin a good all-year school program without waiting to develop the flexibility in the regular school year described above. A school can begin what could be called a regular school year with a flexible summer program. Teachers (or a school) who are reluctant to risk the innovation of flexibility in the regular school year may choose to introduce it during the summertime.

The idea of the summertime being a safe time for flexibility and innovation was alluded to by Charles H. Boehm, Superintendent Emeritus of the Pennsylvania Department of Public Instruction, at the Second National Seminar on Year-Round Education:

> In [summer], lay people more readily accept new ideas. In the nineteenth century we often used the basement for innovative enterprises. The first science laboratories were constructed in these substandard basement rooms. When they became respectable they moved upstairs and in came the shops and homemaking rooms. In many schools art, music and some commercial classes followed by the same route. In fact the outside toilets were first located in the basement before they were brought upstairs.
>
> In our basementless buildings we have had to use the summer school. We could provide a cheerleaders course in the summer school much easier than during the regular term. In one school the practical arts teacher taught the seventh grade program to fifth and sixth graders during the summer. The program was so successful that a fundamental shift in curriculum is now under way in that area. We found that we can teach everyone to swim in six or eight weeks in the summer. Instruction in skiing too will require a flexible winter schedule. Driver education has often been introduced in the summertime.[7]

A school district that operates a summer school could easily introduce concepts of flexible scheduling and the use of an array of planned courses during the summer and, as Boehm suggested, move these practices into the regular school program when they become respectable.

This chapter has focused largely on the secondary program because the major hangup is in finding ways to maintain credibility and accountability at the level where graduation credits are involved. The flexible use of the planned course retains credibility because all courses have stated objectives and expected outcomes. Attainment of these outcomes is always assessed by a professional educator certified to teach in the area being measured. Accountability is maintained because students receive academic credit only for the work they accomplish, and the scheduling of courses is designed to meet all state academic requirements.

The basic principles of flexibility apply to the elementary level as well; the reader is referred to books like Hasset and Weisberg, *Open Education: Alternatives within Our Tradition*[8]; *The Elementary School—Humanizing? Dehumanizing?*[9]; Don Glines, *Creating Humane Schools*[10]; and Jack Edling, *Individualized Instruction, A Manual for Administrators*[11].

Beginning Flexibility with Individualized Reading

One of the major concerns of teachers and parents is the teaching of the basic reading skills. Techniques of self-selection of reading materials are commonly used in many schools today, and can become the nucleus for individualizing other subjects as well. Children given a wide choice of reading whatever they want tend to select books that relate to what they are studying in science, social studies, and other subjects. Teachers who individualize the reading program soon find that programs in the other subject areas integrate with reading, almost automatically becoming individualized themselves. (For a presentation on individualized reading made by this author in 1962 to the parents of a second grade class, at the time the teacher was introducing the program in her classroom, see Appendix C.)

The teacher's managerial role is to help students learn what they need to know, whenever they need to learn it, and in whatever ways they can learn it best. This certainly is not a new concept. Few teachers will admit to starting all the students at the beginning of the textbook and pacing them rigidly through the book to finish at the end of the semester or school year. Most teachers do introduce some flexibility into the classroom: they divide students into subgroups or committees for various activities; they assign special projects to individual students; they use printed materials in addition to or in place of the textbook; they use a variety of multimedia instructional resources to enrich the course of study; they call on the talents of the human resources of the community. The multiple use of planned courses is just one more step ahead. Planned courses can be designed to be pursued in large groups, small groups, or on an individual basis. A teacher can easily manage a situation in which individuals and/or small groups of students pursue different courses while he focuses his attention on the major group.

Given the options provided by planned courses that can be pursued individually or in groups in varying blocks of time, any student can plan his schedule so as to tie up loose ends whenever he needs to depart from school, then reenter any time he is ready. Once this flexibility in scheduling is established, the school can operate continuously without the rigidity of start and stop schedules of the whole school or sections of students. The quarter, trimester, quinmester, and other schedules for major sections of students would be unnecessary and unduly limiting. The transition will be completed, and the flexible all-year school will have evolved.

Notes

1. By official action of the state legislature, the Pennsylvania Department of Public Instruction is now called the Pennsylvania Department of Education and the title Superintendent of Public Instruction has been changed to Secretary of Education.

2. Public School Code of 1949, amended July 3, 1969 (Act no. 80).

3. Regulations of the State Board of Education of Pennsylvania, General Curriculum Regulations, chapter 7, adopted by the State Board of Education on March 17, 1969.

4. Contained in articles of agreement between Pennsylvania Department of Education and Clarion State College.

5. Educational Policies Commission, American Education and the Search for Equal Opportunity (Washington, D.C.: National Education Association, 1965), p. 11.

6. Ibid.

7. Charles H. Boehm, "Year-Round Use of Schools as They Relate to the Needs of Youth," opening address, Proceedings of the Second National Seminar on Year-Round Education, Harrisburg, Pennsylvania, April 5, 1972, p. 10.

8. Joseph D. Hasset and Arline Weisberg, Open Education: Alternatives Within Our Tradition (Englewood Cliffs, N.J.: Prentice-Hall, 1972), p. 141.

9. *The Elementary School—Humanizing? Dehumanizing?* (Washington, D.C.: National Association of Elementary School Principals, NEA, 1971), p. 168.

10. Don E. Glines, *Creating Humane Schools* (Mankato, Minn.: Campus Publishers, 1971), p. 281.

11. Jack Edling, *Individualized Instruction, A Manual for Administrators* (Corvallis, Ore.: Oregon State University, Continuing Education Publications, [1971]), p. 137.

9 ✻ Role of the State in Year-Round Education

Attempts were made during the Constitutional Convention of 1787 to allow the federal government legislative power over education in this country. George Washington, Charles Pinckney, and James Madison called for a national university, national seminaries for learning, and national public education institutions.

The Constitution of the United States adopted in 1788 made no mention of public education, however. Furthermore, the Tenth Amendment, adopted as part of the Bill of Rights, provides: "The powers not delegated to the United States by the Constitution, nor prohibited by it to the States, are reserved to the States respectively, or to the people." By interpretation of this amendment, education remained a residual power retained by the states. Most state constitutions recognize education expressly as a responsibility of the state, and the legislatures in all states have enacted statutory authority for appropriations to administrative agencies to provide for the education of children and youth of the state.

Local school districts, legally, are an administrative convenience to maintain public schools as a state function. The districts are quasi corporations, and their school board members are technically officers of the state who are selected locally under state law. The Indiana Supreme Court held in 1890 that local school boards derive all their authority from state statutes and can exercise no powers except those granted or those that arise from the necessary implication of a granted power.[1]

In accordance with the federal Constitution, state constitutions also vest primary responsibility for public education in the states. State legislatures have delegated responsibility for direct operation of most schools to local educational agencies and have established a state educational agency to administer the program. (Hawaii has a single state school system with no delegation of authority, and other states administer some schools directly.) The "general welfare clause" of article I, section 8, of the federal Constitution provides the basis for the increasing number of federally funded programs to support public education; but public education is clearly the responsibility of the states.

The Politics of Year-Round Education

Public education is an integral part of local, state, and federal governments and is involved in all three branches of each: legislative, executive, and judicial. It is widely believed, however, that the purposes of education are best served when it is somewhat removed from partisan politics and political patronage. Nevertheless, the continued increase in cost of operation is making education more and more subject to political control and direction. The recent *Serrano* case in California and similar cases in several other states are likely to have far-reaching impact on operation of the schools. Court judgments in these cases have declared that a system of financing education that is based on local property taxes is unconstitutional because it is biased in favor of the rich (providing greater opportunity for quality education in the wealthier districts). It appears that alternative tax systems that provide greater equality in educational opportunity must be devised. School financing is likely to be a political issue that may greatly affect the relationship between local and state educational agencies. It can also have major impact on the structure of schools and the all-year school movement.

The state education department typically operates under pressure from local educators and citizens, on the one hand, and from the governor and the legislature, on the other. Governors and legislators, under strong pressure from tax lobbyists with considerable power and influence, often seek to hold down state financial assistance to local schools and to find ways to economize on the operation of the educational program.

With educators supporting year-round education as a way to improve the quality of education and, at the same time, increase the economic efficiency of operation, state legislatures across the country are now considering the possibility of legislation to implement full use of school buildings. This greatly increases the need for strong leadership, particularly by state departments of education, to make sure the legislatures are fully informed about the pros and cons of year-round education and the educational, social, and economic implications of each of the various plans.

On the surface the matter seems simple and clear. The school buildings are not used during one-fourth of the year. Economic efficiency could be gained by full use in either of two ways: (1) have the children go to school longer and graduate in fewer years (the eleven-month plan), or (2) divide the students into four sections and schedule three of the sections to attend school each of the four quarters of the year (the mandated four-quarter plan). As the discussion in previous chapters indicates, the matter is far more complex than most people realize. Unless the state departments of education provide strong and positive leadership, legislatures are likely to make hasty decisions that can complicate rather than improve educational programs and economic efficiency.

New York Developments

The New York legislature was the first to take a major step forward in examining year-round education. In doing so, however, it assumed that the eleven-month plan or some modification of it was the logical solution to full utilization of the schools. In 1963 the legislature directed the state Department of Education to

design demonstration programs and conduct experimentation to discover the educational, social, and other impacts of rescheduling the school year from the present thirteen year system to a twelve or eleven year system but still providing as many instructional hours or more than are now available under the present thirteen year system.[2]

A Coordinator for Rescheduling the School Year was employed by the Department of Education for a six-year period to carry out this legislative mandate. Several experimental designs were developed, and four school districts conducted pilot programs to test the plans: Central School District #2, Syosset; Union Free District #10, Commack; Cato-Meridian Central School, Cato; and Hornell School District, Hornell. None of the programs is currently in operation, and the legislature never passed a law that would allow ongoing programs.

Florida Developments

The Florida legislature passed a bill in 1972 authorizing and directing its state Department of Education to develop a detailed plan for implementation of "an extended school year of 200 days of instruction divided into four quarters of 50 days to allow a condensation of the thirteen school years (kindergarten through grade 12) into twelve years without a loss in total instructional time."[3] The plan is to be developed in conjunction and cooperation with the college of education of a state university. A pilot program is expected to begin in 1973-74.

Texas Developments

The Texas legislature is the only one to date that has enacted a statewide change in the basic structure of the schools. Its 1971 law mandated that all school districts in Texas operate on the quarter plan, but they are not required to conduct a fourth (summer) quarter program.

Before the adoption of this law the Speaker of the Texas House of Representatives appointed a committee to study the feasibility of adjusting the schools to a (mandated) four-quarter system. The committee held public hearings in Amarillo, Dallas—Fort Worth, Houston, Odessa, and San Antonio. At the outset of each meeting the people were assured that no student would be required to attend school more than nine months a year, no teacher would be required to teach more than nine months a year, and all members of a family could attend the same nine months on request. The meetings were open to questions and comments from the audience. On the basis of these hearings the committee concluded that (1) the curriculum should be divided into sixty-day quarters, (2) state financial assistance should be allowed for school attendance during any quarter (but no additional state assistance should be provided for students in attendance more than nine months), and (3) any school district should be permitted but not required to operate a fourth quarter. These recommendations became the essence of the new law. It provided:

The Central Education Agency shall prepare a reorganized curriculum based on operation of the schools on a quarter basis. The revision shall be so structured that the material covered during the present school year of two semesters is covered in three three-month quarters. The agency shall distribute this restructured curriculum to each school district in the state in sufficient time so that the new curriculum can be put into operation beginning with the 1972-73 school year.

The tentative guidelines prepared by the Texas Education Agency for implementation of this law are included in Appendix C. After specifying that no district was required to stay open all four quarters, the law stated:

(a) A school district may choose to operate all or some of its schools for all four quarters of the year. This choice shall be approved or disapproved by the district school board in a regularly scheduled open meeting. If a district so chooses, no credit for average daily attendance under the Foundation School Program may be given to the district for attendance by any one student more than three quarters during any one school year. Attendance by a student for his fourth quarter must be financed either by the student on a tuition basis or by the district from its own funds at the option of the district.

(b) A district operating all four quarters of the school year shall decide which students are to attend school during which quarters. However, schedules shall be so arranged that all members of a family attending the schools of a district may attend the same three quarters. Children who had not attained age six on or before September 1 of a current school year may enroll for the next quarter in which a beginning class is offered immediately following their reaching the age of six during that year.

Michigan Developments

The Michigan legislature appropriated $100,000 in 1968 for

grants to school districts for feasibility studies to be conducted by districts for extending the regular school year beyond the present required amount of time, no one district's grant to exceed $20,000. No grants shall be made for summer school programs. Grants shall be made in accordance with rules of the State Board of Education.[4]

Forty-seven school districts or groups of school districts submitted applications to conduct the feasibility studies. Grants were awarded to six projects: Ann Arbor, Freeland, Northville, Port Huron, Utica, and Okemos, East Lansing, and Haslett, cooperating in one study. The legislature appropriated an additional $87,000 for the continuation of five of the studies for the 1970-71 school year.

As an outcome of these feasibility studies the following recommendations were made for changes in legislation so that

the Extended School Year concept could become a viable option for local school districts: (1) allow kindergarten children to enter school on the first day of the next scheduled instructional time unit after their fifth birthday, (2) provide for 180 day *equivalency*, and distinguish between days of student instruction and days of school district operation for instructional purposes, (3) stipulate that no student shall be absent for more than two consecutive segments of the school district's established calendar, (4) modify the State School Aid Act to provide for additional funding to school districts operating all-year school programs, and (5) lay the legal basis for changing Child Accounting Rules and Regulations.[5]

Two pilot programs are currently in operation, one in an elementary setting and the other in a high school setting. Others are awaiting legislative appropriation.

Pennsylvania Developments

The leadership role performed by the Pennsylvania Department of Education, described in chapter 8, is unique in the nation. Recognizing the frustration resulting from conflicting reports about the various plans, the Bureau of Curriculum Development and Evaluation of the Pennsylvania Department of Education called a meeting of the national "spokesmen" for different plans in October 1969. The participants sought some "common ground" from which to develop guidelines for state and local school systems in studying the issue. As chairman of the Pennsylvania State Committee on Year-Round Education, the author synthesized the thinking of this group into a proposed position paper, *A Statement on Year-Round Education* (see chapter 2 for the text), and presented it to the Second National Seminar on Year-Round Education in Harrisburg, Pennsylvania, in April 1970, which unanimously approved it. The paper subsequently was widely distributed and approved by other groups. It has been published by the Education Commission of the States, the Council of

State Governments, and numerous journals and reports on year-round education. In Pennsylvania it has been approved by the Department of Education, Committee on Year-Round Education; the Governor's Council on Human Services, Committee on Children and Youth; and the Council on Year-Round Education.

The statement makes the basic assumption that school time structures need change but that no one plan is the right answer for everybody. Three recommendations are directed specifically at the state level and need to be implemented by each state if the all-year school movement in the United States is to mature. It is recommended that each state (1) take appropriate action to provide enabling legislation and/or policies permitting flexibility of programming so that various patterns of year-round education may be explored at the local level, (2) take appropriate action to provide state school aid on a prorated basis for extended school programs, and (3) encourage experimental or exploratory programs for year-round education through financial incentives or grants.

As described in chapter 8, the Pennsylvania Board of Education revised the curriculum regulations to provide maximum flexibility in curriculum planning; the legislature established 990 hours as a school year; the Department of Education established the Pennsylvania Center for Year-Round Education and a research-demonstration model of the flexible all-year school at Clarion State College; and the legislature approved a budget of $500,000 a year to encourage pilot programs in year-round education. At this writing, there is a bill pending in the legislature to provide state financial support on a prorated basis for student attendance beyond the standard 180 days (990 hours) in approved all-year school programs.

Virginia Developments

Virginia is developing a program similar to that of Pennsylvania. The Virginia Polytechnic Institute and State University and the state Department of Education are developing an Institute for the Study and Development of Year-Round Education. The primary purposes of the institute will be to conduct research, to provide development and evaluation services to schools, to disseminate information and research findings, and to develop a preparatory program.

The Virginia Board of Education adopted a position paper on year-round education in January 1972, encouraging exploratory programs using various approaches:

Feasibility studies of year-round education conducted by the State Department of Education in conjunction with a number of local school divisions suggest that full use of the calendar year to promote more effective educational programs is a valuable resource for improving the quality of education in Virginia. However, policy decisions relative to the possible adoption of year-round school programs require firm evidence of the merits of the various plans for year-round operation of schools. The State Board of Education provides professional support and encourages local school divisions to undertake research and development projects to provide this evidence. Funds have been requested to support research and development projects on year-round education during the 1972-74 biennium.

Many scheduling arrangements are possible in a year-round school calendar. However, realization of the potential for better education through year-round school programs entails more than changes in calendars and schedules. Prominent among the desirable changes in policies and practices are provisions for shorter courses of instruction, fewer sequential courses, and a change in emphasis from hours of instructional time to the achievement of instructional objectives. If these conditions have a reasonable chance of being achieved, the year-round operation of schools has great potential for improving education through more effective use of time, staff, and facilities. The development of greater breadth, depth, and flexibility in the curriculum is facilitated, as well as the development of more individualized instructional strategies and techniques. More effective use of the instructional staff can be achieved through optional contracts, greater differentiation of staff roles, and wider use of paraprofessionals. Year-round use of school facilities has obvious advantages: their availability for instructional purposes is increased, and capital expenditures can be reduced. Although some of these benefits can be realized in the traditional nine-month school year, the potential flexibility inherent in year-round school programs can greatly facilitate their achievement.

The statement described both fixed and optional attendance plans and recommended the 45-15, the optional four-term, and the continuous-term plans as prototypes for research and development studies. Studies of other plans were also encouraged.

A decision to undertake a research and development project should be preceded by a careful assessment of the feasibility of each plan as it relates to the community's educational needs and resources. The ultimate value of year-round education as a resource for improving the quality of education will be determined by the evidence gained from carefully designed and thoroughly executed research and development studies.

The Virginia Department of Education is also funding feasibility studies and pilot programs.

Conclusion

Each state department of education is unique, just as each local community is unique and each person is unique. Each department has unique circumstances and must deal with the issues of year-round education in ways appropriate to its situation. There are three major functions that a department of education should perform, however, regardless of its specific problems and promises.

The department should have personnel who are well informed about the issues of year-round education as well as the factors within the state that impede or facilitate the all-year school movement.

The department of education should work closely with the state board of education and the legislature, presenting adequate and accurate information about year-round education and providing leadership to encourage prudent decisions in implementing the all-year use of the school facilities.

The department of education should disseminate research and implementation information about year-round education, carefully selected for accuracy and pertinence, to local school systems and the interested public so that they may become better informed and make wise decisions in restructuring their schools.

The future of the United States depends on its education system, and public education is the responsibility of the state.

Notes

1. State ex rel. Clark v. Haworth, 122 Indiana 462, 23 N.E. 946 (1890).
2. New York Education Law, section 3602-a, paragraph 16.
3. Information obtained from O. E. Daugherty, Assistant Division Director, Division of Elementary and Secondary Education, Florida Department of Education, in response to inquiry by the author.
4. As reported by Bob R. Sternberg, Coordinator of the Extended School Year Feasibility Studies, Michigan Department of Education, Proceedings of the Fourth National Seminar on Year-Round Education, San Diego, California, February 23, 1972, p. 23c.
5. Ibid.

10 * Strategies for Implementing Change at the Local Level

Strategy is the art of employing an effective plan to achieve a specific objective. Any person, committee, or agency contemplating year-round education as a possible alternative to the existing program is confronted with two broad strategic considerations: the feasibility of change and a plan for implementation. The basic strategy for implementing change at the local level is not really any different from that at any other level, though the details of implementation will vary in each situation.

In its simplest form any systematic approach to solving a problem, whether large or small, individual or group, involves six basic steps: (1) identifying unmet needs, (2) identifying the resources that are or may be made available to meet the needs, (3) considering the alternative ways the resources may be used to meet the needs, (4) selecting the most appropriate alternative, (5) making a commitment to a specific change, and (6) executing the plan of action. The first four steps may be described as a feasibility study; the last two as a plan for implementation.

In order to take action on each of these steps, it is essential to develop an adequate information base. This requires obtaining the appropriate data, analyzing and synthesizing the information, and interpreting and disseminating the findings.

It is assumed that the democratic process, respecting the rights of the individual, will be applied. This means that the people who will be affected by the change or failure to change should have an opportunity to participate in considering those aspects of the problem that affect them.

It should be recognized that the issue of year-round education involves not just one problem or unmet need, but many. It involves not just the students, teachers, and parents but also the total community. It involves not just one change, but many. The solution to one problem creates new conditions that may pose new problems. People who plan changes in the school year should be aware that they are dealing with an important and complex issue.

The implementation of an all-year school program to replace the traditional, ongoing program is a long-range process normally requiring a minimum of two years. It takes many short steps to reach the goal. The recognition and attainment of short-range goals will help to sustain the interest of those involved as well as solve facets of the broad problem along the way.

The first broad consideration is whether year-round education is feasible at the particular time and place. A feasibility study to determine this should be distinguished from a study of the pros and cons of year-round education in general. In fact, the person proposing that a feasibility study be made should already have some knowledge of all-year school concepts. The feasibility study should be a comprehensive analysis of local school needs, the impact an all-year school program would have both in meeting those needs and in creating new needs, and the reaction to any proposed changes by the people concerned. The study will entail considerable community involvement and discussion, uncovering many stereotyped misconceptions about the meaning of year-round education and its impact on budgets and people.

The board of education should have some concept about the impact a feasibility study is likely to have on the community before it agrees to undertake such a study. No matter how comprehensive the effort to disseminate accurate information, there are bound to be some misinterpretations and misunderstandings. There is no reason for a community to undergo such an experience unless the school board and administration are seriously considering year-round schooling as an alternative to the present schedule.

Year-round education should not be seen as an end in itself but as a possible way to meet specific needs of people in the community. A feasibility study on year-round education provides a wonderful opportunity for the school personnel and the community to analyze the total operation of the school with the open question, "How can we improve it?" A carefully planned and executed study, involving those who are concerned about the school, can lead to numerous improvements in its operation, even in a short timespan, and can strengthen the relationship between the school and the community. On the other hand, a poorly executed study can be interpreted as a wild idea the school administration is trying to force on the faculty and the community.

The Feasibility Study

Before beginning the feasibility study, the initiating group should consider who is going to do what, when it is to be done, and why. If the study is initiated by the school administration, a committee needs to be formed. If the study is initiated by a group of interested citizens, they should work closely with the school administration to obtain the data needed to conduct the study.

The school board and the chief school administrator should support the idea of conducting the feasibility study or it should not be initiated. This does not mean that they should endorse the idea of year-round education for their schools before the study is begun; that decision should come after the study is completed. It does mean, however, that they should be open to considering year-round education as an alternative and willing to proceed with plans for implementation if it proves to be the most feasible alternative to achieve the objectives.

The Coordinator and the Steering Committee

How a local school district conducts the study depends on the resources available to it. First of all, it is important that one specific person be responsible for organizing and managing the study. This should be someone who has time to do the job well, but that does not necessarily mean it will be a full-time job. A member of the central administrative staff may have part of his time allocated to the study; a building principal who has a particular interest in the issue may be willing to allocate some of his time to leading the project; a teacher may be given released time for this purpose; someone may be employed specifically to conduct the study, if funds are available; or someone outside the school, such as a graduate student writing a research paper or a citizen who has enough interest and time, may volunteer to do it without pay.

The coordinator should be interested in conducting the study, willing to put in the effort necessary to do a good job, and able to seek the most appropriate solutions to the problems with an open mind, whatever the outcomes. He should be capable of collecting and organizing data and recognizing what is pertinent to the study. Finally, he should be able to work well with other people, both the school district personnel who will be contributing to the study and the volunteers serving on the general study committee and various subcommittees.

The project coordinator should be selected before the basic study is undertaken. His responsibilities and authority should be carefully defined by the administration, if this is an official school undertaking. The administration also should assure the cooperation of the central staff with the coordinator in collecting and analyzing pertinent data about the district itself. The coordinator, in turn, should have a steering committee to assist in preparing initial plans for conducting the study and to give overall direction as the study proceeds. The coordinator may be the chairman of the committee, or he may serve as its executive secretary. (In terms of the democratic process, the latter is probably more open-ended.) Members of the steering committee are likely to have limited time to give to the study. Therefore, detailed data-collection and analysis tasks that are objective in nature (not dependent on the opinions of individuals) should be done by paid staff rather than the committee.

The administration or board of education has the prerogative to determine the size of the committee and the groups to be represented. If committee members are to be selected through the representative process, the groups to be represented may include the teachers' association (the official bargaining agency, if there is one), the parent-teachers association or its counterpart, perhaps the ministerial association, the student association, the chamber of commerce, a leading union, the press, and any other significant groups (which will vary from community to community). The specific groups represented and the procedures used in selecting the committee members will probably depend on the local situation as well as the philosophy of the administration and the school board. An authoritarian administration, for example, may want to select the members itself, whereas an equalitarian administration may favor allowing each interest group to select its representative. If a strong pressure group is attempting to force a specific plan on the community, the administration may want to take a more forceful role in the whole study, in order to keep it more open-ended, than if the study is initiated for the purpose of examining all alternatives.

If the committee is appointed by the administration it will be recognized as an administrative committee, not a representative committee. If a person on the committee is to *represent* the teachers' association or bargaining unit, for example, the selection should be made by that organization, not the school administration.

The advantage of an appointed committee is that the administration can select people who are opinion-molders in the community and who have the interest and competence to conduct the study. The advantage of a representative committee, however, is that it has a built-in structure for communicating with large numbers of people, to disseminate information about the study, obtain reaction to it as it progresses, and select additional persons to serve on subcommittees of the project.

At the onset of the study, the administration should clearly define for the committee the basic goals of the project, the authority and responsibility of both the coordinator and the committee, their relationship to each other, and the general procedures to be followed in the study. If funds have been allocated for the study, the committee should know how much money is available and how it can be used. The committee should have the authority to establish subcommittees, drawing on the human resources of the community, as needs develop in conducting specific aspects of the study. All subcommittees should be responsible directly to the steering committee. Information about the operation of the committee should be public and open to the press, but the committee should not call public hearings or conduct opinion surveys in the name of the school district *without express authorization to do so.* Such meetings and surveys are essential parts of a feasibility study, of course, and will be discussed later in this chapter. It is desirable for the committee to have some operating funds, including funds for consultants. It is normally not desirable, however, to have a consulting firm come into the community and conduct the feasibility study for the committee. The district may employ outside help to collect and interpret basic data and advise the committee about options it may have, but it should remember that *community problems can be solved by and in the community.* This requires building horizontal bonds among the groups that are concerned with and affected by the problems and their solutions.

Step 1: Identifying Unmet Needs

The study should begin by carefully defining the needs or problems to be analyzed. The most common problem that stimulates studies on year-round education is the inadequacy of the existing school buildings to accommodate all the students, using standard scheduling procedures. The issue is whether to build new schools or additions to schools, or to modify the schedules. Related to this, of course, is the overall problem of economic efficiency. Another common problem that has stimulated all-year school studies, at least in the last few years, is the need to provide quality education for all students with equality in educational opportunity. The issues are complex; they relate, essentially, to techniques of increasing the appropriateness and the options of curriculum content, instructional processes, and use of time. A third reason for initiating an all-year school study—although, to date, few studies have been initiated for this reason—may be the incompatibility of the school time structures with changing life-styles of people in the community. This is likely to receive greater community attention in the future. These three broad areas—economic efficiency, quality education, and compatibility with changing life-styles—are basic and should be included in any comprehensive analysis of year-round education. The steering committee may wish to establish a subcommittee in each area to determine the needs and characteristics of the particular school district. If a key factor in the study is building needs, the committee must obtain and analyze accurate information about enrollment trends and building use. If there is no problem about the adequacy of the school buildings, this aspect of the study can be avoided.

For each and every problem that is identified the committee should attempt to answer these questions:

1. What is the most accurate definition of the problem?
   a. What is the intrinsic importance of the problem?
   b. At what rate is the problem increasing in magnitude and/or intensity?
2. What causes the problem?
3. What are the effects of the problem?
   a. What harm is being done by failing to solve it?
   b. To what extent is the damage irreversible if immediate action is not taken?
   c. What individuals or groups are most directly affected by the problem?

Step 2: Identifying Available Resources

Basic to the formulation of any plan of action is the identification of significant resources that may be used to meet the identified needs. When the problem is an overcrowded school building, for example, there are three major categories of resources that should be considered: (1) additional funds from local taxes, (2) use of the building at times when all or part is not now being utilized, and (3) alternative places where students may study part of the time without occupying the building.

If the community has an adequate tax base and the people are willing to increase taxes, the construction of a new school or addition may be a simple solution. If the school district is already bonded to the maximum legal level or if the people are unwilling to increase the tax rate, additional funds from taxes are not a significant available resource. Of course it is possible to attack the problem that people are unwilling to increase taxes, learn why they are resistant, and proceed to develop better support for the school. The possibility of increasing funds up to the legal limit exists, and this should be considered a possible resource.

The visible resource that stimulates the all-year school movement is the underutilization of the school facilities, particularly in the summertime. The buildings could also be used more fully at night and on weekends. At the secondary level, class schedules and the number of students using each classroom during the day are factors to consider. There may be many classrooms with many empty seats during many periods of the day, particularly in advanced classes with small enrollments. (Not only is the building underutilized in this case, but so is the teacher.) When each teacher has his own classroom and has one or two "free periods" a day for planning purposes, the classrooms are often unoccupied during these periods. This can easily create a 15 to 20 percent underutilization of space during the school year.

The basic concept of the storefront school is that learning takes place in the total environment, and much of what is taught in school can be learned outside of school as well as or better than in school. To the extent that this concept can be applied, the community is a resource for reducing building needs.

There are constraints or conditions on how each of these resources may be used satisfactorily to meet the need (in this case, the overcrowding of the school). In addition to identifying the available resources, the study committee should also identify these constraints or conditions.

A constraint on using the school in the summer, for example, may be the heat. A way to remove that particular constraint may be air conditioning, but a major constraint on that may be the cost.

For each identified need or problem in step 1 of the study, a list of resources and the constraints on their use should be compiled.

Step 3: Considering Alternative Uses of Resources

Perhaps the most creative part of the study is the step of considering alternative ways of using the resources to meet the needs. The steering committee and any subcommittees that have been established are responsible for "dreaming up" adequate and acceptable solutions to the problems being studied. The resources are the raw materials, the building blocks of change; solutions to problems are the goals. Each possible resource and the constraints on its use must be examined, and the committee must fit them together somehow into the best solution.

This whole process may be likened to a man who drives into a remote mountain forest and has a flat tire. This is no great problem, he thinks; he has changed flat tires before, when no service station or other help was available. He opens the trunk of his car and, to his dismay, discovers he has no jack. He looks around him to see what resources are available that might be used to raise the wheel off the ground so he can change the tire. He finds a rock he can use as a fulcrum to support a lever to lift the car. He walks a short distance in the woods and finds a sapling tree that has died and fallen to the ground; this can be used as a lever. He takes it back to the car and, with the rock as the fulcrum, gets the wheel with the flat tire off the ground by placing his own weight on the end of the pole. When he gets off the pole to go change the tire, the car falls back to the ground. He needs three resources: a fulcrum, a lever, and a weight on the end of the fulcrum. There is an alternative to using his own weight. He finds a log that he can drag to his car. He places his weight on the fulcrum, raises the car, and then pulls the log over the end of the pole to hold it down. He changes his tire and proceeds happily on his journey in the quiet solitude of the forest, whose many resources enrich man's life. Step by step he has identified his need, identified the available resources, selected the best alternative use of the resources, committed himself to a plan of action, and executed the plan.

The responsibility of developing plans to improve the educational system of our society is far greater than that of changing a tire, and the task is far more complex; but, if we look at the issue of education with the same clarity of purpose and commitment to change, we can soon find ways to resolve our educational dilemma.

Each of the various all-year school plans is a proposed way to capitalize on the unused resource of the empty schoolhouse in the summer. The committee studying the feasibility of year-round education must know and understand these plans. It must know what specific needs each plan is designed to fill. It must know the constraints commonly associated with the implementation of each plan. It must know the anticipated outcomes of each plan and the reaction to each alternative by the people who will be affected by the change.

Step 4: Selecting the Most Appropriate Alternative

From the list of alternatives the committee needs to forge the best set of plans it can devise to meet the educational needs of the community. In step 1, many needs were identified. No one plan of action will meet all these needs; multiple approaches must be used. Many needs or problems may be solved by preliminary measures without adopting a change in the school calendar. In fact, some interim steps must be taken before an all-year school program can be implemented. The achievement of short-range goals and a step-by-step progression toward the long-range goals helps to keep the committee viable and the general public interested.

There are many issues that the committee needs to think through before it can select the most appropriate plan of action. Specific questions that need to be considered are listed in chapter 2. After the committee has determined answers to these and other questions relating to the local community, and has weighed each alternative course, together with its inherent constraints and roadblocks, it should select the plan of action that the members feel offers the greatest measure of benefit to the students and the community in general.

It is important for the steering committee to build credibility with the groups of people who will be affected by the change. This can be done in the initial phases by using an open approach to all issues that arise during the feasibility study. At the time the committee is established, the school administration should make it clear that the committee will only study the problem and that no change will be made until the people have been informed about the possibilities, have had a chance to react to them, and have indicated their general acceptance of the proposed plan.

Of course, no such promise should be made unless it is true. But no all-year school plan is feasible, no matter how good it looks on paper, unless the people accept it. So part of the task of selecting the most appropriate alternative entails the assessment of community reaction to the plan. The people cannot react intelligently, however, unless they are adequately informed about the issues and how each issue will be resolved.

To build a broad base of understanding the committee needs the support of individuals who have the opportunity to reach large numbers of people and who will transmit their knowledge and conviction to others. Ideally, the committee itself and its subcommittees are composed of such individuals. If the steering committee contains key people representing the major segments of the community, each member has the opportunity to report back to his constituency.

It should be made clear, *by the action of the committee,* that consideration will be given to all facets of the issue. No opinion surveys asking whether people favor year-round education should be made until after the people have had a chance to learn about the plan or plans proposed for the community.

A broad approach is needed in order to inform the public adequately about the plan. The Northville, Michigan, public schools presented a comprehensive information program before they conducted a survey of community opinion about the mandated four-quarter plan. They employed a public relations firm to direct this phase of their project. It included (1) specific publications that dealt with operation of the mandated four-quarter plan, (2) a direct mailing to all citizens, (3) news releases, (4) public appearances by speakers at civic, professional, and other community meetings, (5) a slide presentation relating the needs of the community to the building program, and (6) everyday news articles reported in the papers. They stressed an open-minded "inform" approach rather than a "sell" approach. The initial issue of *Opening School Doors,* a newsletter designed to inform the community about the program, is reproduced in Appendix D. The Utica, Michigan, public schools conducted a similar information program and then took a community survey of five groups: the business and industrial sector, the certified teaching staff, the students, the school administrative staff, and the general community. The surveys are presented in Appendix E.

A flow of information about the entire project from its inception is essential. Often people automatically oppose something they do not understand, and public apathy is nearly as detrimental to effective implementation as unfavorable attitudes. Understanding is a valuable weapon for attacking both hostility and apathy. Moreover, people are unlikely to become proponents of a proposal or be identified with a cause unless they thoroughly understand both the problem and the proposed solution. But once a core of knowledgeable people is created, those people will actively communicate information to others to help promote implementation of the recommendations.

The Implementation Plan

Step 5. Making a Commitment to Change

Once it appears certain that the community accepts the proposed plan as the most suitable alternative, an official commitment should be made by the board of education to enact such a program and to initiate a plan for implementation.

Implementation requires careful planning. A step-by-step analysis needs to be made of the total transition necessary to make the new plan operational. Each major component of the transition—curriculum revision, in-service training, modification of the building, procurement of curriculum materials, revision of contracts with employed personnel, revision of bus schedules, etc.—should be outlined and a target date established for each phase of the components. A budget should be set to provide the personnel, consultants, teacher released time, materials, equipment, and other items necessary to conduct the transition and make the new program operational.

The commitment is not really made until the board of education officially takes these actions.

Step 6. Executing the Plan of Action

If the steering committee has done its job well and a step-by-step plan of action has been approved, executing the plan becomes a procedural matter. This does not mean the tasks ahead are easy. On the contrary, this is when the real work begins. The biggest job is likely to be revision of the curriculum and instructional procedures. All personnel affected must participate in various aspects of the change as the program matures. It can be an exciting and rewarding experience for all concerned if the feasibility study and the plan for implementation have been managed well.

Implementing change, no matter how important the cause and how logical the proposed plan, has many hazards. Psychological characteristics or outside forces may cause administrators, board members, teachers, or the entire community to resist change. Criticism, implied in the idea that the instructional system must be improved, is likely to be resented by those who are a part of the existing system, unless the rationale for the recommended changes is also presented. (Rationale for educational change along with logical and legitimate defense of the past are emphasized throughout this book, particularly in chapter 5 on quality education.) Most people oppose change when it threatens their security or endangers their position. Unless constructive action is taken to overcome the obstacle of this resistance, individuals and groups will probably exert influence either to maintain the status quo or to take regressive action.

Another obstacle to implementation is the inability or the failure of the proponents to marshal all their potential allies. A broad-based steering committee and subcommittees involving many community leaders help marshal the support of major and influential groups, but effort should be exerted to contact personally all key agencies and civic, fraternal, religious, and professional organizations that may be concerned about operation of the schools. The steering committee needs to seek their opinions sincerely and keep them informed as the feasibility study and implementation program progress.

Failure to recognize opposition to the study or to its proposed outcomes is another pitfall that should be avoided. It is important to identify those who actively oppose the program and to understand the reasons for differences in opinion. Few critical issues produce unanimity; there is usually someone to stand in opposition to any change. Meeting this obstacle honestly and openly is important. The committee must entertain questions and comments at public hearings or meetings. Each dissenting comment should be accepted as an expression of legitimate concern and should be analyzed in terms of the best way possible to achieve goals and resolve differences.

In expanding the curriculum and establishing new educational programs, funding is definitely a potential obstacle. The steering committee members should be well informed about the amounts and purposes of needed funds, and should be able to interpret the need for change to all those concerned with the outcome.

Sources of Implementation Information

When initiating the feasibility study, and as the study progresses, the steering committee will want to know what other school districts are doing or how they solved a particular problem. The annual conference of the National Council on Year-Round Education and the periodic seminars on all-year community schools sponsored by the AASA National Academy of School Executives provide good opportunities to share ideas with others and to seek the advice of those who have already gone through the process.

A comprehensive bibliography on year-round education is contained in the back of this book; in addition a school district undertaking a feasibility study will want to obtain the most current information and the literature most pertinent to its particular problem. Such information may be obtained from the National Council on Year-Round Education and from the following agencies:

National School Calendar Study Committee
P.O. Box 37
Horseshoe, North Carolina 28742

Pennsylvania Center for Year-Round Education
Clarion State College
Clarion, Pennsylvania 16214

Institute for the Study and Development of Year-Round
   Education
College of Education
Virginia Polytechnic Institute and State University
Blacksburg, Virginia 24064

Studios for Educational Alternatives
School of Education
Mankato State College
Mankato, Minnesota 56001

The three most commonly considered all-year school plans, in addition to the flexible all-year school discussed in chapter 8, are the 45-15 plan, operating at Francis Howell School District, St. Charles, Missouri, and the Valley View School District, Romeoville, Illinois; the optional four-quarter plan, operating at Atlanta Public Schools, Atlanta, Georgia; and the optional quinmester plan, operating at Dade County Schools, Miami, Florida. Statements about each of these plans by the people operating them are given in Appendix F.

11 * Variables, Constants, and Conundrums

What should be the units of measure to determine when a student has completed basic education? The traditional measure of progress in school and readiness for graduation is the school year:

12 school years = 1 graduation

How long is a school year? Historically, this has been a variable. As was discussed earlier, in 1918 the North Carolina school year was 120 days in length. In 1933 it was changed to 160 days, and in 1943 it was changed again to 180 days. This is typical; the length of the school year has gradually increased in all states.

If the 1918 school year were used as a constant unit of measure to determine how many days a student has to go to school to graduate, the amount of time would be:

12 years x 120 days = 1,440 days = 1 graduation

If students were accelerated by going to school a longer number of days, say 180 days, they could graduate sooner and reduce the budget. In fact, they could graduate in eight years, thus reducing the size of the school by one-third:

8 years x 180 days = 1,440 days = 1 graduation.

The basic problem with this plan of acceleration is that the number of days in a school year has been a *variable*, not a constant. Can we assume that the 180-day school year is a constant today? Can we plan to have students complete twelve years of work in ten years by going to school eleven months a year instead of nine?

12 years x 180 days = 2,160 days = 1 graduation
10 years x 220 days = 2,200 days = 1 graduation + 40 days

Or will our society decide that children should be in school longer than 180 days? If it does, what happens to our acceleration plans (the continuous four-quarter plan or the eleven-month school year plan)?

The four-quarter plan and its derivatives, the 12-4 plan and the 45-15 plan, are also based on the assumption that 180 days are a constant measure of a school year (or three quarters).

180 days ÷ 3 = 60 days = 1 quarter

Under the four-quarter plan, school operates four quarters or 220 days of the year, but each student attends three of those four quarters, or 180 days. The one quarter of vacation is taken in different ways under the various plans—three months all at once in the four-quarter plan, a month at a time after a quarter of study in the 12-4 plan, and three weeks after nine weeks of study in the 45-15 plan.

What would happen if society decided that children should be in school 210 days a year instead of 180? Could the four-quarter system work?

210 days ÷ 3 = 70 days = 1 quarter
4 quarters x 70 days = 280 days of school operation

Are there actually 280 school days in a year? A week has five school days.

52 weeks x 5 days = 260 days

There are not enough school days in the year for the four-quarter plan or any of its derivatives to work if the school year for each student is 210 days. All these plans would be obsolete. But does the number of school days in a week have to be a constant five? Children could go to school six days a week if necessary. Or is the length of the school day variable? Can we extend each school day to complete 210 days' work in 180?

A law recently passed in Pennsylvania defines a school year as 990 hours. This is based on a 5.5-hour school day and 180 days:

180 days x 5.5 hours = 990 hours

If we assume the unit of measure of one school day is 5.5 hours, how many hours a day would a student need to go to school to attain 210 days' work in 180?

210 days x 5.5 hours = 1,155 hours
1,155 hours ÷ 180 days = 6.4 hours

So, using 6.4-hour school days, the four-quarter plan could still function. In fact, if the school day were 6.5 hours instead of 5.5, children could complete the traditional thirteen years (including kindergarten) in eleven years without going to an all-year school, and still cut the budget more than by adopting the four-quarter plans.

All this is not really about the days and hours a child spends in school, but about the amount of time he could be in school—if he weren't sick and were enrolled all the school year. The amount of time a child must actually spend in school in order to complete a school year is really quite variable.

One might ask on what basic assumptions these standards for school graduation are built. Can it be assumed that a measure of time in school is a measure of knowledge? No. What a person learns depends on a great many factors besides time in school. Can it be assumed, then, that the primary function of the school is to keep a student busy for a specified period of time and that knowledge is not important? This cannot be assumed either. A student must "pass" or "fail" at the end of each year (or semester or quarter). At the secondary level, this is measured by subject, and each subject is assigned a specified amount of credit. Generally four credits represent one year's work. Does this mean that there is a specified body of knowledge to be mastered for graduation, and that time is used as a measure only to keep students busy at acquiring that body of knowledge? The answer to both parts of the question is no.

The amount of time children are expected to spend in school has been dependent on two factors. When they were *needed* to do something else (work on the farm, for example) the school time was short. When it was important to get the children "out from under mother's feet" or off the labor market, the time they were required to be in school increased. It is not generally acceptable to let a student graduate too early, even if he masters the body of knowledge, because the next step is not ready for him—he is not wanted on the labor market.

What is the body of knowledge to be mastered? Is this a constant? Is it the same from state to state or from school to school or from student to student within a school? What a child is expected to learn at school varies greatly. There are common basic skills that are taught in all schools, but the level of performance varies greatly among individuals. The capacity to learn varies among individuals. The amount of time it takes to learn varies. What they need to know and what they learn outside of school varies not only among individuals at a given time and place, but also in general among groups. The knowledge a person needs in one region of the nation may vary somewhat from what he needs in another region. What he needs to know at one time in history varies from what he needs at another time.

In summary, the following factors are *variables* and therefore should not be used as *constant* measures.

1. The amount of time a child is expected by society to remain in school—the number of hours, days, and years.
2. The amount of knowledge a child must acquire to graduate from school.
3. The amount and kind of knowledge a child learns outside of school.
4. The rate at which a child learns, in or out of school.
5. The things he really needs to know and be able to do in order to live as a self-directed, contributing member of society.

What, then, are the constants? Life is constant for the individual; from the time he is born until he is dead, a human being is growing and changing as an entity and interrelating with his environment. Change is constant. Each hour, day, and year that an individual lives he changes; so do the conditions for living—the environment in which he lives. Adaptation to change is constant. All living things must adapt to change or die.

In a society that is changing only slowly, a child can learn from his parents and others in an informal way what he needs to know as he grows up, and school is not necessary. The more rapid the change, the more difficult it becomes for one generation to transmit in an informal way the knowledge, skills, and attitudes needed by the next generation. The school is therefore developed to provide in a *formal* way, in an organized curriculum, what a person needs to know but does not acquire in his informal environment.

The American school has changed as the characteristics of our society have changed. In the early days there were no schools. As our society became more complex and as the rate of change of our society accelerated, the school grew and changed with the changing needs of society. In our complex, technologically advanced, rapidly changing society today we need to quit playing numbers games with hours, days, and credits.

It is time for our democratic society, living in an economy of abundance, to recognize human variables and the dignity and worth of the individual human being.

It is time for school to be developed as an educational service center, to provide the services members of our society need in order to adapt to the rapid changes that are taking place and to help give direction to change so that man may survive. Such a school must be *flexible*, available at all times of the year to those who need it, and able to deal with the broad spectrum of educational needs of the learners who use it.

It is time for our society to develop a flexible, all-year school.

Appendix A * Port Huron Feasibility Study

The Cost of the Four-Quarter Plan

At best, an estimated budget of a school district's expenses is only approximate. Estimating a budget for a plan of operation not actually in use presents many opportunities for honest errors. In order to reduce the possibility of error and to provide a fairly sound basis for comparing the cost of four-quarter operation with that of a nine-month operation, the expenditure budgets for two years were worked out for both plans of operation. Those budgets appear in Tables IX and X. The budget of expenditures and revenues for the school year 1968-1969 is complete and, although the yearly audit has not been finished, its figures are fairly accurate. In addition, using the 1968-1969 budget is facilitated because it is known how many students, teachers, buildings, and classrooms were used in that school year. This information is essential in establishing a good estimation of the cost of a four-quarter school.

Although the school year 1969-1970 had not yet begun when this estimate was written, most of the needs of the 1969-1970 school year have been well established. The number of students for the 1969-1970 school year have been taken from the estimated enrollments. The number of teachers and classrooms needed for year-round school operation were computed from the simulation of student placement. As was noted in the section on that simulation of student placement, ideal savings were not realized. The number of teachers and classrooms that would have been needed in the 1968-1969 school year had Port

From *The Four-Quarter Plan and Its Feasibility for the Port Huron Area School District, 1970,* by Sami J. Alam. Reprinted by permission of the author.

Huron been on a four-quarter plan was computed by assuming the same percentage of savings would have occurred as did in the simulation. Table IX compares the cost of the 1968-1969 school year as it occurred and the estimated cost of year-round operation for that year. Table X compares the projected 1969-1970 costs for the nine-month school year to the estimated cost of year-round schools for 1969-1970.

Table IX. 1968-1969 General Fund Expenditures for the Regular School Year and Simulated Four-Quarter Expenditures

	Actual*	Four-quarter
Instruction—Elementary		
Salaries		
Principals	$ 234,793	$ 267,664
Supervisors and Consultants	115,144	133,567
Teachers	2,180,287	2,335,086
Substitutes	43,865	49,589
Librarians	18,569	23,397
Clerical	81,776	94,042
Others	63,114	78,892
Contracted Services	15,989	16,489
Teaching Supplies	48,058	40,849
Library Books	18,927	16,088
Audio-Visual Supplies	9,572	8,136
Office Supplies	5,980	5,980
Travel and Mileage	7,955	7,955
Recruitment	1,000	1,000
Miscellaneous Supplies	913	913
Total Instruction—Elementary	$2,845,942	$3,079,647
Instruction—Intermediate and Secondary		
Salaries		
Principals	$ 222,125	$ 242,116
Supervisors and Consultants	59,043	70,000
Teachers	2,640,898	2,695,300
Substitutes	65,687	70,764
Librarians	97,861	123,129
Guidance	264,683	238,214
Clerical	163,300	182,896
Others	115,569	144,461
Textbooks	2,525	2,525
Contracted Services	653	653
Teaching Supplies	56,488	47,450
Library Books	24,842	24,842
Audio-Visual Supplies	19,609	16,668
Miscellaneous Supplies	264	264
Office Supplies	11,313	11,313

*All figures shown are prior to audit.

	Actual	Four-quarter
Instruction—Intermediate and Secondary (continued)		
Student Teachers	1,072	1,072
Recruitment	797	797
Rentals	158	158
Travel and Mileage	15,632	15,632
Printing	2,720	2,720
Miscellaneous Expenditures	13,931	13,931
Total Instruction—Intermediate and Secondary	$3,779,170	$3,904,905
Instruction—Special Education		
Salaries		
Supervisors and Consultants	$ 60,444	$ 65,944
Teachers	234,997	234,997
Substitutes	1,679	1,679
Psychological	31,400	31,400
Clerical	8,950	8,950
Aides	940	940
Contracted Services	473	473
Teaching Supplies	6,026	6,026
Library Books	24	24
Office Supplies	677	777
Mileage	8,418	8,418
Miscellaneous	5,573	5,573
Total Instruction—Special Education	$ 359,601	$ 365,201
Instruction—Summer School		
Salaries		
Director	$ 1,267	- 0 -
Teachers	21,113	- 0 -
Guidance	968	- 0 -
Aides	1,670	- 0 -
Other (instructional)	730	- 0 -
General (instructional)	698	- 0 -
Office Supplies	34	- 0 -
General (mileage)	114	- 0 -
Miscellaneous Expenditures	107	- 0 -
Total Instruction—Summer School	$ 26,701	- 0 -
Instruction—Evening School		
Salaries		
Director	$ 3,695	$ 3,695
Teachers and Other	12,589	12,589
Printing	92	92
Miscellaneous	5	5
Total Instruction—Evening School	$ 16,381	$ 16,381

	Actual	Four-quarter
Instruction—E.I.P. Program		
Salaries		
Consultants	$ 31,449	$ 35,852
Teachers	89,032	96,690
Substitutes	1,276	1,383
Clerical	4,006	4,006
Mileage	1,001	1,001
Miscellaneous Expenditures	328	328
Capital Outlay	2,111	2,111
Total Instruction—E.I.P. Program	$ 129,203	$ 141,371
Administration		
Salaries		
Superintendent	$ 23,100	$ 23,100
Assistant Superintendents	56,077	56,077
Business Administration	44,637	44,637
Personnel Office	25,190	25,190
Research	17,664	17,664
Clerical	89,214	89,214
Others (S.C.R.)	14,500	14,500
Printing and Publishing	4,157	4,157
Legal Services	7,752	7,752
School Elections	17,137	17,137
School Census	2,632	2,632
Auditor	14,215	14,215
Office Supplies	21,880	21,880
Travel and Mileage	11,913	11,913
Rentals	1,541	1,541
Printing and Publishing	3,758	3,758
Miscellaneous Expenditures	7,343	7,343
Total Administration	$ 362,710	$ 362,710
Attendance		
Salaries		
Attendance Officer	$ 5,022	$ 6,277
Visiting Teachers	51,032	48,225
Child Accounting	5,538	5,538
Office Supplies	526	526
Travel and Mileage	2,348	2,348
Miscellaneous Expenditures	90	90
Total Attendance	$ 64,556	$ 63,004
Health Services		
Salaries: Nurse	$ 7,038	$ 8,868
Contracted Services and Supplies	7,053	7,053
Travel and Mileage	224	300
Miscellaneous	10	10
Total Health Services	$ 14,325	$ 16,231

	Actual	Four-quarter
Pupil Transportation		
Salaries		
Supervision	$ 15,529	$ 17,029
Drivers	148,192	145,192
Contracted Services, Rentals, Gasoline,		
Oil, Tires, Parts, Repairs	68,112	68,112
Miscellaneous Supplies	1,063	1,063
Travel and Mileage	451	451
Transportation Insurance	5,960	6,543
Secretary (salary)	4,929	4,929
Overtime	14	14
Miscellaneous Expenditures	1,630	1,630
Total Pupil Transportation	$ 245,880	$ 244,963
Plant Operation		
Salaries		
Engineers	$ 95,011	$ 135,011
Custodians (schools)	396,225	396,225
Custodians (grounds)	18,319	18,319
Overtime and Miscellaneous Help	58,575	58,575
Others (bus drivers, PBX, warehouse,		
overtime)	28,132	28,132
Contracted Services	32,489	32,489
Vehicle Supplies	56	56
Heat (coal, gas, oil)	118,280	118,280
Others—utilities	139,256	222,810
Custodial (grounds) and Miscellaneous		
Supplies	43,291	43,291
Travel and Mileage	404	404
Rental of Equipment	1,127	1,127
Miscellaneous Expenditures	53	53
Total Plant Operation	$ 931,218	$1,054,772
Plant Maintenance		
Repairs of Grounds, Equipment, and		
Other Miscellaneous Repairs	$ 63,356	$ 63,356
Overtime	1,646	1,646
Contracted Services (grounds, roofs,		
decorating, boiler, heat, elec-		
tricity, plumbing, miscellaneous		
building, equipment, and vehi-		
cle repair)	86,341	86,341
Maintenance Supplies	35,974	40,291
Replacement of Equipment	16,798	16,798
Total Plant Maintenance	$ 204,115	$ 208,432
Fixed Charges		
Employment Retirement and FICA	$ 1,709	$ 1,709

	Actual	Four-quarter
Fixed Charges (continued)		
Property and Other Insurance	123,266	123,266
Interest	5,461	5,461
Rental—Educational Data Processing	24,810	24,810
Miscellaneous Fixed Charges	11	11
Total Fixed Charges	$ 155,257	$ 155,257
Capital Outlay		
Site Acquisition	$ 18,925	$ 18,925
Remodeling	1,626	1,626
Furniture and Equipment	35,073	271,000
Total Capital Outlay	$ 55,624	$ 291,551
Transfer to Other Funds		
Tuition	$ 678	$ 678
Miscellaneous	5,933	5,933
Total Transfer to Other Funds	$ 6,611	$ 6,611
GRAND TOTAL	$9,197,294	$9,911,036

Because of the apparent differences in the actual expenditures for 1968-1969 and the simulated expenditures for the same academic year on a year-round basis, it is essential that thse items of discrepancy be explained. Accordingly, the rest of this section will mainly be devoted to explaining those differences.

The 1968-1969 Budget—An Explanation of Expenditures

I. Instruction—Elementary

A. Salaries

1. Principals: The increase from $234,793 to $267,664 is based upon the fact that elementary principals' salaries would have to increase by 14 percent due to the increase in the contracted number of weeks for that position from forty-two weeks to forty-eight weeks.

2. Consultants and Supervisors: The increase here from $115,144 to $133,567 amounts to a 15 percent increase resulting from a change in the number of weeks worked by those in that category.

3. Teachers: An increase in the teachers' salaries equivalent to about $154,000 is necessitated using the rationale that teachers' salaries were reduced initially by 15 percent because at least that much reduction in elementary staff was computed by the simulation. Since each teacher worked 240 days in place of 189, the salaries were then multiplied by 1.26. It is important to remember, however, that this figure would have to be negotiated with the Port Huron Education Association.

4. Substitutes: An increase of about $6,000 was necessitated in this area on the basis that substitutes' salaries had to be increased initially by one-third because the teachers will be working one-third more days of school each year. This salary figure was then reduced 15 percent because the elementary staff would have been reduced by at least that amount.

5. Librarians: It was assumed that the same number of librarians would be retained at the elementary level for year-round operation of schools. Accordingly, the salary of a librarian was increased by 26 percent to account for the extra number of days worked by the librarian.

6. Clerical: The increase of about $13,600 in the area of clerical salaries is equal to 23 percent. This is a justifiable amount of increase due to the fact that elementary secretaries were working the same number of weeks as were their principals. Additional secretarial and/or clerical help were considered in this figure.

7. Others: This category includes noon hour supervisors, aides, and other contracted salaries. An increase in salaries of 12 percent was estimated to be a fair increase with only the fact that school will be in operation for a longer period of time taken into consideration.

B. Contracted Services includes salaries for consultants for in-service days and other activities. This item was increased by 3 percent although it is not certain that any increase would occur.

C. Teaching Supplies were reduced 15 percent because it is expected that there will be 15 percent fewer teaching stations. It must be remembered that this is a compromised figure. Nonconsumable items such as physical education equipment and science supplies could be reduced by 25 percent because 25 percent of the students are on vacation. Consumable items such as paper and chalk would remain the same because eventually the same number of students would use them.

D. Library Books: This area was reduced 15 percent. Since only 75 percent of the students will be in school at any one time, a smaller inventory of books will be required. It is felt that a 15 percent reduction instead of a 25 percent reduction will permit continued upgrading of our school libraries. Audio-visual supplies would have been reduced approximately 15 percent because there would be about that many fewer teaching stations.

II. Instruction—Intermediate and Secondary

A. Salaries

1. Principals: These salaries have been increased only for the intermediate principals by 9 percent because of the increase in the number of weeks for which they are contracted.

2. Supervisors and Consultants: The increase in this figure of about $11,000 is necessitated by the fact that supervisors' and consultants' salaries are prorated representing a percentage of the supervisors' salaries. The percentage reflects the part of the supervisors' time spent on secondary and intermediate education.

3. Teachers: The increase is a result of the fact that at the intermediate and high school level it was simulated that we would have 19 percent less teachers. Accordingly, what the teachers receive for the regular 1968-1969 school year was reduced by 19 percent. Since those teachers left would be working an additional fifty-one days, a 26 percent increase in their salaries was necessitated. Again, it must be remembered that this item is to be negotiated with the Port Huron Education Association.

4. Substitutes: Substitutes' salaries were increased by 33 percent for the extra sixty days substitutes might be needed and reduced by 19 percent because there would be 19 percent fewer teachers to substitute for.

5. Librarians: The same number of librarians would be needed. Their salaries would be increased by 26 percent due to the increase in the number of days worked.

6. Guidance: Guidance salaries were reduced by 25 percent because 25 percent of the students would be on vacation, thus requiring 25 percent fewer guidance personnel. The salaries of those remaining were then increased by 20 percent to account for the extra days the counselors will be working.

7. Clerical: The increase in clerical salaries reflects the increase in the number of days worked by the clerical staff. Not all clerks and secretaries presently work the same number of days. It was estimated that the average increase would be equivalent to 12 percent.

8. Others: Other salaries were increased 25 percent in expectation of additional services required by the longer year. The increase was not computed to be 33 percent because fewer students will be served.

B. Teaching Supplies were reduced 16 percent using the same logic as that used in the case of the teaching supplies for the elementary level.

C. Audio-Visual Supplies were reduced using the same logic as that utilized at the elementary level.

III. Instruction—Special Education

A. Salaries

1. Supervisors and Consultants: An increase in this item is noted in proportion to the extra days supervisors and consultants in this area will be expected to work. Average increase is equal to 9 percent.

2. Teachers: Because students are in a homogeneous classroom setting and because it is recommended that special education students be granted the same vacation quarter, no change in salaries will be expected.

IV. Instruction—Summer School

The cost of the 1968-1969 summer school was equivalent to $26,701. Since the four-quarter plan would eliminate the need for a separate summer school program, a savings equivalent to that amount would be realized.

V. Instruction—Elementary Internship Program

A. Salaries

1. Consultants: An increase of 14 percent in the salaries of consultants would be needed to adjust to the fact that the working days of those consultants would be increased on a four-quarter plan.

2. Teachers: Since about 15 percent less teachers would be required at the elementary level with the four-quarter plan, the cost of teachers' salaries for 1968-1969 was reduced by that amount. Since teachers' salaries would increase by 26 percent because of the increase in the length of the year, the product was multiplied by 1.26 to arrive at the new figure of $96,690 for teachers' salaries.

3. Substitutes: With the reduction in the number of teachers, the number of substitutes would be reduced proportionately. With the increase by one quarter of the working year of the teacher, an increase of 26 percent was then made to adjust for the salaries of the substitutes in this area.

VI. Attendance

A. Salaries
1. Attendance Officer: The salary of the attendance officer would be increased by 26 percent because of the extra days worked. There is only one officer; accordingly, there can be no reduction in personnel in this area.
2. Visiting Teachers: The number of visiting teachers was reduced 25 percent because of the smaller number of students in school at any one time. The salaries were then increased 26 percent because of the extra days worked.

VII. Health Services

A. School Nurse's salary: The school district has only one nurse. The school nurse's salary would be increased by 26 percent due to the increase in the length of the school year.
B. Travel: Travel is increased by 33 percent because of the extra quarter in which travel would occur.

VIII. Pupil Transportation

A. Salaries
1. Supervisors: An increase in the cost of supervision would be expected due to the need for two additional part-time supervisors.
2. Drivers: There would be a decrease in this item since there would be fewer buses to be driven because only 75 percent of the students needing bussing would be attending school at any one time. This reduction is based on the estimate of the supervisor of the transportation department.
B. Transportation Insurance: This item would be expected to increase because of the increase in the length of time buses would be operating.

IX. Plant Operation

A. Salaries of Engineers: There would be an increase in this item upon the recommendation of the supervisor of maintenance. This increase represents salaries of five extra men with special maintenance training.
B. Utilities: A substantial increase is expected in the consumption of electrical power due to the use of the proposed air conditioners.

X. Plant Maintenance

A. Maintenance Supplies: Maintenance supplies are increased by 12 percent. This increase represents less than 33 percent (the number of extra days schools are in use) because some supplies are year-round expenses. Besides, some buildings are projected to be closed.

XI. Capital Outlay

The substantial increase in this item is accounted for by an estimated cost of $271,000 to air condition 542 rooms that are presently without air conditioning in the school district. By selecting a unit for each room, this was considered the most expensive way to air condition. The real cost would certainly not exceed this figure. This expense is a one-time expense that need not be repeated.

The 1969-1970 Budget—An Explanation of Expenditures

As stated earlier, the budget of expenditures for the 1969-1970 regular school year does not represent the actual amounts spent for each item on that budget. However, the projected 1969-1970 expenditures were again simulated for a 1969-1970 four-quarter school. (See Table X.)

Table X. Projected 1969-1970 General Fund Expenditures
for the Regular and Four-Quarter School Years

Instruction—Elementary	Budgeted*	Four-quarter
Salaries		
Principals	$ 276,951	$ 276,951
Supervisors and Consultants	95,000	100,000
Teachers	2,354,185	2,519,097
Librarians	16,647	20,975
Clerical	92,904	106,840
Others	42,898	51,480
Contracted Services	4,000	4,000
Teaching Supplies	79,600	68,456
Library and Audio-Visual Supplies	19,500	16,575
Office Supplies	5,000	5,000
Travel	7,450	7,450
Miscellaneous	600	600
Substitutes	49,000	49,744
Recruiting	1,000	1,000
Rentals	200	200
Total Instruction—Elementary	$ 3,044,935	$ 3,228,368
Instruction—Intermediate and Secondary		
Salaries		
Principals	$ 240,600	$ 240,600
Supervisors and Consultants	146,605	165,000
Teachers	3,062,500	3,135,080
Librarians	88,884	111,993
Others	88,740	98,425
Guidance	320,293	288,264
Clerical	134,590	150,740
Contracted Services	4,000	4,000
Travel	12,300	12,300
Bookstore (fees and book rental) K-12	78,181	78,181
Library	7,296	7,296
Audio-Visual Supplies	5,000	5,000
Teaching Supplies	41,496	41,496
Substitutes	74,000	79,966

*These figures are tentative and preliminary.

	Budgeted	Four-quarter
Instruction—Intermediate and Secondary (continued)		
Recruiting	500	500
Rentals	250	250
Miscellaneous	2,500	2,500
Office Supplies	4,000	4,000
Total Instruction—Intermediate and Secondary	$ 4,311,735	$ 4,425,591
Instruction—Special Education		
Salaries		
Supervisors	$ 43,319	$ 46,000
Teachers	268,206	268,206
Psychological	19,773	19,773
Clerical	10,105	10,105
Others	- 0 -	- 0 -
Contracted Services (teachers)	11,500	14,490
Teaching Supplies	5,304	5,304
Office Supplies and Res. Library	650	650
Travel and Mileage	10,550	10,550
Miscellaneous	- 0 -	- 0 -
Substitutes	2,000	2,053
Aides	1,200	1,500
Total Instruction—Special Education	$ 372,607	$ 378,631
Instruction—Evening School		
Salaries		
Principal	$ 3,500	$ 3,500
Teachers and Consultants	16,500	16,500
Clerical	800	800
Teaching Supplies and Expense	700	700
Total Instruction—Evening School	$ 21,500	$ 21,500
Instruction—E.I.P. Program		
Salaries		
Teachers	$ 87,300	$ 94,598
Consultants	33,716	38,436
Substitutes	3,300	3,526
Clerical	4,304	5,380
Contracted Services	2,500	2,500
Instructional Supplies	800	800
Travel	1,860	1,860
Capital Outlay	4,929	4,929
Miscellaneous	150	150
Total Instruction—E.I.P. Program	$ 138,859	$ 152,179
Administration		
Salaries		
Superintendent	$ 24,422	$ 24,422

	Budgeted	Four-quarter
Administration		
Salaries (continued)		
Assistant Superintendents	53,038	53,038
Business Administration	48,700	48,700
Clerical	99,968	99,968
Personnel Department	32,000	32,000
Printing and Publishing	4,659	4,659
School Elections	10,000	10,000
Contracted Services and Rentals	2,000	2,000
Office Supplies and Other Expenses	20,000	22,000
Travel and Mileage	10,000	12,000
Miscellaneous	4,850	5,000
Research	7,866	7,866
S.C.R. Director	16,500	16,500
Legal Services	10,000	10,000
Auditing	12,000	12,000
Rentals	1,500	1,500
Printing and Publishing	5,750	5,750
Total Administration	$ 363,253	$ 367,403
Attendance		
Salaries	$ 20,144	$ 20,144
Office Supplies and Expenses	500	500
Travel	2,625	3,500
Miscellaneous	100	100
Attendance Office	5,285	6,600
Child Accounting	5,981	5,981
Visiting Teachers	84,237	90,217
Total Attendance	$ 118,872	$ 127,042
Health Services		
Contracted Services and Supplies	$ 5,100	$ 5,100
Travel	350	350
School Nurse	7,000	8,750
Miscellaneous	100	100
Total Health Services	$ 12,550	$ 14,300
Transportation		
Salaries		
Supervision	$ 15,500	
Drivers	158,300	
Contracted Services and Rentals, Gasoline, Oil, Tires, and Parts	64,000	
Insurance	7,000	
Supplies and Other Expenses	1,600	
Replacement of Vehicles	50,000	
Travel	400	
Secretary	6,125	
Miscellaneous	950	

	Budgeted	Four-quarter
Transportation (continued)		
Salaries		
Supervisors		$ 18,000
Drivers (including extra miles)		154,800
Garage Mechanics and Employees		25,000
Travel		500
Clerical Salaries		6,000
Contracted Services		- 0 -
Gasoline, Oil, Grease		17,500
Tires, Tubes, and Batteries		2,500
Vehicle Repair Parts		20,000
Supplies and Expenses for Garage		
Operation		6,500
Miscellaneous Supplies		1,000
Travel and Mileage		900
Salaries		1,525
Transportation Insurance		6,543
Repairs on Garage Equipment		500
Bus Drivers' Physical Examination		
Costs		500
Bus Drivers' License Costs		172
Bus License Costs		10
Replacement of Vehicles (six)		49,200
Replacement of Garage Equipment		450
Office Supplies		400
Total Transportation	$ 303,875	$ 312,000**
Plant Operation		
Salaries		
Engineers and Maintenance	$ 105,465	$ 148,000
Custodians	443,457	443,457
Others (PBX, truck drivers,		
warehouse)	29,856	29,856
Contracted Services and Rentals	36,500	36,500
Fuel	124,000	124,000
Utilities	148,000	236,000
Supplies and Other Expenses and		
Vehicle	47,000	47,000
Custodians (grounds)	20,965	20,965
Miscellaneous Help (summer)	5,164	- 0 -
Overtime	46,783	40,000
Total Plant Operation	$ 1,007,190	$ 1,125,778
Plant Maintenance		
Contracted Services (grounds, main-		
tenance, decorating)	$ 33,000	$ 33,000
Equipment (contracted)	15,000	15,000

**Assuming a warehouse is provided.

	Budgeted	Four-quarter
Plant Maintenance (continued)		
Supplies and Other Expenses	37,000	41,000
Repairs on Grounds and Equipment	76,117	76,117
Miscellaneous (not planned)	20,000	20,000
Vehicle Repairs	3,500	3,500
Replacement of Equipment	20,500	20,500
Travel and Mileage	500	500
Total Plant Maintenance	$ 205,617	$ 209,617
Fixed Charges		
Insurances		
Employment Retirement and FICA	$ 2,000	$ 2,000
Property	10,500	10,500
Employee	102,700	102,700
Interest (bus cost)	6,625	6,625
Miscellaneous	200	200
Rental (data processing)	32,000	32,000
Total Fixed Charges	$ 154,025	$ 154,025
Expenses to Other School Districts	$ 6,000	$ 6,000
Transfer to Other Funds	$ 1,000	$ 1,000
Capital Outlay (Site, Remodeling,		
Equipment, and Miscellaneous)	$ 100,000	$ 120,000
GRAND TOTAL	$10,162,018	$10,643,434

The following outline will attempt to explain the items which, in the judgment of the writer, might raise questions:

I. Salaries

It is noted that the principals' salaries for elementary, intermediate, and secondary instruction remain the same for both plans. This is due to the fact that the principals will work year-round in the 1969-1970 school year regardless of whether school is nine months or year-round. Teachers' salaries were increased again by 26 percent for the extra days worked. The number of teachers was computed from the simulation of student placement under the nine-month plan for the 1969-1970 school year. It was projected that 245½ teachers will be needed for the K through 5 program, and 320 for the 6 through 12 program. These figures compare with 208½ teachers for the K-5 program needed for the same number of students using a four-quarter plan in 1969-1970, and 260 teachers in grades 6-12 for the same four-quarter plan. With these figures available, the average teacher's salary was found by dividing the regular budgeted amount by the number of teachers projected for 1969-1970. This procedure was used for teachers in the elementary, intermediate, and secondary areas respectively.

II. Attendance

Due to a change in the accounting procedures in the Port Huron Area School District, supervisory salaries under this heading were placed under special education for the purposes of the 1968-1969 budget. For the 1969-1970 school year, special education and attendance share these salaries to reflect the responsibilities of the directors in these areas. It must also be noted that the increase in the salaries of the visiting teachers represents a decrease in the number of visiting teachers contracted for the 1969-1970 regular school year plans for six visiting teachers. Reducing this by 25 percent due to the fact that 25 percent of the students will be on vacation at any one time, would leave four and one-half visiting teachers. The budget for year-round visiting teachers is figured as five visiting teachers earning 26 percent more due to working more days each school year.

III. Transportation

Figures for a four-quarter plan of transportation have been supplied by the transportation department and are based on the acquisition of a central warehouse service area. This budget is also based on the simulated bus routes presented by the transportation department for the four-quarter school.

In comparing the cost of the nine-month school plan with the year-round plan, it should be noted that comparable situations would not exist between the two plans. The nine-month school would be overcrowded during the 1968-1969 and the 1969-1970 academic years. The latter year would be more crowded than the former. The year-round schools, by contrast, would not be overcrowded. There would be space to spare. As the figures for the two operational plans are examined, this very important difference must be kept in mind.

With the above in mind, let us then compare the costs of the two operations. The cost of the 1968-1969 regular school year amounts to $9,197,294. In revenues, the Port Huron Area School District received $4,154,655 from the State Department of Education. The difference, using a state equalized valuation for the Port Huron Area School District for the 1968-1969 school year of $188,463,053, amounted to an expenditure equivalent to 26.75 mills. By contrast, operating the schools of the district on the four-quarter plan would cost approximately $9,911,036. Since the same revenue would have been received from the State Department, the cost for the taxpayer would have been equivalent to 30.55 mills. Accordingly, the difference in the cost of operating the 1968-1969 school year on a four-quarter basis would have been equal to 3.87 mills in extra operational millage. Almost two mills of that amount of difference is accounted for by the installation of air conditioning in the district schools. The rest is due to increased salaries and maintenance costs because of the increased length of the school year.

For the 1969-1970 school year, the preliminary budget prepared by the Port Huron Area School District estimates expenditures at $10,162,018. The estimated expected revenues from the State Department of Education amount to $4,857,825. The differences in revenues will amount to an expected expenditure of 27.31 mills for the above year. The cost of the 1969-1970 four-quarter year on the other hand was projected to be $10,643,434. Since the revenues received from the State Department for a regular school year would not be any different from those received for a four-quarter year, the difference between the two plans would cost the taxpayers an extra 2.49 mills in operational levy.

As one considers the expected increase in the cost of operating schools on a four-quarter plan, it must be remembered that the Port Huron Area School District schools are overcrowded and that the needs justifying the requirement of an $11.8-million bond issue are still with us. It must also be remembered that the cost of construction has increased by about 12 percent in the past year. With this in mind, it is estimated that the buildings, rooms, and additions costing $11.8 million in December of 1968 would cost $13,216,000 at this time. It is then appropriate to consider the alternative cost of building and adding to our existing school facilities. In order to do that, the interest rate on municipal bonds as of September 8, 1969, was obtained from a bonding attorney. The figure quoted was 6.37 percent. Equipped with this figure, an historical pattern of the increase in the state equalized valuation of the Port Huron Area School District was then developed. An average increase in the state equalized valuation was determined to be 2.28 percent per year. Accordingly, the state equalized valuation of the Port Huron Area School District was projected for a period of thirty years, starting with the 1969-1970 academic year. The cost of borrowing $13,216,000 for buildings and sites was also determined per year. In order to retire a mortgage of $13,216,000 in the maximum allotted time of thirty years at an interest rate of 6.37 percent, it was determined that it would cost $988,889 in principal and interest per year. Dividing this figure by the state equalized valuation for each of the thirty years required to retire the bond, the cost in mills for each of the thirty years needed to pay off this mortgage was then determined. With these figures computed, an average of 3.75 mills per year in buildings and sites levy for a period of thirty years would be required. To this amount, it is estimated that the cost of maintaining the additional facilities would amount to 1.8 mills per year.

Assuming no major and drastic increase in the population of the Port Huron Area School District, the rate of increase of 200 per year, which has been our rate of growth for the past four years, would then be expected. The four-quarter plan could then reasonably forestall a major building program in the school district for a period of ten years. Comparing the projected cost of operating the facilities mentioned in the study on a year-round basis to the cost of building and operating the needed facilities for a regular plan of school year operation, it would appear that the taxpayers could be saved a minimum of three mills per year. The cumulative savings amount approximately to $6,463,000 in ten years.

Another important item to remember is that the alternative of constructing the proposed new high school, two elementary schools, and one intermediate school would require operating those schools as well. Accordingly, as new buildings are constructed, those buildings have to be equipped and staffed. Both of these items are also costly. Since one of the schools proposed at the North Road area calls for the construction of an eleven-room elementary building, the cost of operating the Negaunee School (the most equivalent of our schools to the proposed North Road area school) was computed. This cost amounts to $143,202 for the 1968-1969 school year. It would then be safe to assume that a school equivalent to the Negaunee would have cost approximately the same amount of money to operate on a regular school year basis during the year 1968-1969. The bond issue also calls for the construction of a seventeen-room elementary building at Allen and West Water Roads. The Michigamme School, a seventeen-room elementary building, cost the Port Huron Area School District $185,262 to operate in 1968-1969. This same bond issue called for the construction of a 500-pupil intermediate school in the Garfield area. The cost of operating the Howard D. Crull Intermediate School with a student population of about 500 was $318,456 for 1968-1969. A high school was also slated for construction to house 1,800 students. Port Huron Northern High School, which is designed for 1,800 students, cost the school district $1,173,923 to operate for the 1968-1969 school year. The above examples are given to indicate that once the building is constructed, it costs money to operate that building and the cost of operating newer buildings must also be taken into consideration as one decides on the merits of the four-quarter plan.

One final point that should be taken into consideration concerns the long-range cost of constructing buildings for a four-quarter school year. Any new additions in buildings and sites under a four-quarter plan would have to consider the fact that a building designed for two semesters would have the capacity for 25 percent more youngsters under a four-quarter plan. It is reasonable then to expect that the cost of school buildings under a four-quarter plan would be 25 percent cheaper than constructing them for a regular school year.

Sami J. Alam
Director for Research and
Evaluation

Appendix B * General Curriculum Regulations

Regulations adopted by the State Board of Education on March 17, 1969, pursuant to Section 1317 of the Administrative Code of 1929. These regulations shall become effective July 1, 1969.

7-100. GENERAL PROVISIONS

7-110. General Policy—It shall be the policy of the State Board of Education through the Superintendent of Public Instruction to delegate to a Board of School Directors the greatest possible flexibility in curriculum planning consistent with a high quality of education for every pupil in the Commonwealth.

7-111. Exceptions to the Curriculum Regulations—The Superintendent of Public Instruction may grant exceptions to individual regulations contained in this chapter, where necessary to adapt these regulations to school district curriculum needs.

7-112. Experimental Programs—The Superintendent of Public Instruction may waive any or all of the regulations contained in this chapter for experimental programs. Such experimental programs shall be evaluated by the Superintendent yearly and may be terminated at the Superintendent's discretion.

7-120. DEFINITIONS

The following definitions shall apply:

From Regulations of the State Board of Education of Pennsylvania, Chapter 7.

7-121. Schools

a. *Elementary School.* An elementary school shall be defined as kindergarten or grade 1 through grade 6, or a school approved as an elementary school by the Superintendent of Public Instruction.

b. *Secondary School.* A secondary school shall be defined as grades 7 through 12 or a school approved as a secondary school by the Superintendent of Public Instruction.

c. *Middle School.* A middle school shall be defined as a school with at least three consecutive grades from 5 through 8 or a school approved as a middle school by the Superintendent of Public Instruction.

d. *Junior High School.* A junior high school shall be defined as grades 7 through 9 or a school approved as a junior high school by the Superintendent of Public Instruction.

e. *Senior High School.* A senior high school shall be defined as grades 10 through 12 or a school approved as a senior high school by the Superintendent of Public Instruction.

7-122. Unit of Credit

For general course planning purposes only, a unit of credit shall be defined as a planned course of 120 clock hours. Special attention shall be given by school authorities to varying the clock hour requirements in accordance with Sections 7-130 and 7-140 of these regulations.

7-123. Courses

a. *Planned Course*—A planned course shall consist of at least:
1. a written statement of objectives to be achieved by students;
2. content to be used to reach objectives for which credit is awarded at the junior high and senior high levels;
3. expected levels of achievement;
4. procedures for evaluation.

b. *Course Offering*—The term course offering, as applied to Section 7-233, shall be defined as a planned course which shall be taught in each secondary school where there is sufficient student demand. Sufficient student demand shall be determined according to either Section 1604 of the Public School Code of 1949, as amended, or school district policy which does not conflict with Section 1604.

c. *Authorized Course*—An authorized course, as applied to Section 7-234, is defined as a planned course approved for inclusion in the secondary school curriculum.

7-124. Others

a. *Principal*—The term principal shall mean the building principal and not the supervising principal.

b. *Superintendent of Public Instruction*—The term Superintendent of Public Instruction shall mean the Superintendent or his designate.

7-130. AWARDING CREDIT

7-131. Course Completion—Satisfactory completion of planned courses shall be determined by the principal in consultation with the teacher.

7-132. Fractional Units of Credit—Courses may be planned on the basis of fractional credit at the discretion of the principal in consultation with the teacher.

7-133. Laboratory Work—Laboratory hours in arts, English, social studies, mathematics, science, business education and modern foreign languages may be equated with classroom hours.

7-134. Exception to Hours of Instruction as a Basis for Awarding Credit—At the discretion of the principal in consultation with the teacher, credit may be awarded for the satisfactory completion of a planned course as defined in Section 7-123a, regardless of the time actually spent in class, in accordance with policies established by the Board of School Directors.

7-135. Credit by Examination—Credit may be awarded by the principal in consultation with the teacher to regularly enrolled students who successfully pass an examination which assesses mastery of a planned course, as defined in Section 7-123a, regardless of the time spent receiving formal instruction in the course, in accordance with policies established by the Board of School Directors.

7-136. Summer Schools—Summer school courses may be offered for credit or noncredit according to a plan approved by the Superintendent of Public Instruction.

7-137. Standard Evening High School—Credit for Standard Evening High School courses shall be granted on the same basis as the regular school program as provided in Sections 7-122, 7-123a, and 7-130.

7-138. Transfer of Credit—Credits granted by an approved secondary school shall be accepted by all public secondary schools in the Commonwealth upon the transfer of a student.

7-140. INDIVIDUALIZING INSTRUCTION

7-141. Independent Study—Independent Study courses may be offered for credit.

7-142. Course Credit Flexibility—Students may earn course credit through correspondence study, attendance at summer school, Saturday classes, study at summer camps, or in any other manner considered appropriate by the principal and approved by the Superintendent of Public Instruction.

7-143. College Advanced Placement—College level advanced placement courses may be offered as part of the senior high school program of studies.

7-144. Parttime College Enrollment—High school students may enroll part-time in college with the approval of the high school principal.

7-145. Fulltime College Enrollment—Exceptionally able students may leave high school prior to the senior year to attend approved colleges fulltime at the discretion of the school district. The high school diploma shall be awarded to these students upon successful completion of the freshman year of college.

7-146. Pupils 14 Years of Age or Over Not Benefitting from the Existing Program—Any pupil 14 years of age or older who is not benefitting from the regular program as determined by his teacher may, with the permission of his parents and the school principal, have an individualized schedule containing those subjects from which he can profit to prepare him for an occupational skill. All such programs shall include appropriate instruction in citizenship and communication skills.

7-150. SPECIAL INSTRUCTION TO BE PROVIDED IN THE CURRICULUM OF ALL SCHOOLS

7-151. **Racial and Ethnic Group History**—In each course in the history of the United States and of Pennsylvania taught in the elementary and secondary schools of the Commonwealth, there shall be included the major contributions made by Negroes and other racial and ethnic groups in the development of the United States and the Commonwealth of Pennsylvania.

7-152. **Conservation and Outdoor Education**—Conservation and outdoor education shall be a part of the instructional program in every school. This instruction may be presented in separate planned courses or integrated into other courses.

7-153. **Secondary Social Studies**—During grades 7 through 12, six units of social studies shall be offered, of which four units shall be required.

The four required units shall consist of two units of World Cultures and two units of American (U.S.) Culture which shall be interdisciplinary studies taken from the social sciences (anthropology, economics, geography, history, philosophy, political science, psychology and sociology). The two units of electives may be either single-discipline or interdisciplinary courses.

Of the six units, at least two units shall be taught in grades 10 through 12 and be required for graduation.

7-154. **Intergroup Education**—Intergroup education concepts shall be included in appropriate areas of the instructional program of every school.

7-200. SCHOOLS

7-210. Elementary Schools

7-211. Elementary Curriculum

a. *Kindergarten*—Kindergarten curriculums are exempted from the provisions of Section 7-211, b through j. Kindergarten curriculums shall meet standards established by the Superintendent of Public Instruction.

b. *Fine Arts*—Planned courses in art and music shall be taught in each year of the elementary school.

c. *Health*—Health education content shall be taught as a part of the instructional program each year of the elementary school.

d. *Language Arts*—A planned course in the language arts shall be taught in each year of the elementary school. This course shall emphasize skills in listening, speaking, reading, and writing, and shall include instruction in language, literature, and composition. Priorities for instruction shall be in the skills of speaking, reading and composition.

e. *Mathematics*—A planned course in mathematics shall be taught in each year of the elementary school. The content of this planned course shall consist primarily of the study of the fundamental number operations. In addition an emphasis shall be given to the study of informal algebraic and geometric concepts.

f. *Modern Foreign Languages*—Planned courses in modern foreign languages may be taught as part of the elementary school curriculum.

g. *Physical Education*

1. A planned course in physical education shall be taught daily in every grade of the elementary school, or

2. A planned course of adapted physical education shall be taught in every elementary school.

h. *Practical Arts*—Structured industrial arts content and home economics content may be a part of the program each year of the elementary school.

i. *Science*—A planned course in science, including laboratory type experiences, shall be taught in each year of the elementary school.

j. *Social Studies*—A planned course in the social studies shall be taught in each year of the elementary school. The content of this program shall include anthropology, economics, geography, history, political science and sociology. These may be combined into one general area known as social studies.

k. *Integration of Courses*—Any planned course listed within this section may be integrated with other courses or may be taught separately.

7-220. MIDDLE SCHOOLS

7-221. Middle School Curriculum

The curriculum of the middle schools shall be exempted from the requirements for the Elementary Curriculum, Section 7-211, and the Junior High School Curriculum, Section 7-231. The school districts shall submit to the Superintendent of Public Instruction a written request for approval to establish a Middle School Curriculum.

7-222. Written Request for Approval of Curriculum

Written requests shall contain:

a. A precise statement of the objectives of the school.

b. A description of the characteristics of the children to be served by the school.

c. A description of the curriculum to be offered which meets both the objectives and the needs of the children served by the school.

d. A plan for the evaluation of the curriculum at least biennially.

7-223. Subject Placement

All or part of any planned course usually considered to be part of the elementary or secondary school may be taught in the middle school.

7-230. SECONDARY SCHOOLS

7-231. Junior High School Curriculum

The junior high school curriculum shall include, as a minimum, the following planned courses:

a. *Adapted Physical Education*—A planned course of adapted physical education shall be taught in every junior high school. This may be given in place of Section 7-231i.

b. *Developmental Reading*—A planned course for developing reading skills in the content areas. Completion of this course may be accelerated for able pupils. Time spent by pupils in remedial reading courses may be counted toward this requirement.

c. *English*—Two planned courses with content selected from language, literature, and composition. One of the two courses may be speech. The first priority for instruction shall be language study.

d. *Fine Arts*—One planned course in art and one planned course in music, each equivalent to three-fifths of a unit. These courses may be concentrated within one year or divided among the junior high years.

e. *Health Education*—A planned course which may be taught three periods per week for one year, or one period per week in each of grades 7, 8 or 9, or the equivalent scheduling approved by the Superintendent of Public Instruction.

f. *Industrial Arts or Homemaking*—One planned course of both, taught in either grade 7 or grade 8 or the equivalent divided between grades 7 and 8. Industrial arts and homemaking shall be a required offering in grade 9.

g. *Laboratory Science*—Two planned courses.

h. *Mathematics*—Two planned courses with content selected primarily from arithmetic, algebra, geometry, trigonometry, and probability and statistics. An understanding of the structure of mathematics shall be emphasized.

i. *Physical Education*—A planned course given at least two separate times weekly in each of the grades of junior high.

j. *Social Studies*—Planned courses in accordance with Section 7-153.

k. *Additional Planned Courses*—Three planned courses with content selected to reflect student needs. At the discretion of the school district planned courses authorized to be taught in either the senior high school or the elementary school may be taught in the junior high school.

l. *Modern Foreign Languages*—Planned courses in modern foreign languages may be taught as part of the junior high school curriculum.

m. *Unit of Credit Provisions*—The unit of credit provisions of Sections 7-122 and 7-130 shall apply to the junior high school curriculum.

n. *Integration of Courses*—Any planned courses listed within this section may be integrated with other planned courses or may be taught separately.

7-232. Senior High School Graduation Requirements

Thirteen planned courses for credit in grades 10, 11 and 12 shall be required for graduation for all students and shall include the following:

a. *English*—Three planned courses. One of the three planned courses may be speech.

b. *Health Education*—A planned course which may be taken three periods per week in any one year or one period per week in grades 10, 11 and 12.

c. *Mathematics*—One planned course.

d. *Physical Education*—A planned course given at least two separate times weekly in each of grades 10, 11 and 12.

e. *Science*—One planned course.

f. *Social Studies*—Two planned courses in accordance with Section 7-153.

g. *Subject Acceleration*—At the discretion of the school district, courses offered below the senior high school level may be used to meet graduation requirements if the standards for awarding credit are equal to those used in the equivalent senior high school course.

h. *Other Requirements*—Other requirements for graduation may be established at the discretion of the school district so long as such requirements do not conflict with those cited in this section.

i. *Integration of Courses*—Any course listed within this section may be integrated with other courses or may be taught separately.

7-233. Offerings in Senior High Schools

In addition to the planned courses actually required for graduation as set forth in Section 7-232, every senior high school shall have other course offerings. The term "offerings" is defined in Section 7-123b. These offerings shall include the following:

a. *Adapted Physical Education*
b. *Business Education*
c. *Conservation and Outdoor Education* in accordance with Section 7-152.
d. *Consumer Education*
e. *Fine Arts* including instrumental music, vocal music, music appreciation, studio art, art appreciation and related arts.
f. *Foreign Languages* in each school system at least two foreign languages, one of which shall be a modern foreign language given in a minimum four-year sequence.
g. *Home Economics and Family Studies*
h. *Industrial Arts* including concepts of manufacturing and construction, power technology, and visual communications.
i. *Laboratory Sciences* including biology, physics and chemistry.
j. *Mathematics*—at least three years acceptable for college admission.
k. *Personal and Family Survival* included as a part of a related planned course.

7-234. Authorized Courses

In addition to course titles mentioned in Sections 7-210, 7-220, and 7-230, the school district may offer such additional courses as authorized by the Superintendent of Public Instruction in accordance with Section 7-123c in the general areas of mathematics, social studies, foreign languages, humanities, English, fine arts, vocational-technical education, home economics, science, industrial arts, family studies, driver education and aviation education.

7-300. APPROVAL OF SCHOOL PROGRAMS BY THE SUPERINTENDENT OF PUBLIC INSTRUCTION

7-310. Preapproval

Approval by the Superintendent of Public Instruction shall be obtained prior to the following actions:

a. Changing a grade pattern in a school system.
b. Establishing a new secondary school.
c. Establishing a middle school.
d. Constructing new housing, in whole or in part, for any school.
e. Scheduling half-day sessions, in grades 1 through 12.
f. Conducting an experimental program as outlined in Section 7-112 of these regulations.
g. Initiating a program requiring a curriculum exception as outlined in Section 7-111 of these regulations.

7-320. Approval of Secondary School Programs

7-321. Responsibility for Standards for Approval—Standards for approval of secondary schools shall be established by the Superintendent of Public Instruction.

7-322. Periodic Evaluation and Approval—All schools—public, nonpublic, non-profit and private—shall be subject to periodic evaluation by the Superintendent of Public Instruction for the purpose of program approval. Secondary school program approval may be granted a school which meets any of the following:

a. Standards established by the Superintendent of Public Instruction.

b. Accreditation by the Middle States Association of Colleges and Secondary Schools.

c. Any other evaluation approved by the Superintendent of Public Instruction.

7-323. Secondary School Approval—Secondary school approval shall certify that the school qualifies for state reimbursement and that the diplomas issued by such schools constitute valid pre-professional credentials.

7-324. Continuing Approval—Each approved secondary school shall submit annually to the Superintendent of Public Instruction a secondary school report in such form and at such time as determined by the Superintendent of Public Instruction. This report shall be reviewed for compliance. Approval may be revoked for non-compliance.

7-400. SCHOOL LIBRARIES

7-410. Book Collection—By September 1970, each school district shall have a library book collection of no less than ten carefully selected titles per elementary and secondary pupil or a collection of 10,000 titles per school, whichever is smaller. Books borrowed from non-school libraries may not be counted in this total. Schools constructed after September 1968 shall be given four years to comply with this regulation.

7-420. Elementary School Librarian—Each school district shall employ a fulltime, certified elementary teacher or school librarian to provide leadership in the development of an effective elementary library program. An individual appointed to this position must secure certification as an elementary school librarian before September 1973.

7-430. Secondary School Librarian—Every secondary school shall employ a fulltime, certified school librarian.

7-440. School Library Program—By September 1973, every school district shall have in operation a comprehensive library program, including printed material and non-printed media. This program shall encompass kindergarten or grade 1 through grade 12 and shall meet standards established by the Superintendent of Public Instruction.

7-500. CREDENTIALS EVALUATION

7-510. Commonwealth Secondary School Diploma

7-511. Requirements for Issuance—The Commonwealth Secondary School Diploma may be issued to an applicant who is a resident of Pennsylvania and who meets the following requirements:

a. A passing score as determined by the Superintendent of Public Instruction on the high school level Tests of General Educational Development, or

b. Presentation of evidence of full matriculation and the satisfactory completion of a minimum of one full year (30 semester hours) in an accredited college.

7-512. Restriction on Issuance—The Superintendent of Public Instruction shall not issue a diploma until after the class of which the applicant was a member has been graduated.

7-513. Recognition of GED Tests—The Superintendent of Public Instruction may recognize passing scores on the high school level Tests of General Educational Development as fully meeting the requirements on the secondary level for Certificates of Preliminary Education.

7-520. CERTIFICATE OF PRELIMINARY EDUCATION

7-521. Requirements for Issuance—An applicant may be issued a Certificate of Preliminary Education upon presenting:

a. Evidence of graduation from a state approved senior high school with sixteen units of credit in grades 9, 10, 11 and 12 or its equivalent as determined by the Superintendent of Public Instruction, or

b. Evidence of full matriculation and the satisfactory completion of a minimum of one full year in an accredited college or university, or

c. A Commonwealth Secondary School Diploma, or

d. Evidence of completion of the requirements for a Commonwealth Secondary School Diploma as set forth in Section 7-510 except that it will not be required that the applicant be a resident of Pennsylvania.

7-522. Additional Means to Meet Requirements—The following means may also be used to meet the requirements for the Certificate of Preliminary Education:

a. Attending an approved secondary school (day, evening, summer);

b. Through examinations administered by the State Education Agency of another state or the designated agents of that agency.

7-523. Veterans—Veterans of World War II or applicants who are on active duty or who have been on active duty after 1946 in a branch of the armed forces may earn secondary school credit in the following manner:

a. By completing courses listed in the USAFI (United States Armed Forces Institute) catalogue, or

b. By passing USAFI examinations administered in the service, or

c. By completing courses listed in the Guide to the Evaluation of Educational Experiences in the Armed Services.

7-524. Foreign Students—Foreign students without educational credentials may earn the Commonwealth Secondary School Diploma, by meeting the requirements set forth in Section 7-510, or may earn the Certificate of Preliminary Education by meeting the requirements set forth in Section 7-520.

7-530. EVALUATION OF WORK IN NONAPPROVED SECONDARY SCHOOLS

7-531. **Nonapproved Secondary Schools of Pennsylvania**—Courses completed in a nonapproved secondary school for professional purposes may be approved through the subsequent graduation from an approved secondary school after the satisfactory completion in such approved secondary school of advanced courses in the fields of English, mathematics, science, and social studies. These requirements may be met by a minimum of unit courses in English and science and one-half unit courses in mathematics and social studies.

7-532. **Nonapproved Secondary Schools of Other States**—An applicant who has been graduated in another state from a high school that is not on an approved list of secondary schools may clear this work by passing an examination administered by the State Education Agency of that state, or the designated agents of that agency, or by meeting the requirements set forth in Sections 7-510 or 7-520.

7-540. EQUIVALENT COLLEGE CREDIT

7-541. **Subject Areas**—College credit may be accepted toward meeting the requirements for preliminary education in these subjects: Literature, Latin, French, German, Spanish, Russian, Italian, history, mathematics, advanced space science, physics, biology, chemistry, English composition or in any other academic or technological subjects if the requirements set forth in subsection a, b, c, and d below are satisfied:

a. When any or all of these subjects are offered in an approved secondary school and specially designed and taught at the college-freshman level.

b. When the student has passed the required examination prescribed as part of the program or if the student has passed the College Advancement Placement Examination in the subject.

c. If the college admitting the student will accept the advanced college credits as part of the requirements for the associate or bachelor's degree.

d. When a record of the courses with credit allowed by the College has been submitted to the Department of Public Instruction by the college.

7-542. **Acceptance of Examinations**—The Superintendent of Public Instruction may accept as equivalent college credit examinations on the college level offered by institutions of higher learning for preliminary education for the professions.

7-550. USAFI COURSES

The Superintendent of Public Instruction may accept for purposes of meeting preliminary education requirements, USAFI college course credit granted by an approved college or university.

7-600. RELATED CURRICULUM AREAS

7-610. General Extension Education—Extension education programs may be approved according to standards established by the Superintendent of Public Instruction.

7-620. Summer Schools—Summer school programs may be established according to standards established by the Superintendent of Public Instruction.

7-630. Standard Evening High School—Standard evening high school programs may be established according to standards established by the Superintendent of Public Instruction.

Appendix C * Individualized Reading in Our Second Grade

We invited you here tonight because we thought you would be interested in knowing more about the way Miss Philpot is teaching your children to read.

The procedure she is using is known nationally as individualized reading. The term "individualized" is not meant to imply that each child works entirely by himself. To the contrary, the program is designed to give added meaning and interest for each child in a group setting where the teacher helps the children plan tasks that are purposeful and important. The term "individualized" is used because the program is designed as a way of providing for *every individual* the kinds of experiences that will give him an opportunity to achieve success and to grow at his own rate of development.

The central value of democracy is respect for the individual. It is incumbent upon the American school to foster those capacities that will enable each human being to become the best person he is capable of becoming. Such an undertaking must have two fundamental characteristics—universality and diversity. It must be universal because every individual has a right to self-fulfillment. It must be diverse because every child is unique. This approach to reading, then, is called individualized reading because it is designed as an attempt to fulfill the democratic commitment to the individual.

During the past several decades reading has probably received more attention by teachers and parents than any other subject. We tend to view with suspicion any change in the techniques of teaching reading. A common complaint of the critics of the modern school is that we fail to teach phonics. This is exemplified

---

Address given at Wisconsin State College, La Crosse, December 4, 1962.

by the wide publicity received by the book *Why Johnny Can't Read,* by Rudolph Flesch.

Phonics is the analyzing of the sound structure of words. It involves being able to hear and know the sounds in words, and recognizing the printed symbols for the sounds. I do not know of any reading program that does not include the teaching of phonics as one of its integral parts. A major difference between the McGuffey readers and the Scott Foresman readers, for example, is not *which* phonetic skills are taught but *when* they are taught. Prior to the publication of the McGuffey readers in the 1860s, there were no books for children to read. In the McGuffey program children were taught the sound structure (phonics) first, then used this information to learn to recognize words. In the modern approach, children learn to recognize a limited number of words first, then, by using and analyzing these words, they learn the sound structure in context. This approach is educationally and psychologically sound, but still has not escaped the critics' claim that phonics is not being taught.

Phonics cannot be and never has been the only basic skill in reading. Closely related to phonetic analysis is structural analysis, which is the recognition of a new word made from a familiar word plus an ending or a beginning. We learn to recognize words by their general shape or word-form. We also are able to decide what a word is from the rest of the sentence, through contextual clues. Word recognition—being able simply to recognize a word by sight—is ultimately necessary to develop fluent reading. Individualized reading, like any other good reading program, provides a definite procedure for teaching phonetic analysis, structural analysis, word-form clues, contextual clues, and for developing an ever-increasing sight vocabulary.

There are some basic differences between individualized reading and the more widely used approaches, however. For example, the materials that are used as the basic teaching tools, and the way they are used, are different. To explain this, let me relate an experience I had a few years ago. A teacher, who happened to be a third grade teacher, challenged me to show her an answer to a real dilemma. She had twenty-eight children in her classroom. Their reading achievement ranged from the 1.6 grade level to the 6.5 grade level with the others scattered all the way between the two extremes. (See Table 1.) This, incidentally, is a

Table 1. Reading Gradeplacement Scattergram of a Third Grade Class

Grade level	Grade 1 0-1-2-3-4-5-6-7-8-9	Grade 2 0-1-2-3-4-5-6-7-8-9	Grade 3 0-1-2-3-4-5-6-7-8-9-0
Pupil placement	1	2-1-1-3-2-2	2-2 1-1 1

Grade level	Grade 4 0-1-2-3-4-5-6-7-8-9	Grade 5 0-1-2-3-4-5-6-7-8-9	Grade 6 0-1-2-3-4-5-6-7-8-9-0
Pupil placement	1 1 3 2	1	1

normal classroom situation and every teacher is really faced with this same type of problem. She wanted to know how to organize her class into three reading groups, or even four or five, to make them fit into the third grade reading program, which was centered around third grade reading textbooks designed for the 3.0 to 3.9 grade level range. She wanted to know how the children who were not yet up to the third grade level of reading could use these books. She also wanted to know how she could challenge those children who were already reading at a higher level of achievement than the book covered. Since I did not have a good answer, we studied the literature to see what help we might find in research, and we discovered individualized reading. Several other teachers joined us and we began using individualized reading in some of my schools. I have been involved in careful research concerning this approach to teaching ever since.

The answer to my teacher's question, of course, was *not* to use basic textbooks that were designed for that particular grade level, but to use many good materials with reading levels ranging low enough for the slowest child to have successful reading experiences and high enough to challenge the most advanced children.

Individualized reading is different in other ways, too. Until very recent years, about the only source of material with a limited vocabulary for primary children to read was textbooks. Most "children's books" were designed to be read *to* children. Now, however, there is a wealth of highly motivating materials designed to be read *by* children.

We know people learn best when they are interested in what they are doing. With a wide range of good materials available we can now let children select for themselves the books they want to learn to read. This opportunity for a child to make decisions in selecting his own reading materials, then pursuing them independently, provides experience in assuming responsibility for his own actions and developing criteria as a basis for making decisions.

Sometimes a child may select an easy book to read just for pleasure, which helps to increase fluency in reading. At another time he may select a book so hard that he cannot read it. He may put it back and get an easier one, or he may, if the motivation is strong enough, get as much out of it as he can. Actually, as adults, we do much the same thing. We do not always read the most difficult book we are capable of reading. We read for many different reasons and so do children when they are given a choice. With wise and subtle guidance from the teacher, children learn to make wise selections.

The word-attack skills are taught in context, based on the knowledge that children can learn to read by reading. As children read, they get help from the teacher and sometimes from each other. This on-the-spot help with new words is a continuous, all-day process because reading is an integral part of all the subject areas of learning. In addition to on-the-spot help, the teacher plans to meet one or more times a week with each child, the exact frequency and length of time depending on the individual's needs. She listens to him read, discusses his reading pattern with him, helps him to make plans for study, and teaches the word-attack skills as they are needed. Although there is no planned order in which the skills are taught, every skill is so commonly needed that it is bound to be confronted *repetitiously* until it is learned.

Through this one-to-one teacher-pupil relationship the teacher gets to know each child better, which makes her better qualified to teach him. It also helps the child to feel that what he is doing is important and that he himself is important enough to have the teacher's undivided attention.

When a child finishes reading a book he is expected to evaluate it and in some way share his feelings about it with others. This provides an opportunity to develop critical thinking and to stimulate interest in reading. This high level of interest often leads to much wider reading interests and to a greater amount of reading for pleasure. The demand for library books at the public library has greatly increased in communities where this reading approach is used.

To summarize, the characteristics of individualized reading are: (1) a wide range of reading materials used instead of basic textbooks, as such; (2) children select the materials they want to read rather than being placed arbitrarily in an ability or achievement group; (3) the word-attack skills are taught as needed instead of being presented to all children in a prearranged sequence; (4) the teacher provides personal and direct guidance for each child through the teacher-pupil conference; and (5) children have an opportunity to react to what they have read and to share their feelings with others.

When we first began this work in my schools several years ago we were concerned about two major questions. First, we wondered if we could maintain proper pupil control when we gave the children this much freedom, and secondly, we wondered if they would learn to read. The answer to these questions are quite well researched now, but at that time there was very little in the literature about it.

We learned the answer to our first question in two ways. We asked Dr. James McDonald, who had developed the McDonald-New York University scale for measuring environment in a classroom, to measure the environment in four situations: (1) where basic textbooks were used with *no* supplementary materials; (2) where basic textbooks were used with *few* supplementary materials; (3) where basic textbooks were used with *many* supplementary materials; and (4) where individualized reading was used.

The classrooms with individualized reading had the best learning environment, according to the results of the study. The individualized reading situation was significantly better than the first two groups but statistically was not significantly better than the group that used many supplementary materials.

We also learned the answer to the question about pupil control simply by observing. We could see that children were busy at purposeful work.

To answer our second question we had a reading specialist administer a battery of reading tests to our individualized reading groups and to an equal number of control groups at the beginning and end of the year. The increase in achievement for both groups was the same. This held true for all levels of ability. (See Table 2.)

On the basis of these data we could say that one approach seems to be as good as the other for teaching the reading skills. But we are concerned about other things related to children, too. There appear to be many other promising things about the individualized approach. We know that almost all children who have been taught by both methods prefer the individualized approach. We still want to know what effect each approach has on children in regard to:

1. One's perception about himself and his environment;
2. The relationship between social acceptance by the peer group and reading achievement;
3. Long-range reading habits;
4. Broadened general knowledge and vocabulary;
5. One's approach to solving problems and ability to think critically;
6. Self-direction and self-control.

Table 2. Comparison of Achievement between Individualized and Achievement-grouped Approaches to Reading Growth in Years of Grade Placement (length of time between tests = 0.8 years)

I.Q. range	Number of pupils		Gray Oral		Wide Range Vocabulary		Composite	
	Individual	Grouped	Individual	Grouped	Individual	Grouped	Individual	Grouped
120 and above	8	19	1.3	1.2	1.0	1.1	1.15	1.15
110-119	16	14	1.1	1.1	0.8	0.8	0.95	0.95
100-109	17	10	0.9	0.8	0.9	0.8	0.85	0.85
Below 100	7	5	0.9	0.9	0.7	0.7	0.8	0.8

We have reason to believe that in each of these areas children benefit most through the use of the individualized approach.

The Lakeshore Curriculum Study Council, centered at the University of Wisconsin-Milwaukee, developed a longitudinal study to examine these questions. Setting up such a study involved several steps. First, we developed demonstration centers where other teachers could see the program in action. Then we sponsored summer workshops and other in-service activities to help teachers begin to use this approach. After we had enough teachers using individualized reading to carry out the study and had carefully developed the research design, we began our long-range project. We began with first grade children in fifty different classrooms in sixteen different school systems. Half of these children are being taught to read through the individualized approach and the others are being taught through the use of basic textbooks with many supplementary materials. This particular part of the study is in its second year and the children are now in the second grade. I mention this program because it had a direct effect on our getting started here. I was chairman of the research committee that designed the study and director of the workshops used to train the teachers, and I had developed the demonstration centers in my schools. I have all of the materials we used in training the teachers at the University of Wisconsin-Milwaukee.

As you know, Miss Philpot was injured at the beginning of the school year, and needed a rather long period to convalesce. During this time she read everything we had used previously, and more too, because there is much more in print about individualized reading now. In fact, she read just about everything available on the subject. She was interested in seeing the program in action so she visited classes in South Milwaukee, where I had worked, and at the Campus School at the University of Wisconsin-Milwaukee where *all* the grades are now using individualized reading.

I am happy to say that Miss Philpot has begun to use this technique in her classroom. I feel very confident she is doing an excellent job and I feel sure that your children are going to enjoy it very much.

I have merely hit the high spots to indicate what individualized reading is and some of the ideas behind it. Miss Philpot will tell you more about the things she is doing with her class, then we would like to answer any questions you may have.

John D. McLain
Director, Campus School

Appendix D * Opening School Doors

Opening School Doors

NORTHVILLE PUBLIC SCHOOLS

| Northville, Michigan | Vol. 1, No. 1 | October, 1969 |

FOUR-QUARTER PLAN EXAMINED HERE IN STUDY OF YEAR-ROUND SCHOOLS

It has been felt by taxpayers and businessmen that the long period during the summer when school buildings stand idle or receive only partial use, represents inefficient and expensive luxury that would not be tolerated in business. Most school officials agree.

Breaking a tradition, however, that was the result of an agricultural society's need for the assistance of young people during the summer harvest, is not an easy task. As we changed to an urban industrial society, summer closing of the schools continued and most workers received their short summer vacation to coincide with this period.

Most of the reasons which led to the long closing of schools during the summer months are no longer valid. Year-round employment is now available to students on vacation. Most families now enjoy extensive recreation time together and family breadwinners receive three and four week vacations. Recreation has become a year-round activity with winter sports and travel in the south competing with the traditional July and August vacation period.

At the same time, the demand for better, more extensive education requires complex, well equipped schools. With the cost of construction soaring and taxpayers reluctant to assume any greater burden, it seemed an appropriate time to reappraise the traditional school year.

In a growing community such as Northville, there· is even greater urgency for finding some method of holding down the cost of the many schools that will be needed in a short period of time.

Recognizing the need to meet this problem, your school board adopted a resolution to study the feasibility of year-round school operation back in December of 1967. A committee of interested citizens, school administrators and teachers was formed. They were charged by the Board to "encompass a thorough evaluation of all available information and research on the year-round school, the areas of the present instructional program which would be affected by a change to the year-round school approach, the development of the necessary steps to be taken in a transition to this program, and a thorough cost analysis of the opera-

tion of a year-round school versus that of our program, both present and future."

Many months were spent by this committee in studying the various plans under which year-round schools can operate. Methods used by other school districts to put some form of year-round school into operation were examined and the advantages and disadvantages evaluated.

Under each plan studied, consideration was given to the effect it would have on our curriculum, because the Committee was determined that above all, the plan adopted must offer improvements in our educational programs.

Secondly, the plan that would be chosen for Northville had to offer greater utilization of our existing facilities and reduce the need for future building construction.

The plan which most closely meets all these goals is the four quarter or quadrimester plan. It has been recommended by the Study Committee as the plan which will be explained to the residents of Northville and the one on which they will be asked to make a decision.

SIGNIFICANT FINDINGS TO BE REPORTED

by Raymond E. Spear, Superintendent

Superintendent Spear

In the fall of 1967 the Northville Board of Education inquired, "Where are·we and where should we be going?"

This was the first of many questions which have been asked of your School Superintendent.

A complete evaluation of our District revealed one basic fact: the Northville Public Schools are growing and will continue to grow for the next 10 to 15 years.

With this knowledge came the adoption of a Resolution on December 11, 1967, which established that "the Northville Board of Education, in cooperation with the Administration, teaching staff and citizens of the community, undertake a thorough study of the feasibility of adopting the Year-Round School Program."

We have been doing just that for the past two years and are now ready to report some of our most significant findings.

This issue of "Opening School Doors" is brought to you in an attempt to bring about a better understanding of what we are studying and why.

Reprinted by permission of the Superintendent, Northville Public Schools, Northville, Michigan.

HOW QUADRIMESTER WOULD WORK

If adopted by the Northville Schools, the quadrimester, or four-quarter plan, would basically work this way.

The school year would be divided into four quarters of 60 days each. (Tentative dates for the four quarters are shown in the box.)

All students would be required to attend three of the four quarters. To work efficiently and save anticipated building costs, an equal or nearly equal number of students must attend each quarter.

One fourth of the student body would be on vacation during each quarter. Determining which quarter a student takes his vacation would be the most difficult part of implementing the plan.

Students would probably be asked to pick their first and second choice. If first choices did not result in equal distribution among all four quarters, some students would have to accept their second choice. An attempt would be made to give all children in a family a vacation during the same quarter. If it should turn out that an insufficient number of students would accept vacations dur-

SUGGESTED FOUR-QUARTER SCHOOL YEAR

1st Quarter:	August 3 to October 23
2nd Quarter:	October 28 to January 29
3rd Quarter:	February 3 to April 28
4th Quarter:	May 3 to July 23

ing any one quarter, then the year-round school plan would just not work in Northville.

Other than taking vacations at different times of the year and registering for classes three times a year rather than twice, the year-round plan should not be too different for the students.

All students would receive a Christmas and Easter vacation. They would also receive a ten day vacation, along with the teachers, between the fourth and first quarters, July 23 to August 2. There would be two day vacation periods between each quarter.

Of course, the above dates are not part of any final proposal. Much of this planning will depend on the information received from the community survey to be conducted in December.

PLAN REQUIRES CURRICULUM REVISION

One of the major goals in conducting the year-round school study was to find a means of improving the quality of our educational programs. It was felt that such drastic changes in the school routine must be accompanied by better educational opportunities, or year-round school could not be justified.

Research by the Study Committee and Miss Florence Panattoni, Northville's Curriculum Coordinator, indicates that the four-quarter plan adds flexibility to the curriculum which will allow a wider choice of courses, better instruction and the opportunity for greater comprehension.

Presently the school year is divided into two semesters of nearly equal length totaling 181 days of instruction. Students are able to select courses twice a year, but once started they are locked into them for 90 days and in many cases 180 days.

Under the quadrimester plan the school year is divided into four quarters of 60 days each. Every student must attend three of the four quarters. This allows students to select courses three times a year rather than twice.

A complete revision of the current curriculum would be necessary

before this plan could go into effect. Subject matter would have to be designed to fit a 60 day block of time rather than the current 90 day unit. Credits for graduation would also have to be geared to quarter units rather than semester units.

Building courses of 12 weeks in length, with as many as possible standing by themselves, without a need to extend into other quarters, would require a major study of the curriculum and a detailed plan for each subject taught. Such a study would require the time and efforts of students, teachers, administrators, parents and board members.

The results could have a far-reaching effect, by making subject matter more interesting, by utilizing time to better advantage and by more efficient use of teaching equipment and textbooks.

Students attending three of the four quarters are not the only ones that could benefit from this plan. There is the built-in capacity for offering remedial work for students that need it during their vacation quarter and of eventually developing an accelerated curriculum for those students who would profit by it.

Student Graduation Transfers Affected

One of the frequent questions asked about year-round school is its affect on students transferring in or out of the school system during the year. Could a student make the switch from a two semester plan to the four quarter plan without suffering some penalty in placement or without losing some of the subject matter?

School officials do not anticipate any greater problem in transferring into or out of a school using the four quarter plan is now encountered under our two semester plan. This area, however, is in the final part of the study under the State grant and all possible transferring situations have not been thoroughly studied as yet.

Graduation from high school is an important step for a youngster and his family. There is no doubt that with the quadrimester plan in full operation, some students will be completing their work at the end of each quarter. Leaving school four separate times a year should make finding a college or acquiring a job a much easier task.

It has not been decided whether there would be but one graduation exercise a year in Northville or whether more would be scheduled. This could be determined by the students when the plan becomes a reality.

SURVEY PLANNED

A thorough and extensive survey of every home in the Northville School District is planned for December. A personal interview will be conducted and a questionnaire filled out concerning your opinions and reactions to the plan for year-round school.

School officials would like everyone in the community to become aware of all the advantages and disadvantages of year-round school operation, in order that the survey can accurately gauge the desires of all residents.

Your cooperation in giving this matter some thought and discussion in your home, and your help in completing the survey when the interviewer calls, will be of great assistance in making the study successful.

Year-Round School Has Potential
For Savings In Construction Costs

One of the most attractive features of the quadrimester plan is its potential for saving the taxpayers in Northville large sums of money in construction costs. For example, under the current two semester plan, Northville Schools have a total capacity of about 3,300 students. Under the quadrimester plan we could house up to 4,400, or an additional 1,100 students. We have projected building costs, per pupil, this school year to be $4,000. The quadrimester plan could show net savings in providing accommodations for these additional students alone of about $450,000 in one year.

It is in the long range building program, however, that the real savings in the quadrimester plan seems apparent. The year-round school study has projected the growth of the Northville School District for the next five years. If the maximum projection of population expansion holds true, we could save some 40% of anticipated construction and bond interest costs which could amount to over $7.5 million.

If we were to look at the ultimate population projections for this school district, covering the next 20 years or so, the anticipated savings could amount to 25 to 30 million dollars.

Operational costs, the day to day expenses of running the schools, which include things such as salaries, teaching supplies, heat, light and transportation, would also be affected initially by a switch to the quadrimester plan. There would be some additional costs involved in adjusting work schedules, conducting in-service training for all staff members, upgrading of curriculum standards and generally making the transition from the two semester system to the four quarter plan. The exact amount of these conversion costs is currently under study.

However, the Study Committee has determined, that once this conversion has been completed and the year-round school is fully implemented, operating costs per pupil would be no higher than they are under the present plan. Even during this period the committee could foresee no per pupil increase in the cost of transporting a student to school or of maintaining the buildings.

In fact, the committee felt very strongly that an operational cost saving, per pupil, would be realized due to the increased efficiency in operations, transportation, maintenance and administration. Having fewer buildings to staff, administer, operate and maintain and being able to program each of these items on a "full production" basis rather than the current "stop-start" procedure, could enable us to employ systems of efficiency not now economically feasible. The committee further observed that on a full time basis, teachers could be measured by more normal business procedures and that their rate of compensation could then be established more in line with other professions and industries.

From a cost standpoint, based on full use of all our facilities, equipment, and staff the ultimate saving in money, time and efficiency could be enormous under the year-round operation of our schools. If money alone were the only factor to be considered, schools would have been operated on a year-round basis for a good many years.

Many Basic Routines Affected By Year-Round School

Cafeterias in Northville High School and in the Junior High, now serving meals September through June, would be operating on a year-round basis on a four quarter school year.

Northville's school buses, now a familiar sight during the traditional school year, would be in continuous operation all year long, under a quadrimester school plan.

YEAR - ROUND SCHOOL AFFECTS COMMUNITY LIFE

The major part a school system plays in the life of a community becomes more evident when the effects of year-round school operation are studied. Local business and industry would most certainly have to make some major adjustments to accommodate year-round school operation.

For one thing, there might be requests by many employees for a change in their vacation schedule. If children receive vacations in fall, winter and spring, many of their parents might desire a vacation pe-

riod to coincide with their children's vacation.

Student employment p a t t e r n s would also be altered. Rather than flood local employers with a large student labor force during the summer, there will be a steady 25% of the student body available all year long for part or full-time jobs. Graduating quarterly would also be a great aid in locating permanent work or in gaining entrance to a college of the student's choice.

Representatives of business and

industry in Northville and the Detroit area will be contacted to determine their reaction and degree of cooperation in making year-round school work.

Not only would business and industry require some adjustments, but recreational facilities in the area would have to provide some year-round activities. With 25% of the students on vacation at all times, organizations such as the Park & Recreation Department of the City, Boy and Girl Scouts, Little Leagues and church sponsored recreation, would have to provide year long activities rather than concentrated summer programs.

Even school sponsored extracurricular activities, such as, clubs, dances, athletics and band, will have to make some revisions in order to make all activities available to all students, regardless of whether they are in or out of school.

Northville High

Could These Schools Operate Year-Round?

These Northville public schools, traditionally closed during the summer months, would be in operation all year long under a proposed four-quarter school year.

Junior High

Amerman Elementary

Moraine Elementary

Main Street Elementary

Year-Round School Presentation Planned

Every resident of the Northville School district is going to have the opportunity to see and hear a detailed explanation of how the year-round school plan would work. A slide presentation is being prepared and will be available for every social, civic, school, religious, and service organization in the community at their request.

The presentation will be given by school personnel and members of the Study Committee who are knowledgeable about all facets of the quadrimester plan and will give you plenty of opportunity to ask questions.

Showing of the presentation will probably begin the middle of November.

NORTHVILLE PUBLIC SCHOOLS

405 W. Main Street, Northville, Michigan 48167

Telephone: 349-3400

BOARD OF EDUCATION

Robert Froelich, President

Richard Martin, Vice President

Eugene Cook, Secretary

Andrew Orphan, Treasurer

Stanley Johnson

Orlo Robinson, M.D.

Glenn Deibert

Appendix E * Utica Community Schools Surveys

Cover Letter

To Whom It May Concern:
   The Utica Community Schools is one of six school districts that have received a grant from the Michigan Department of Education, financed by the Michigan State Legislature, to study the possibility of beginning a twelve-month school year.
   The Utica study revolves around a four-quarter year-round school program. Under this proposal, students would be required to attend school three out of four quarters each year.
   Would you please assist the school district in its study by filling out the enclosed survey and returning it in the enclosed envelope? In addition to surveying business and industrial firms in the community, the opinions of community residents, school district teachers and administrators, and the students, are also being sought.
   Your responses to the enclosed survey are important in helping the Board of Education decide whether or not to continue the study for our school district.
   The complete year-round schools study will be finished by the end of the school year. If there appears to be genuine popular support for this system, the school district would probably wish to try it first as a pilot program, as it does with all of its proposed programs.

Year-Round School Study, Utica Community Schools, Utica, Michigan. Reprinted by permission of the Superintendent, Utica Community Schools.

The Utica-Shelby Chamber of Commerce has approved the enclosed survey. Your responses to the questions will remain anonymous. The cooperation you can give by filling out the enclosed survey and returning it in the enclosed envelope at your earliest convenience will be appreciated.

Business and Industrial Survey

Information about Respondents

1. Type of business or industry
   ☐ Manufacturing
   ☐ Professional or Technical
   ☐ Retail
   ☐ Office or Service
   ☐ Other   Specify _____

2. Name and address of your business or industry

   _____

   Name of business or industry

   _____

   Address   City

3. Approximate number of employees _____

4. Approximate number of hourly employees _____

5. Approximate number of salaried employees _____

6. Estimated percentage of employees who live in the Utica Community Schools area (the northern two-thirds of Sterling Heights, all of the city of Utica, and all of Shelby Township).
   ☐ Under 10%
   ☐ 11-25%
   ☐ 26-50%
   ☐ 51-75%
   ☐ 76-100%

Instructions: Please check the appropriate box or fill in the blanks revealing your opinions about the questions that follow.

1. Please rank on the basis of 1, 2, 3, and 4 the seasons when your hourly workers take their vacations. One would be the season when the greatest number of employees vacation, 2 the second busiest, 3 the third busiest, and 4 the season used least for vacations.
   _____ Winter
   _____ Spring
   _____ Summer
   _____ Fall

2. Please rank on the basis of 1, 2, 3 and 4 the seasons when your salaried workers take their vacations. One would be the season when the greatest number of employees vacation, 2 the second busiest, 3 the third busiest, and 4 the season used least for vacations.

   _____ Winter
   _____ Spring
   _____ Summer
   _____ Fall

3. Would it help your business/industry if your hourly employees wanted to take their vacations at a time other than during the summer?
   ☐ Yes
   ☐ No
   ☐ Undecided

4. Would it help your business/industry if your salaried employees wanted to take their vacations at a time other than the summer?
   ☐ Yes
   ☐ No
   ☐ Undecided

5. If a four-quarter year-round school program were started, I would allow my hourly employees to take their vacations at any season of the year.
   ☐ Yes
      How long ahead of time would you need to know the vacation plans of your employees to arrange proper manpower scheduling?
      ☐ Less than one month
      ☐ One to three months
      ☐ Three to six months
      ☐ Six months to a year
      ☐ A year or more
   ☐ No
   ☐ Undecided

6. If a four-quarter year-round school program were started, I would allow my salaried employees to take their vacations at any season of the year.
   ☐ Yes
      How long ahead of time would you need to know the intended vacation plans of your employees to arrange proper manpower scheduling?
      ☐ Less than one month
      ☐ One to three months
      ☐ Three to six months
      ☐ Six months to a year
      ☐ A year or more
   ☐ No
   ☐ Undecided

7. Please indicate the conditions under which your business/industry would approve of a four-quarter year-round school program. You may check all of the answers below, or none of them, as you prefer.

   A. Students would receive about the same education as they do now, but it would cost business/industry less in local school taxes.
     ☐ Yes
     ☐ No
     ☐ Undecided

   B. Additional education would be offered to students for about the same amount of money business/industry now pays in local taxes.
     ☐ Yes
     ☐ No
     ☐ Undecided

   C. Additional education would be offered to students only if there were also some increase in the amount of local school taxes.
     ☐ Yes
     ☐ No
     ☐ Undecided

   D. ☐ I do not favor any of the proposed plans. My reasons are:

_____

_____

_____

_____

8. Do you hire high school students during the school year?
   ☐ Yes
   Approximately how many high school students do you hire during the school year?
     ☐ 0-5
     ☐ 5-10
     ☐ 10-20
     ☐ 20-50
     ☐ 50 or more
   ☐ No

9. Do you believe you would hire more high school students if they were available for work during periods other than the summer?
   ☐ Yes
   Which type of work would you hire more students for?
     ☐ Part-time
     ☐ Full-time

Also, during what periods of the year would you hire more high school students if they were available?
- ☐ Winter
- ☐ Spring
- ☐ Summer
- ☐ Fall
☐ No
☐ Undecided

10. Do you believe you would hire more qualified high school *graduates* if they became available for work during periods other than the summer?
- ☐ Yes
- ☐ No
- ☐ Undecided

11. Our business/industry would be interested in hiring more students full-time if they attended school year-round and graduated earlier. (A new state law allows firms to hire all persons 17 years of age or older who have received a high school diploma.)
- ☐ Yes
- ☐ No
- ☐ Undecided

12. What do you see as the biggest advantage of a four-quarter year-round school program for your business/industry at this time?

_____

_____

_____

_____

_____

13. What do you see as the biggest disadvantage of a four-quarter year-round school program for your business/industry at this time?

_____

_____

_____

_____

14. Any additional comments about the four-quarter year-round school program or about the Utica Community Schools in general?

_____

_____

_____

_____

Certified Staff Survey

Introduction

The enclosed survey is intended to explore your opinions about a four-quarter year-round school program in the Utica Community Schools. The survey is one of five that will be conducted in the next month or two. Additional surveys will be conducted with residents of the community, business and industrial firms, students, and the school administration.

This teacher survey has been approved by a year-round schools Citizens Advisory Committee for year-round schools and the Utica Education Association. Please check the boxes that describe information about you on the first page and record your opinions regarding implications about year-round schools on the subsequent pages.

This survey will be given to all teachers in the Utica Community Schools. Your responses are important in helping the Board of Education decide whether or not a four-quarter year-round school program is feasible in our school district. After the survey is completed, please return it to your building principal.

The Utica Community School District year-round school study will be completed by the end of this school year. If there appears to be genuine popular support for the system, the school district would probably wish to try it first as a pilot program, as it does with all of its new proposed programs.

The Atlanta schools are presently attempting a modified four-quarter year-round school plan. Officials there report it took a total of five years to get their program under way. If our study reveals that a local year-round school program is possible, it would be several years before it would have a major impact on our construction and personnel needs.

Information about Respondents

1. Employment level
   ☐ Elementary school
   ☐ Junior high school
   ☐ Senior high school

2. Sex
   ☐ Male
   ☐ Female

3. Years of teaching experience
   ☐ 0-1
   ☐ 1-2
   ☐ 2-3
   ☐ 3-5
   ☐ 5-7
   ☐ 7-10
   ☐ 10 or more

4. ☐ Married
   ☐ Unmarried

5. Highest degree held
   ☐ Bachelors degree
   ☐ Masters degree
   ☐ Educational specialist

6. Do you live in the school district?
   ☐ Yes
   ☐ No

Instructions: Please check the appropriate box or fill in the blanks revealing your opinions about the questions that follow.

1. Would you be interested in working year-round?
   ☐ Yes
   What are your major reasons for wanting to work year-round? Mark as many as you feel appropriate.
   ☐ Extra pay and/or benefits to be determined
   ☐ Potential curricular advantages
   ☐ Students need more education these days, and I feel a professional responsibility to help them get it by working longer each year if necessary
   ☐ Better utilization of buildings
   ☐ It would reduce criticism that teaching is not a full-time profession
   ☐ Other   Specify _____

   _____

   _____

   ☐ No
   What are your major objections to working year-round? Mark as many as you feel appropriate.
   ☐ Only want to teach ten months a year
   ☐ Concerned about air conditioning in buildings during the summer
   ☐ Want to spend more time with the family
   ☐ Want to take advanced courses during the summer
   ☐ Want to supervise my children's activities
   ☐ Want to supplement my income with another kind of job
   ☐ Want to travel
   ☐ Record keeping
   ☐ Teaching assignment
   ☐ Other   Specify _____

   _____

   _____

2. If the Utica Community Schools were to begin a four-quarter year-round school program, when would you prefer to have your vacation? Rank your preferences for the following seasons on the basis of 1, 2, 3, and 4. One would be your strongest preference, 2 your next strongest, etc.

_____ Winter
_____ Spring
_____ Summer
_____ Fall

3. Rate your preferences 1, 2, and 3 for the following possible plans for arranging school on a four-quarter year-round basis.

☐ School would be open for four consecutive quarters and you would be required to teach for three of the four quarters.

☐ School would be open for four consecutive quarters, but for a longer period of time each day. You would be required to teach for three of the four quarters. You would receive an additional one-month vacation in the summer.

☐ School would be open for four consecutive quarters, but each school day would be a little longer. You would be required to teach for three of the four quarters. You would receive an additional week of vacation between each quarter.

☐ Undecided

4. Would you be interested in working year-round if the fourth quarter were spent on professional tasks other than your normal classroom duties? This could include curriculum improvement, educational research, conferences, seminars and workshops, and supervising enrichment programs.

☐ Yes
☐ No

5. I would agree to taking a vacation other than the summer if the following members of my family could get away at the same time.

☐ Student members
☐ Other wage earners in my family
☐ Both student members and other wage earners in my family
☐ None of the above appeal to me

6. What do you see as the biggest advantage of a four-quarter year-round school program?

_____

_____

_____

_____

_____

7. What do you see as the biggest disadvantage of a four-quarter year-round school program?

_____

_____

_____

_____

_____

8. Do you have any other comments about the Utica Community Schools or about the proposed four-quarter year-round school program?

_____

_____

_____

_____

_____

Student Survey

Introduction

The enclosed survey is intended to explore your opinions about a four-quarter year-round school program in the Utica Community Schools. The survey is one of five that will be conducted in the next month or two. Additional surveys will be conducted with residents of the community, business and industrial firms, teachers, and the school district administration.

The student survey has been approved by the Intra-School Student Council. Please place a checkmark in the boxes below that describe information about you and your opinions about the year-round school on the other pages. Fill in the blanks when asked.

This survey is being given to all ninth and eleventh grade students in the Utica Community Schools and at St. Lawrence High School, and eighth graders at Trinity Lutheran School. Your responses are important in helping the Board of Education decide whether or not to consider starting a four-quarter year-round school program in our school district.

After the survey is completed, please return it to your classroom teacher.

The complete year-round schools study will be finished by the end of the school year. If there appears to be genuine popular support for this system, the school district would probably wish to try it first as a pilot program, as it does with all of its proposed new programs.

The Atlanta, Georgia, schools are presently attempting a modified four-quarter year-round school plan. Officials there reported it took a total of five years to get their program under way. If our study reveals that a local year-round school program is possible, it would probably be several years before it would have a major impact on our construction and personnel needs. Thank you for your cooperation.

Information about You

Please check appropriate boxes in all three columns.

School	Grade	Sex
☐ Stevenson High School	☐ 8th grade	☐ Male
☐ Utica High School	☐ 9th grade	☐ Female
☐ St. Lawrence High School	☐ 11th grade	
☐ Trinity Lutheran Elementary School		
☐ Davis Junior High School		
☐ Sterling Junior High School		
☐ Shelby Junior High School		
☐ Eppler Junior High School		

1. Have you held a part-time job while you are in school?
   ☐ Yes
   ☐ No

2. What do you usually do during your summer vacation?
   ☐ Summer school
   ☐ Full-time work
      If you work full-time, when do you work?
      ☐ During the day
      ☐ During the evening
      ☐ During both the day and evening
   ☐ Part-time work
      If you work part-time, when do you work?
      ☐ During the day
      ☐ During the evening
      ☐ During both the day and evening
   ☐ No school or work

3. Do you usually leave town for some time during the summer?
   ☐ Yes
      ☐ All summer
      ☐ A week or two
   ☐ No

4. If the Utica Community Schools were to begin a four-quarter year-round school program, when would you prefer to have your vacation from school? Rank your preferences for the following seasons on the basis of 1, 2, 3, and 4. One would be your strongest preference, 2 next strongest, etc.
   _____ Winter
   _____ Spring
   _____ Summer
   _____ Fall

5. Rate your preferences 1, 2, and 3 for the following possible plans for arranging school on a four-quarter year-round basis.
   ☐ School would be open for four consecutive quarters and students would be required to attend classes for any three of the four quarters.
   ☐ School would be open for four consecutive quarters, but each school day would be a little longer. Students would attend school for any three of the four quarters. Everybody would receive an additional one-month vacation period in the summer.
   ☐ School would be open for four consecutive quarters, but each school day would be a little longer. Students would attend school for any three of the four quarters. All students would receive an additional week of vacation between each quarter.
   ☐ Undecided

6. Would you approve of some type of year-round school program whereby you could attend the summer session strictly on a tuition basis to broaden or accelerate your education?
   ☐ Yes
   ☐ No
   ☐ Undecided
   If yes, which of the following types of courses would you like to take during the summer quarter? (Answer as many as you feel are appropriate.)
   ☐ Trade and Industrial Education
   ☐ Academics such as English, Math, History, Social Studies, etc.
   ☐ Business Education
   ☐ Home Economics
   ☐ Retailing and Marketing courses
   ☐ Enrichment courses such as Art, Drama, Mythology, etc.
   ☐ Languages
   ☐ Physical Education and Recreation, including swimming
   ☐ Other   Specify_____

7. If a four-quarter year-round school program is established, should special privileges regarding school attendance be given to students who are involved in junior varsity and varsity sports?
   ☐ Yes
      Which one of the following two possible special privileges should be given to these students? (Mark one.)
      ☐ They should be given a choice on what quarters of the year they attend school.
      ☐ They should be allowed to participate in sports even if they are not attending school at the time.
   ☐ No
      Should these students be allowed to participate in sports even if they are not attending school at the time?
      ☐ Yes
      ☐ No

8. If a four-quarter year-round school program is established, should special privileges regarding attendance be given to students involved in such extra-curricular activities as Student Council, clubs, yearbook, and newspaper staff, etc.?
   ☐ Yes
   Which one of the following two possible special privileges should be given to these students? (Mark one.)
   ☐ They should be given a choice on what quarters of the year they attend school.
   ☐ They should be allowed to participate in extra curricular activities even if they are not attending school at the time.
   ☐ No
   Should these students be allowed to participate in extra curricular activities even if they are not attending school at the time?
   ☐ Yes
   ☐ No

9. Do you have any other comments about the Utica Community Schools or about the proposed four-quarter year-round school program?

   _____

   _____

   _____

   _____

   _____

   _____

Community Attitude Survey

Introduction by Interviewer

Hello, my name is _____ .
I am helping the Utica Community Schools conduct a survey of attitudes regarding four-quarter year-round schools. As you may know, the school district has received a grant from the State of Michigan to study whether or not it would be possible to begin a four-quarter year-round school program here.
The school district is going to rely heavily on the feelings of residents in deciding whether to continue the study. The survey I have is designed to find out what people in the school district think about year-round schools. Would you mind if I asked you a few questions?

Information about Respondents

1. What elementary school is nearest your home? (Circle correct number.)

   1. Auburnshire   8. Flickinger   16. Plumbrook
   2. Burr   9. Gibbing   17. Schwarzkoff
   3. Collins   10. Harvey   18. Sterling
   4. Crissman   11. Kidd   19. Switzer
   5. Disco   12. Magahay   20. Walsh
   6. Dresden   13. Messmore   21. West Utica
   7. Ewell   14. Monfort   22. Wiley
                          15. Morgan

2. Are you
   ☐ Married
   ☐ Unmarried (Includes persons who are single, widowed, divorced, separated, etc.)

3. Do you have children?
   ☐ Yes
   ☐ No
   If yes, do you have
   ☐ Preschoolers
   ☐ Elementary School Children (grades kindergarten to six)
   ☐ Junior High School Children (grades seven to nine)
   ☐ Senior High School Children (grades ten to twelve)
   If you have children in high school, are any of them involved in varsity sports?
   ☐ Yes
   ☐ No
   If you have children in high school, are any of them involved in such extra curricular activities as student council, clubs, newspaper or yearbook staff, etc.?
   ☐ Yes
   ☐ No
   ☐ Children attend a parochial or private school.
   ☐ Children have graduated or left school.

4. Sex
   ☐ Male
   ☐ Female

5. How long have you lived in the school district?
   ☐ Less than two years
   ☐ Two to four years
   ☐ Four to six years
   ☐ Six years or more

6. How many times have you moved in the past ten years?
   - ☐ Not at all
   - ☐ Once
   - ☐ Twice
   - ☐ Three times or more

7. Are you registered to vote?
   - ☐ Yes
   - ☐ No

8. Do both the husband and wife work in your family?
   - ☐ Yes
   - ☐ No

Name of person interviewed _____

Address _____

Telephone number _____

Name of interviewer _____

Instructions: Please check the appropriate box or fill in the blanks revealing your opinions about the questions that follow.

1. In general, how well would you rate the present educational programs of the Utica Community Schools?
   - ☐ Above average
   - ☐ Average
   - ☐ Below average
   - ☐ Undecided

2. In your opinion, how well are our high school graduates being prepared to take additional training or courses after high school if they wish?
   - ☐ Very well prepared
   - ☐ Fairly well prepared
   - ☐ Poorly prepared
   - ☐ Undecided

3. Now, how about our high school graduates who plan to immediately take a job in business or industry after graduation. How well are they prepared?
   - ☐ Very well prepared
   - ☐ Fairly well prepared
   - ☐ Poorly prepared
   - ☐ Undecided

4. How well do you feel we are using our school buildings, considering that regular educational programs are offered during the day for all students and other types of adult education, enrichment and recreation programs are offered in the evening and summer?
   ☐ Very good use
   ☐ Adequate use
   ☐ Poor use
   ☐ Undecided

5. If the Utica Community Schools were to begin a four-quarter year-round school program, when would you prefer that students (including your children) have their vacation? Rank your preferences for the following seasons on the basis of 1, 2, 3, and 4. One would be your strongest preference, 2 next strongest, etc.
   _____ Summer
   _____ Fall
   _____ Winter
   _____ Spring
   If summer is your strongest preference (1):
   Why do you prefer to continue summer vacations for students (including your children?) Answer as many as you feel appropriate.
   ☐ Satisfied with current school calendar
   ☐ Recreation opportunities for children
   ☐ Breadwinner vacations during the summer
   ☐ Tradition
   ☐ Want to travel with children
   ☐ Don't like the possibility that my children will be on vacation at different times
   ☐ Other   Specify_____

   _____

6. I would approve of a four-quarter year-round school program in the Utica Community Schools if (answer as many as you feel appropriate):
   ☐ Students would receive about the same education as they do now for less in school taxes
   ☐ Students would receive more educational opportunities for the same amount of local taxes
   ☐ Students would receive more educational opportunities, although it would cost more in local school taxes
   ☐ None of the above possibilities appeals to me
   ☐ Undecided

7. Would you approve of some type of year-round school program whereby students could attend the summer session strictly on a tuition basis to broaden or accelerate their education?
   ☐ Yes
   ☐ No
   ☐ Undecided

8. Rate your preferences 1, 2, and 3 for the following possible plans for arranging school on a four-quarter year-round basis.

☐ School would be open for four consecutive quarters and students would be required to attend classes for three of the four quarters.

☐ School would be open for four consecutive quarters, but each school day would be a little longer. Students would be required to attend school for three of the four quarters. Everybody would receive an additional one month vacation period in the summer.

☐ School would be open for four consecutive quarters, but each school day would be a little longer. Students would be required to attend school for three of the four quarters. All students would receive an additional week of vacation between each quarter.

☐ Undecided

9. In your opinion, if a year-round four-quarter program is started in the Utica Community Schools, and the number of courses is increased, what kinds of courses should we offer more of? Answer as many as you feel appropriate.

☐ Trade and Industrial Education
☐ Academics such as English, Math, History, Social Studies, etc.
☐ Business Education
☐ Home Economics
☐ Retailing and Marketing courses
☐ Enrichment courses such as Art, Drama, Mythology, etc.
☐ Languages
☐ Physical Education and Recreation
☐ Other   Specify_____

10. If a four-quarter year-round school program is established, should special privileges regarding school attendance be given to students who are involved in junior varsity and varsity sports?

☐ Yes

Which one of the following two possible special privileges should be given these students? (Mark one.)

☐ They should be given a choice on what quarters of the year they attend school.

☐ They should be allowed to participate in sports even if they are not attending school at that time.

☐ No

Should these students be allowed to participate in sports even if they are not attending school at the time?

☐ Yes
☐ No
☐ Undecided

11. If a four-quarter year-round school program is established, should special privileges regarding attendance be given to students involved in such extra curricular activities as Student Council, clubs, yearbook and newspaper staff, etc.?

☐ Yes

Which one of the following two possible special privileges should be given these students? (Mark one.)

☐ They should be given a choice on what quarters of the year they attend school.

☐ They should be allowed to participate in extra curricular activities even if they are not attending school at the time.

☐ No

Should these students be allowed to participate in extra curricular activities even if they are not attending school at the time?

☐ Yes

☐ No

☐ Undecided

12. Do you have any other comments you would like to make regarding the Utica Community Schools or the proposed four-quarter year-round school program, or any other educational issue in this community?

Administrative Staff Survey

Introduction

The enclosed survey is intended to explore your opinions about a four-quarter year-round school program in the Utica Community Schools. The survey is one of five that will be conducted with residents of the community, business and industrial firms, students and teachers.

The administrative survey has been approved by the Steering Committee of the Year-Round Schools. On the following pages, please check the boxes that describe information about you on the first page and your opinions regarding implications of the year-round schools on the subsequent pages. Fill in the blanks when asked.

This survey is being given to all administrators in the Utica Community Schools. Your responses are extremely important in helping the Board of Education decide whether or not a four-quarter year-round school program is feasible in our school district. After the survey is completed, please return it to Cass Franks, Administrative Assistant for School-Community Relations.

The complete year-round schools study will be finished by the end of the
school year. If there appears to be genuine popular support for this system, the
school district would probably wish to try it first as a pilot program, as it does
with all of its proposed new programs.

The Atlanta Schools are presently attempting a modified four-quarter year-
round school program. Officials there reported it took a total of five years to get
their program underway. If our study reveals that a local year-round school
program is possible, it would probably be several years before it would have a
major impact on our construction and personnel needs.

Thank you for your cooperation.

Information about Respondents

1. Position _____

    If you are a principal, are you an
    ☐ Elementary school principal
    ☐ Junior high school principal
    ☐ Senior high school principal
    If you are an assistant principal, are you a
    ☐ Junior high school assistant principal
    ☐ Senior high school assistant principal

2. Years of experience as an administrator
    ☐ Less than two years
    ☐ Two to five years
    ☐ Five or more years

Note: This question should be answered by all administrators. The next four
questions (2, 3, 4 and 5) should be answered only by administrators who work
fewer than 52 weeks a year.

1.. Considering your on-the-job tasks, what things would be most difficult to do
    if schools were kept open for twelve months? Explain in detail and attach
    additional pages if necessary.

_____

_____

_____

_____

_____

_____

_____

_____

_____

_____

The following four questions should be answered only by administrators who work fewer than 52 weeks a year.

2. Would you be interested in working year-round, with the extra pay or benefits to be determined?
   ☐ Yes
   ☐ No
   If yes, what are the major reasons?
   ☐ Additional salary and/or fringe benefits
   ☐ Recognize need for students to be in school longer each year in order to keep pace with the educational needs of today
   ☐ School facilities and services should be used for a longer period of time each school year
   ☐ Other   Specify_____
   If your answer is no, what are your major objections to working year-round?
   ☐ Concerned about air conditioning in buildings during the summer
   ☐ Want to spend more time with the family
   ☐ Want to take advanced courses during the summer
   ☐ Want to supervise my children's recreational activities
   ☐ Want to supplement my income with another kind of job
   ☐ Want to travel
   ☐ Other   Specify_____

3. If the Utica Community Schools were to begin a four-quarter year-round school program, when would you prefer to have your vacation? Rank your preferences for the following seasons on the basis of 1, 2, 3, and 4. One would be your strongest preference, 2 next strongest, etc.
   _____ Winter
   _____ Spring
   _____ Summer
   _____ Fall

4. Would you be interested in working year-round if the fourth quarter were spent on such professional tasks as curriculum improvement, educational research, conferences, seminars, and workshops, etc.?
   ☐ Yes
   ☐ No

5. I would agree to take an off-season vacation if the rest of my family could get away at the same time.
   ☐ Yes
   ☐ No

This question can be answered by all administrators.

6. Do you have any other general concerns about a year-round school program? If so, please explain in detail and attach additional pages, if necessary.

   _____
   _____
   _____

Appendix F * Plans in Operation

1. The 45-15 Year-Round School

Overview of Operational Plans for Becky-David Elementary School

Becky-David Elementary Schools, located in Francis Howell School District, only thirty minutes from St. Louis, Missouri, have the capacity of housing something over 1,300 students. It became apparent in the fall of 1968 that the debt limit of the school district would make it impossible to build elementary classrooms to meet the population growth (about 12 percent per year). This being the case, Dr. Gene Henderson, District Superintendent, commissioned a task force of school personnel to find an answer to the monumental problem of housing 1,500 to 1,600 students in a school built for 1,300 without sacrificing educational excellence.

Within a few weeks numerous possibilities were narrowed to three. First, it was proposed to change the junior/senior high campus to double sessions with all sixth year students in the district, including those from Becky-David, being transferred to the junior high. Under this plan tenth through twelfth year students would attend school from 6:00 a.m. till noon, and sixth through ninth graders would attend school from 12:30 p.m. to 6:30 p.m. This idea was discarded primarily because the length of bus routes would have necessitated some students boarding buses before 5:00 a.m. and others getting home after 7:30 p.m.

Reprinted by permission of the author.

Second, serious thought was given to converting World War II buildings located on the junior/senior high campus into classrooms and again transferring sixth year students to the junior/senior high campus. School officials considered this plan a short-term *solution* and a long-term *waste* of money.

Third, study began on the feasibility of year-round school throughout the district. Finally the year-round idea concentrated on Becky-David schools as a pilot. When a questionnaire sent to parents indicated that 62 percent preferred the year-round plan over the other possibilities, the School Board decided to go ahead with development and implementation for July 1969.

Development

Becky-David is actually two schools—a primary school and an intermediate school. Miss Wilma Cole is principal of the primary school. The two schools are connected by a multipurpose/kitchen complex in the center of the building. With its forty-eight classrooms, Becky-David is one of the larger elementary schools in Missouri.

Though the concept of operating schools for twelve months is not new, the plan developed here is rather unique. The Becky-David plan is neither an extended school year nor summer sessions added to a regular school year. The plan is based upon having three-fourths of the total student population in school at all times. In the past, a few schools have achieved this via a school calendar which gave one-fourth of the pupils a three-month vacation in each of the four seasons. Part of the reason for discontinuance of these plans has been the fact that one-fourth of the students had their vacations in the winter—a rather undesirable time for a three-month vacation.

At Becky-David the students are also divided into four groups according to area. Similarity with most previous plans ends at that point. The geographical area served by Becky-David is divided into four parts designated as Cycles A, B, C, and D. Each of these four areas contains from 400-425 elementary school children. At any given time, three of the four cycles are in school. The uniqueness of the plan lies in the fact that students basically attend school for nine weeks, then have a three-week vacation. This procedure repeated four times will be a thirty-six-week school year for any given group. Since the legal school year must fall between July 1 and the following June 30, one nine-week period had to be broken up into a three and a six week period for Cycles C and D (see illustration on p. 247).

Operation

For the most part, the school's operation has continued as usual. There have been, however, three areas in which changes in operation have taken place: teachers' work schedule, bussing, and student room assignments.

1. *Teachers' work schedule*. Under the new schedule teachers were given the option of being employed for twelve months, nine months, or on the nine-week/three-week schedule. Most of the teachers chose to work on the nine-week/three-week schedule, and therefore stay with the same groups of children throughout the year. Fifth and sixth year teachers are employed on a nine- or twelve-month basis. Each nine weeks they will have a different group of students. Teachers contracted on a full-year basis are required to have a

July 1

June 30

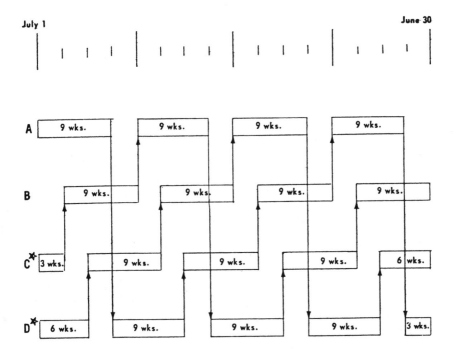

* State statutes require that the school year (174 days of classes) fall between July 1st and June 30th of the following year. For this reason, one 9 week session for cycles C & D was divided into a three and six week session. Ideally, cycle C would have started three weeks after cycle B and cycle D would have begun three weeks after cycle C. It should be noted, however, that after the first year all sessions are in reality nine weeks in length since the three and six week sessions at the beginning and end of cycles C and D join to make up a nine week session.

three-week vacation during the year in addition to Christmas vacation and other vacation days.

2. *Bussing.* As the year-round plan transforms forty-five rooms into sixty rooms, eighteen buses are needed to transport the same number of students, which would require twenty-four buses on a nine-month schedule. The changes required because of the new schedule are twofold. First, bus drivers must learn more than one route since they must change to a different area each time the area they have been transporting begins on its three-week vacation. Second, students ride different buses each nine-week period.

3. *Student room assignments.* Since the classes returning from vacation occupy the rooms vacated by classes going on vacation, it is necessary for each cycle on its return from vacation to be assigned to a different set of rooms. It was a relatively simple task to design a room schedule indicating where students would be each nine weeks. Each time they leave for vacation, students are informed which rooms will be theirs when they return.

Problems

Because the year-round school is new and different and because no model was available to guide its administration, numerous minor problems have arisen. Teachers and other school personnel have almost unanimously agreed, however, that the problems of this year have not been insurmountable. Two problems that are not yet evident may become the most serious—traditionalism and teacher fatigue. Another problem, heat and humidity, can easily be overcome by air conditioning—certainly a necessity if the plan continues.

No one can properly evaluate a program after a few short months. It is apparent, however, that in order to succeed a new approach should have a good beginning. This has been the case at Becky-David School.

> *Alan M. O'Dell*
> Principal, Becky-David
> Intermediate School

2. Atlanta Has Begun

The advantages and disadvantages of operating schools year-round have been discussed for years. A few school systems have experimented with variations from the traditional school year pattern, but most American elementary and secondary schools still adhere to a school calendar that was established to fit the needs of a past era. The time has come to move from discussion to action and to tackle realistically the job of arranging the school year in accordance with the needs of today rather than yesterday.

Education has paid a high price for being a part-time profession. Although it is less true today than in years past, it is still true that many outstanding young people (especially men) do not choose teaching as a profession because of the financial implications of summer unemployment. Many outstanding teachers have left the profession for the same reason. The time has come to solve this problem by providing full-time employment with full-time pay for all teachers and other school employees. It is recognized that some teachers prefer the present nine or ten month school year. The transition to full year school operation can be arranged to accommodate this preference, but as the change is made, it is believed that a great majority of instructional and other school personnel will prefer the annual plan.

As important as questions relating to personnel policies may be, the point of overriding urgency is the fact that a large percentage of school age children and youth are in desperate need of worthwhile summer activities. The public

Reprinted by permission from COMPACT, published by the Education Commission of the United States, Denver, Colorado.

schools have the facilities and the trained personnel to go a long way toward meeting this obvious need. All concerned should begin to explore how the full year school plan can be accomplished for the benefit of children and youth.

Program Goals

Atlanta has begun. In the fall of 1968, a four-quarter school program was implemented in 26 high schools. Unlike similar efforts in other school systems, however, Atlanta's approach was not motivated by the desire to relieve overcrowded school facilities. While such relief is a possible by-product of the Atlanta plan, the major goal was to organize the high school calendar so that year-round educational opportunities could be provided and a more flexible schedule and viable program realized.

The need for a more up-to-date curriculum was evident. More than nine years had passed since completion of a major curriculum revision for high schools. Since that time, profound changes had occurred in social and economic conditions, in the composition of the student body, and in the teaching staff. There was a need for the curriculum to be examined and redesigned to provide each pupil educational opportunities which would be challenging but appropriately adjusted so that he could experience success without becoming either bored or discouraged.

A review of needed curricular improvements brought to the fore the need for a program which would permit pupils to take advantage of job opportunities which were not always available during the summer months. Under a quarter plan an employer could employ four different high school pupils, each in turn working his respective quarter, and have the equivalent of a full time employee. The teaching staff would also benefit from greater flexibility in scheduling their time for teaching, in-service training, college study and vacations. The four-quarter plan was adopted as the vehicle by which major curriculum renovations and greater educational opportunities could be realized.

Two years of intensive planning preceded the actual implementation of the four-quarter plan. This period was devoted to examining and completely rewriting the high school curriculum. Courses were designed as autonomously as possible with minimum dependence upon sequence. The content of each course was selected in terms of learning characteristics of identifiable groups of pupils. More than 860 quarter courses were developed which made possible a much wider option for course selection for Atlanta high school pupils. With the assistance of his parents, classroom teacher and counselor, each pupil arranges his schedule each quarter.

Since the number of courses in each subject category has been greatly increased and since the majority of them are non-sequential, considerable flexibility in scheduling is possible. Very few specific courses are required for graduation, though the number of graduation credits in a given area has not been reduced. Pupils may exercise choices not previously possible in course selection.

State Funds

Designing the courses was only one of the many tasks involved in the transition to the quarter plan. Another problem was related to organizing the school year so that the quarter program could be implemented. The state legislature provides funds through the Minimum Foundation Program for 190-day employment of teachers. Of this number, 180 days are used for instructing pupils and ten days for in-service training. No funds are provided for teachers' salaries beyond the regular school year.

Until the implementation of the four-quarter year, Atlanta operated an eight-week high school summer session on a tuition basis. To make the current program possible, efforts were made to get the school year divided into four quarters of equal length and to secure financial assistance for operation of the summer quarter. The state agreed to shorten the school year for high school pupils from 180 to 177 days provided that a regular program was offered during the summer quarter. Although four 55-day quarters are desired, the calendar currently in operation provides for three 59-day quarters and one 52-day quarter. All sessions operate for a full day. Other than the three-day overlap, no changes have been made in the state's program to assist in financing the summer quarter or in changing attendance requirements for the other three quarters. It is believed that eventually some financial assistance will be made available by the state, but at present the full cost of the fourth quarter is paid from local funds except that certain projects utilize federal funds.

The Teachers

Teachers' salaries are on an index schedule based on 190 days of employment. No one is required to work during the summer quarter as part of his contract. All who volunteer to teach beyond the 190-day period are paid at the same rate as during the previous three quarters. These and other limitations have not permitted a free interchange of quarters for teachers. It is Atlanta's goal, however, to organize the four-quarter program in such a manner as to permit teachers to select the three quarters they wish to teach and to move toward full year employment for those electing it. Legislative authorization to divide the year into four quarters of equal length and with equal state support will help achieve this goal.

Changing administrative procedures and providing necessary in-service programs for teachers were additional concerns. Providing for highly flexible scheduling procedures rather than scheduling prescribed, sequential courses dictated the need for more assistance. The new plan required teachers to assume a more important role in counseling pupils in the selection of courses. The classroom teacher who works closely with pupils is in the best position to assist with the selection of appropriate courses. Filling this role, however, requires in-service training programs designed to assure required teacher competence. Record keeping procedures, pupils' course loads, number of credits for graduation and for a full day, and related areas had to be examined, discussed, evaluated, and redesigned. Systemwide administrators, high school principals, and one counselor from each high school devoted part of their time during two academic years and full time during the summer months working on these problems prior to implementation of the four-quarter plan. Since its implementation, these procedures have been continually re-evaluated and redesigned as needed.

Success of the four-quarter program is in large measure dependent upon the acceptance and understanding of the teaching staff. Changing deeply ingrained attitudes and role expectations of teachers was and continues to be of paramount concern. Teachers, department chairmen, principals, and system-wide personnel who provided the major input in developing materials for the new instructional program received a secondary benefit which in essence was a type of in-service training. These organized activities contributed to a better understanding of the goals, purposes, and potential of the new plan. Each classroom teacher had an opportunity to make suggestions and recommendations about the program for his subject area. Department chairmen met in citywide meetings to discuss and refine the suggestions and proposals thus received. Representatives from each subject area group met with personnel responsible for citywide curriculum development and worked to achieve the desired program balance. Consultants from universities, citizens from the community, and high school pupils assisted with the program's development.

The Students

The program was designed to provide optimum flexibility for pupils. The equivalent of a regular load for three quarters is expected of each pupil. However, each pupil has a choice as to which three quarters he will attend and whether he will take a full or partial load the fourth quarter, or, in fact, all four quarters. A pupil may choose to take off a quarter other than during the summer months if he has attended a previous fourth quarter and accumulated adequate credits. Experience to date indicates that pupils who attend the fourth quarter usually attend the other three also. As the importance of work experience is stressed, it is expected that more pupils will use the flexibility of the four-quarter plan to take advantage of work opportunities. Pupils who take a full load all four quarters usually do so in order to graduate early or to develop a broader understanding in subject areas of special interest. Under the semester organization this goal was frequently impossible because of scheduling difficulties. Also pupils are frequently scheduling vocational and other practical courses which were not undertaken as a part of the two semester academic program. There has been an increase in the number of pupils who exercise the option to attend school year-round in order to complete requirements for graduation in less time than would otherwise be required.

The number of pupils working part time and scheduling work experience as part of the school day has increased rather significantly during the past two years. During the spring quarter of 1970, more than 2,300 high school pupils scheduled work experience as part of their school day. Other pupils held jobs outside of the regular school day which were not reflected in their regular six period schedule. Still other pupils registered for less than full academic load in order to have additional time for extracurricular activities.

Of the 32,000 pupils enrolled in Atlanta high schools during the first three quarters, 12,770 enrolled in one or more courses during the summer quarter of 1969, averaging 2.6 courses per pupil. During the summer quarter of 1970, the number of pupils who enrolled was 10,484, but the average number of courses per pupil had increased to 3.6. The consensus is that the pupils no longer perceive the summer quarter as summer school but now consider it as a quarter equal to the other three.

We have had no major problems in staffing the program. Teachers as well as pupils volunteer to participate. Thus far, there have been more teachers indicating their willingness to work than there have been positions available. There have been no detectable ill effects on either the teachers or the pupils for attending or teaching school on a year-round basis.

Community support has been most favorable once it was understood that pupils and teachers would be able to select the quarters they would attend. In fact, during the earlier days of implementation, businessmen frequently expressed their approval and indicated that they would no longer have to schedule summer month vacations for all their employees.

Despite the progress of the four-quarter program, there are still problems to be considered and solved. Continued effort must be devoted to making the fourth quarter equal in every respect to the other three, thus enabling a teacher who wishes to work only three quarters to have some choice as to the three he prefers. The number of teacher preparations per quarter and per year has increased. Although this requires additional effort, it also contributes to offering more meaningful instruction for pupils. Perhaps the most difficult problem to solve is obtaining adequate single concept instructional materials rather than having to rely on the traditional hardback books. Understandably, textbook publishers and other printing companies are not too eager to change the format of their publications until the market is large enough for the change to be profitable. In the meantime, short assignments from a variety of sources will continue to be substituted for the traditional textbook approach —another advantage of the four-quarter plan.

John W. Letson
Superintendent of Schools,
Atlanta, Georgia

3. Dade County, Florida: Quinmester—Extended School Year Program

The Quinmester Extended School Year design was developed around a calendar that divides the school year into five forty-five-day or nine-week sessions. Pupils in schools operating with the quinmester organization must attend four quinmesters in the five quinmester school year. The student has the option of attending all five quinmesters and accelerating his graduation from high school or electing a vacation quinmester other than the traditional summer vacation period. Each fifth quinmester attended by the pupil could possibly accelerate his graduation from high school forty-five days, although the fifth quinmester may be used by pupils for enrichment and remedial experiences and not result in an accelerated graduation.

This extended school year organization does not radically affect the present operational calendar of the Dade County Schools, and provides the community with the option of an extended school year program while maintaining the present calendar structure for those people in the community who prefer the traditional 180-day school year. The Quinmester Program is designed to be different from the present summer programming in that the summer quinmester is expected to be an extension of the four other terms of the school year and is not considered to be primarily a vehicle for remediation or enrichment. Although these types of programs will be available in quinmester

Reprinted by permission of the author.

schools, the Quinmester Extended School Year Plan makes available regular school programming throughout the calendar year with the exception of a two-to-three week summer vacation period. The above average student could accelerate under this plan while other pupils could more easily repeat grades failed. (Gifted and motivated pupils could complete six years of secondary schooling in five years by attending four summer quinmesters between grades seven and eleven, while less gifted pupils who did fail grades could get their elementary and secondary education in the present normal twelve-year period.) The voluntary feature of this plan permits those who wish to attend a full year to do so and those who strongly object to being in school for an elongated period to attend only the regular 180-day school program.

Quinmester Pilot School Involvement

Seven secondary schools have been identified as quinmester pilot schools. They are Miami Springs Senior High School, Miami Beach Senior High School, North Miami Beach Senior High School, Nautilus Junior High School, Henry Filer Junior High School, Hialeah Junior High School, and Palmetto Junior High School.

All but two of the pilot schools (North Miami Beach Senior High School and Miami Beach Senior High School) offered a quinmester program starting in June 1971. The other two pilot schools started their first quinmester in September 1971.

During the 1970-71 school year, the pilot schools were involved in a comprehensive study of the administrative and curriculum implications of the Quinmester Program, through representation on all the subject area advisory committees and the administrative review and steering committee.

The individual pilot schools in addition to writing curriculum support material for the Quinmester Program, conducted a community information dissemination campaign designed to acquaint the community with the Quinmester Extended School Year Program.

*Plant Utilization Implications of the Quinmester Extended
School Year Program*

The Quinmester Plan theoretically has the potential to increase the capacity of school plants by 25 percent. A school having a capacity of 2,000 pupils could conceivably enroll 2,500 and due to the staggered attendance periods have but 2,000 pupils in attendance during any given quinmester. Increased plant capacity could also be achieved through an acceleration procedure developed under this plan. The fact that the fifth quinmester coincides closely with the Dade County Base Plan for summer school operation is likely to make attendance in summer school for acceleration purposes more appealing. To achieve the maximum benefit from this plan relative to plant utilization four-fifths of the total secondary school population would need to be in attendance each quinmester.

This maximum benefit indicated above could only be achieved by mandating pupil attendance and vacation periods. The *Quinmester Extended School Year* design, as *presently being planned in the Dade County schools does not anticipate this mandatory procedure.*

The prevailing patterns of family and community living and working, although presently undergoing change, militate against the acceptance of any extended school year design by the community that assigns pupils to specific attendance sessions for plant utilization purposes. It is anticipated that as community mores and habits change, the number of families that elect to vacation in a period other than the summer will increase and more students will attend fifth quinmester program that affords them the same academic opportunities that are available in the regular school year program.

Attendance statistics from the 1970 six-week summer session indicate that 34 percent of the potential secondary school population attended an academic summer school for credit. These attendance figures provide some data for a projection of what summer quinmester attendance might become after several years of operation.

It is not projected that attendance at a summer quinmester will always be reflected in an accelerated graduation for students; however, it can be generally assumed that in most cases each summer quinmester attended by a pupil will result in the saving of 25 percent of a pupil station.

The projection of 3,384 pupils attending quinmester programs during the summer of 1971 could conceivably provide a savings of 846 student stations computed at .25 pupil station per student in attendance. The economic benefits derived from savings in operating costs per pupil between ten-month operation and fifth quinmester operation averages about 1 percent. The degree to which pupils avail themselves of the acceleration factor in the Quinmester Plan and the degree to which pupils voluntarily elect a vacation period other than the traditional summer months will in effect represent the sum total of the plant utilization benefits available from the Quinmester Plan.

Numerous references and informational items concerning the Quinmester Program have been published in *Checkpoint* and the school newspapers of the pilot schools. Several of the pilot schools have developed and distributed brochures to their patrons and pupils.

Reach for Relevance

Curriculum development is a "grass roots project" because planning has involved hundreds of teachers serving on curriculum committees to decide course content and objectives. Students also have been used in an advisory capacity. Some 1,600 educators working with subject area consultants have developed and packaged numerous nine-week courses. All the old basics are there, but many have fresh new titles and approaches. In addition there are new courses representative of the system's reach for relevancy. Some 1,300 "quin" titles will be offered in college-like catalogues. Of these, approximately 350 were available this past summer, the full gamut by the summer of 1973.

Under the quinmester plan no longer will a student go to school to take a semester of math or English. Instead, he'll take nine-week "quin" courses in a variety of math topics such as "Practical Statistics" or "Geometric Constructions." English, or language arts, courses will come through as "The Power of Words," "The Art of Satire," "Living Shakespeare," "Suit the Speed to the Road" (reading), "Righting Your Writing," "Rags and Riches in Modern American Literature," and "The Reel Thing."

Some quin courses will be sequential. Before a student takes the nine-weeks course "Pre-Algebra 3," for example, he must already have mastered "Pre-Algebra 1" and "2."

Language arts and social studies will join forces in such courses as "You, Too, Can be a Legislator!"; business education and social studies in such courses as "Bull and Bear: The Stock Market," and "Taxes"; science and social studies in such courses as "Ecopolitics."

The Quinmester is receiving close scrutiny, including an initial evaluation this spring. This and follow-up evaluations will lead to determination of whether the plan should be continued in its present format, redirected, or expanded.

Whatever the results, the things that are tried in quinmester schools and the things that happen in them will have far-reaching implications for the rest of the school system.

Martin Rubinstein
Quinmester Project
Manager, Dade County
Public Schools

Bibliography

This bibliography of approximately 800 titles was compiled as a part of the research work done by the Committee to Study the Feasibility of the Extended School Year.

The Committee wishes to express appreciation to Miss Ellen Tollison, Information Processor for the Research Information Section of the South Carolina Department of Education, for her willing and valuable assistance in the completion of this work.

All materials are listed by year of publication and are categorized under each year's listings as follows: books, periodicals, newspapers, pamphlets, booklets, and reports. The time period covered is from the year 1907 to April 1972.

Joyce Gayden
Director, Extended
School Year
Feasibility Study

Year-Round Schools: A Chronological Selected Bibliography from 1907 to 1972, compiled by Joyce Gayden and Barbara Thornton. Department of Instruction, Richland County School District 1, 1616 Richland Avenue, Columbia, South Carolina.

1907

Periodicals

Wirt, William A. "A School Year of Twelve Months." *Education* 27:619-622.

1913

Books

Cubberly, Ellwood P. "Vacation Schools and Continuous Sessions of Public Schools." *A Cyclopedia of Education,* vol. v. Edited by Paul Monroe. New York: MacMillan Co., 1913.

1918

Periodicals

Corson, David. "The All Year School." *Journal of Education* 88:563-568.

Pamphlets, booklets, and reports

Jackson, B. B. *The All-Year School Plan.* Report. Minneapolis, Minn.: Minneapolis Public Schools, 1918.

1919

Periodicals

"The All-Year School." *Journal of Education,* December 5, 1919.

1921

Periodicals

Clark, W. F. "All Year Elementary Schools." *Elementary School Journal* 22:286-289.

1923

Periodicals

Hebb, Bertha Y. "All-Year Schools Have Many Advantages." *School Life* 8:198.

Pamphlets, booklets, and reports

Webb, F. S. *Bibliography of All-Year Schools and Vacation Schools in the United States.* Washington, D. C.: United States Bureau of Education, 1923.

1925

Periodicals

"The All-Year School." *Journal of Education,* August 13, 1925.

Beverdige, J. H. "Omaha High School on the All-Year Plan." *School Life* 11:22.

Weber, H. C. "Defense through the Educated Quota: The All-Year School." *Addresses and Proceedings of the National Education Association* 63:751-759.

Pamphlets, booklets, and reports

Farrand, Wilson; O'Shea, M. V.; and others. *The All-Year Schools of Newark, New Jersey.* Report. Newark, N.J.: Newark Public Schools, 1925.

1926

Periodicals

"The All-Year School." *National Association of Secondary School Principals' Bulletin,* October 1926.

Farrand, Wilson, and O'Shea, M. V. "Report of the Newark Schools." *School and Society* 23:462-469.

Roe, Warren A. "The All-Year School." *Bulletin of the Department of Elementary School Principals* 6:10-22.

Swan, Edith. "A Mother's View of the Twelve Month School." *Elementary School Journal* 26:428-429.

Weber, H. C. "The All Year School." *Journal of Education* 104:347-351.

1927

Periodicals

Lovell, L. E. "All Year School." *Educational Review* 73:196-202.

Pamphlets, booklets, and reports

Bush, R. H. *The Status of Summer Schools in Secondary Schools in Illinois.* Springfield, Ill.: State Superintendent of Public Instruction, 1927.

Reals, W. A. *Study of the Summer School Contribution to Education,* no. 237. New York: Teacher's College, Columbia University, 1927.

1929

Periodicals

"All Year School." *Elementary School Journal* 30:83-84.

"All-Year School; One Way of Reducing Crime Expenses." *Nation's Schools* 4:34.

"All Year Schools." *School Review* 37:174-175.

Clogston, E. B. "Health and Scholarship in Summer High School." *School Review* 37:760-763.

"Freedom of the Streets versus All-Year Schools." *Nation's Schools* 4:74-75.

Judd, C. H. "Year-Round Schools Urged for More Thorough Education." *American City* 40:140.

Postel, H. H. "Enforced Idleness." *Elementary School Journal* 29:653-654.

Pamphlets, booklets, and reports

Nelson, M. J. *Differences in the Achievement of Elementary School Pupils Before and After the Summer Vacation.* Madison: University of Wisconsin, 1929.

1930

Periodicals

"All-Year Schools." *School Executive* 49:517.
Brinkerhoff, G. L. "The Effects of All Year Schools upon Pupil Advancement." *Educational Method* 10:168-174.
Ellis, R. T. "All-Year Schools." *Texas Outlook* 14:34-38.
"Five Years Experience with the All Year School." *Elementary School Journal* 30:576-585.
McNally, E. J.; and others. "Report on the All-Year School." *Elementary School Journal* 30:509-518.
Odell, C. W. "Summer Work in Public Schools." *University of Illinois Bulletin* 27:1-42.
Page, F. J. "Twelve-Months Rural School." *Journal of Education* 112:320.
Roe, Warren A. "All-Year School." *School Executive* 50:121-123.
_____. "All Year School Organization." *Educational Method* 10:66-69.
_____. "All-Year Schools, A Potential Progressive Educational Improvement." *Educational Method* 10:3-6.
"Something about the All-Year School." *American School Board Journal* 80:67.
"Tentative Opinions about All-Year Schools." *Texas Outlook* 14:19-20.
Vanderslice, H. R. "The All-Year School in Aliquippa, Pennsylvania." *Elementary School Journal* 30:576-585. Same, *Texas Outlook*, 14:7-8.

1931

Periodicals

"The All-Year School." *Review of Educational Research*, June 1931, pp. 237-238.
Brinkerhoff, G. L. "The Effects of All-Year Schooling upon Scholarships." *Educational Method* 10:203-209.
_____. "Effects of All-Year Schooling upon Social Adjustment." *Educational Method* 10:290-294.
Caswell, H. L. "Study of Nashville's All-Year School." *Peabody Journal of Education* 8:323-347.
"New Evidence as to the Efficiency of the All-Year School." *Elementary School Journal* 32:168-172.
Pulliam R. "All-Year School, Who is Right?" *Education* 52:159-162.
Reavis, W. C. "Evaluation of the Various Units of the Public School System." *Review of Education Research* 1:173-199.

Roe, W. A. "Comparative Costs of Integrated All-Year Schooling and of Part-Time Schooling." *Educational Method* 10:350-358.

Pamphlets, booklets, and reports

The All-Year School of Nashville, Tennessee. Nashville, Tenn.: George Peabody College for Teachers, Division of Surveys and Field Studies, 1931.
Survey Report. Nashville, Tenn.: George Peabody College for Teachers, Division of Surveys and Field Studies, 1931.

1932

Periodicals

DeGalan, F. S. "Some Thoughts on Summer School." *Junior-Senior High School Clearing House* 6:524-528.
Lane, Elian N. "The All-Year School—Its Origin and Development." *Nation's Schools* 9:52-59.
Vanderslice, H. R. "Place and Purpose of the All-Year School." *Texas Outlook* 16:23-24.

Pamphlets, booklets, and reports

Year-Round Schools. Newark, N.J.: Newark Public Schools, 1932.

1933

Periodicals

Buster, N. E. "Long Vacation is the Bunk." *Junior-Senior High School Clearing House* 7:281-284.
Vanderslice, H. R. "Five Years' Experience with the All-Year School." *Elementary School Journal* 34:256-268.

1934

Periodicals

Irons, H. S. "Utilizing School Buildings and Instructional Services Twelve Months Annually." *American School Board Journal* 88:17-19.
"Shall We Have Year-Round Schools?" *Virginia Journal of Education* 28:99-100.
Vanderslice, H. R. "All-Year School." *Junior-Senior High School Clearing House* 8:294-297. Summary, *School Management* 3:12.

Pamphlets, booklets, and reports

Reports Concerning the All-Year School. Los Angeles, Calif.: Los Angeles City School District, Office of the Superintendent, February 1934.

1935

Pamphlets, booklets, and reports

Hood, Ralph S. *Economies in the Operation of the All-Year School in the Third Class Districts in Beaver County, Pennsylvania.* Master's thesis, University of Pittsburgh, 1935. (Abstract in University of Pittsburgh, *Abstracts of Theses* 11:278-279.)

1936

Periodicals

"Possible Solution to Emergency School Housing Problems." *Ohio Schools,* May 1936.

1937

Periodicals

Phelps, C. L. "All Year College." *Sierra Education News* 33:22-23.

1939

Periodicals

Hollingshead, Billie. "An Evaluation of Half-Day and Full-Day Sessions in the First Two Grades." *Elementary School Journal* 39:363-370.
"How Long Should the School Year Be?" *Pennsylvania School Journal,* May 1939.

1940

Periodicals

Haislet, E. L., and Simley, I. T. "Should Our Schools Extend the Whole Year with a Modified Curriculum for Summer Months?" *Minnesota Journal of Education* 20:176-177.
Riley, E. C. "Year-Round Schools." *Kentucky School Journal* 19:21.

1942

Periodicals

Chapman, A. L. "Keep the Schools Open All Year." *School Executive* 61:16.
Fink, T. R. "All Year Schools." *High School Journal* 25:158-162.

1943

Periodicals

Robinson, F. P. "Effect of Year Around Attendance on Students." *Journal of Higher Education* 14:441-443.

1945

Periodicals

Peterson, R. G. "Twelve Months Schools." *American School Board Journal* 110:38-40.

Taylor, D. E. "Year Round School." *School Executive* 65:50-51.

1946

Periodicals

Lomax, Dorothy. "Extended Program and Increased Salaries." *Texas Outlook* 30:2.

1947

Periodicals

Gaumnitz, H. "Senior High School Extends Its Program." *Secondary Education* 13:20-22.

Gestie, B. D. "Year-Round Employment." *Elementary School Journal* 48:65.

Pahl, Eleanor. "A Year-Round Program." *Childhood Education* 24:82-84.

Sternig, J. "Glencoe's 12-Month School Year." *School Management* 17:4.

Thomas, M. J. "Year-Round Service and Higher Salaries." *School Executive* 66:63-64. Same, *Minnesota Journal of Education* 27:300-301. Same, *School Management* 17:9.

1948

Periodicals

Clifford, J. M. "Wasteful School Year." *American School Board Journal* 117:24.

Cline, Aleise. "A Twelve-Month Program in Gladewater High School." *Bulletin of the National Association of Secondary School Principals* 32:79-81.

Feather, W., Jr. "How to Relieve Crowded Schools if New Building Is Impossible." *School Management* 18:3.

Katterle, Z. B. "How Schools Can Function in the Summer Months." *School Executive* 67:40-42.

McKinney, L. G. "Teaching: Year Round Profession." *Teachers College Journal* 19:78-79.

Misner, P. J. "Teachers' Role in All-Year Program." *Journal of the National Education Association* 37:500-501.

Studebaker, John W. "Why Not a Year Round Educational Program?" *Journal of Educational Sociology* 21:269-275.

Thomas, Maurice J. "Return on a Year-Round Investment." *Educational Leadership* 5:459-464.

1949

Periodicals

Besley, I. E. N. "School Year." *Journal of Education* (London) 81:74.
Clifford, J. M. "The Wasteful School Year." *American School Board Journal,* September 1949.
Lafferty, H. M. "American School, Open All Year!" *American School Board Journal* 118:17-18.
Moe, M. P. "Lengthened Schoolyear." *Montana Education* 26:20.
"School, Year Round." *Commonweal* 50:331.
Sternig, John. "All-Year Program." *School Executive* 68:66-67.
"Trends in City School Organizations, 1938 to 1948." *NEA Research Bulletin* 27:1-40.

Newspapers

McVey, Frank. "The Gates Open Slowly." Lexington: *University of Kentucky Press,* 1949.

1950

Books

Otto, Henry J. "All-Year School." *Encyclopedia of Educational Research.* Rev. ed. Edited by Walter S. Monroe. New York: MacMillan Co., 1950, p. 375.
————. "Length of School Day." *Encyclopedia of Educational Research.* Rev. ed. Edited by Walter S. Monroe. New York: MacMillan Co., 1950, p. 369.

Periodicals

Palm, Reuben R. "How Effective is the All-Year Secondary School?" *Bulletin of the National Association of Secondary School Principals* 34:63-67.
Ylvisaker, H. L. "How Effective is the All-Year Secondary School?" *Bulletin of the National Association of Secondary School Principals* 34:67-73.

Pamphlets, booklets, and reports

Lewis, Russell L. *The Organization and Administration of Summer Public School Educational and Recreational Programs in Districts within Metropolitan Areas of the United States.* Dissertation. Los Angeles: University of Southern California, 1950.
Paying for Better Schools. Committee on Economic Development, 1950.
The Twelve Months Plan. Houston, Tex.: Houston Independent School District, January 19, 1950.
Wilson, Lytle M. *Report to Pennsylvania State Board of Education.* January 6, 1950.

1951

Periodicals

"All Year School." *Educator's Dispatch*, November 1951.

Lafferty, H. M. "Let's Keep Schools Open in Summer." *Nation's Schools* 48:41-42.

McIntosh, W. R. "Year-Round Programs and Professional Service." *Educational Leadership* 8:286-289.

Shannon, J. R. "Recess from Living." *Education* 71:657-659.

"Should High Schools Go On a Year-Round Schedule?" *Scholastic* 58:9.

Tomancik, Mary. "Administrators Dispute Arguments for All-Year Schools." *Nation's Schools* 47:69-71.

Pamphlets, booklets, and reports

A Study of the Four-Quarter System for Elementary and Secondary Schools. Report. San Mateo, Calif.: Office of the Superintendent, San Mateo County Schools, 1951.

1952

Periodicals

Donovan, E. "Georgia Begins an Extended School Service Program." *National Elementary Principal* 31:22-24.

Faunce, Roland C. "Twelve Months of School." *National Association of Secondary School Principals' Bulletin* 36:25-29.

Fosdick, H. A. "All-Year Schools O.K. but Not on the Quarter Plan." *California Teachers Association Journal* 48:6-7.

Gabbard, H. F. "Extended School Services the Year Around." *National Elementary Principal* 31:2-5.

Klein, H. L. "When a Twelve-Month Plan is Carried Out." *Childhood Education* 28:262-264.

Miles, Dorothy. "Lexington's Year-Round School." *American School Board Journal* 124:27-28.

"Status of Year-Round School Programs; Length of School Year for Professional Employees in City School Systems." *School Executive* 72:82.

Pamphlets, booklets, and reports

Inquiry Concerning the All-Year School. Report. Long Beach, Calif.: Long Beach Public Schools, Office of the Supervisor of Research, 1952.

Kegler, John D. *The Relationship between State Aid for the Support of Public Schools and the Length of the School, with Special Attention to California.* Dissertation. Los Angeles: University of Southern California, 1952.

Status of Year-Round School Programs: Length of School Year for Professional Employees in City School Systems. Washington, D. C.: Educational Research Service, National Education Association, 1952.

Summary of Replies to "Inquiry Concerning the All-Year School." Report. Long Beach, Calif.: Long Beach Public Schools, 1952.

1953

Periodicals

Best, J. W. "Year-Round School Program." *School Executive* 73:56-59.
Hartsell, Horace C. "Twelve-Month School." *Bulletin of the National Association of Secondary School Principals* 37:18-33.
Johnson, R. D. "What are the Evidences of Need for a Year-Round Educational Program?" *Bulletin of the National Association of Secondary School Principals* 37:325-327.
"When Do School Bells Ring for You?" *Childhood Education* 30:23-25.
"Year-'Round High School? Pro and Con Discussion." *Scholastic* 62:7-8.

1954

Periodicals

Hammond, Sarah Lou. "What Happens to the Five Year Olds?" *Educational Leadership* 12:9-14.
Honey, Floyd, and McDonald, E.A., Jr. "How Can the Year-Round Educational Program Serve Better the Needs of Youth?" *National Association of Secondary School Principals' Bulletin* 38:40-43.
Horn, Thomas D., and Smith, Louise L. "Is the Half-Day Session Full Measure?" *Journal of the Association for Childhood Education International*, April 1954.
Potter, Gladys. "Packing Them In." *Educational Leadership*, October 1954.
"A Symposium of the Meaning of the Enrollment Bulge for Secondary Education." *California Journal of Secondary Education*, February 1954.
Young, Mary R. "Double Sessions Are Pressure Points." *Educational Leadership*, October 1954.

Pamphlets, booklets, and reports

The All-Year School. A report by the Committee to Study the All-Year School. Los Angeles, Calif.: Los Angeles Board of Education, July 1954.

1955

Periodicals

Anderson, L. W., and Kehoe, R. E. "Advantages of Extending the School Year." *Michigan Education Journal* 32:415-417.
"Are Year-Round Schools Coming?" *U.S. News & World Report*, November 11, 1955, pp. 100-103.
Leibman, Mary B. "A Simple Answer to the School Problem." *Woman's Day*, October 1955.

'Los Angeles Rejects Plan for Keeping Schools Open Year-Round; Calls it Costly, Inconvenient." *Nation's Schools* 55:120.

MacPherson, Vernon D. "Keeping Schools Open All Year." *Nation's Schools* 56:51-54.

'Opinion Poll. Superintendents Reject All Year School Plan; Teachers and Buildings Need Three Months to Recoup and Repair." *Nation's Schools* 55:6.

'Summer Use of School Facilities." *School Executive* 74:62-71.

Pamphlets, booklets, and reports

An Analysis of the Four-Quarter Plan of School Operation. Report. Flint, Mich.: Flint Public Schools, Flint Board of Education, 1955.

Shrene, Robert H. *A Survey of Selected Schools Currently Operating Extended School Year Programs*. Dissertation. Greeley: Colorado State College of Education, August 1955.

Twelve Month School Program. Report. Detroit, Mich.: Detroit Public Schools, 1955.

1956

Periodicals

'Advantages and Disadvantages of the Four-Quarter Twelve Months Plan of Operation of the Public Schools of Florida." *Changing Times*, April 1956.

'The All-Year School: A Critical Review." *Contra Costa County Taxpayer's Association, Research Bulletin no. 18*, February 1956.

Brown, K. R. "What is a Teacher's Work Year?" *California Teachers Association Journal* 52:8-9.

Brown, Robert S. "A Possible Solution to Emergency School Housing Problems." *Ohio Schools* 34:22-23.

Deacon, James M. "Year Round Program." *Bulletin of the National Association of Secondary School Principals* 40:88-90.

Gaumnitz, Walter H. "Underbuilt or Underused? A Research Analysis of Present Day School Housing." *Clearing House* 30:275-278. Same, *Education Digest* 21:13-15.

Henderson, J. "Why Close Schools in Summer?" *Collier's*, June 22, 1956, pp. 92-97.

Irwin, Constance; and others. "A Discussion of the Year Round School Program." *National Education Association Journal* 45:82-84.

'Los Angeles City Schools Conduct Study to Determine Effect of Twelve-Month Year." *Texas Outlook* 40:28.

MacPherson, Vernon D. "Keeping Schools Open All Year." *Education Digest* 21:11-14.

Ogden, Clyde L. "The Four-Quarter Plan—How Practical an Idea?" *American School Board Journal* 133:19-21.

'Oppose Twelve-Month Plan." *American School Board Journal*, February 1956.

Rich, K. W. "Present Status of the All-Year Secondary School." *California Journal of Secondary Education* 31:18-24.

"Twelve Month School Year? Pro and Con Discussion." *Scholastic* 68:7-8.

"Use the Schools the Year Round?" *Changing Times* 10:13-14.

Wagner, Paul B. "Twelve Month School!" *National Association of Secondary School Principals' Bulletin* 40:218-220.

Pamphlets, booklets, and reports

Experiments with Twelve-month Service for Classroom Teachers. Report. Teacher Personnel Practices, Urban School Districts, 1955-56 (special memo). Washington, D. C.: National Education Association, June 1956.

Hull, Dan J., and Wright, Grace. *The All-Year School: A Bibliography.* Washington, D. C.: U.S. Department of Health, Education, and Welfare, Office of Education, 1956.

Shrene, Robert H. *A Survey of Selected Schools Currently Operating Extended School-Year Programs.* Washington, D. C.: National Education Association, March 1956.

Thomas, George I. *Economy and Increased Educational Opportunity Through Extended School Year Programs.* Albany: New York State Education Department, 1956.

1957

Periodicals

Bailey, Thomas D., and Maynard, Zollie. "Summer School with a Difference!" *National Education Association Journal* 46:297-299.

Berman, H. "Do Our Schools Need More Time?" *American School Board Journal* 135:35-36.

Cardozier, V. Ray. "For a 210-Day School Year." *Phi Delta Kappan* 38:240-242.

Derthick, Lawrence G. "Classrooms Shortage Hurts Children." *Education Digest* 22:20-21.

Derthick, Lawrence G.; Hickey, P. J.; Shull, M.; and Stinnett, T. M. "Year Round School." *School Life* 40:8-10.

"Florida Says 'No' to the All Year School." *School Management* 1:45-47.

Goodlad, J. I. "Year-Round Use of Educational Facilities." *School Review* 65:387.

Harding, R. B. "Supporting Year Round School." *National Parent-Teacher* 52:40.

Moon, James V. "The How and Why of Twelve Month Contracts for Teachers." *School Management* 1:20-23, 72-74.

Ornstein, J. A. "Education in the News." *High Points* 39:70-75.

Robinson, H. M. "Year-Around Schools Again?" *Elementary School Journal* 57:420.

"Shall We Change the School Calendar?" *National Parent-Teacher* 52:12-14, 35.

Shannon, Dan C. "What Research Says about Acceleration." *Phi Delta Kappan* 39:70-72.

"Twelve-Month School Year: Will It Solve Your Building Problems?" *School Management* 1:22-25.

Walker, K. E. "3+3+3 Plan." *Clearing House* 32:201.

"What One Town Learned in Ten Years of Year-Round Schools." *U.S. News & World Report*, August 2, 1957.

Williams, Robert F. "Year-Round Use of Schools." *Virginia Journal of Education* 50:13-14.

Wyman, Raymond. "Full Employment of Teachers and Schools." *American School Board Journal* 135:25-26, 67.

"The Year-Round School." *School Life* 40:8-9.

"Year-Round Schools: An Idea That's Coming Back." *U.S. News & World Report*, March 1, 1957, pp. 32-34.

Pamphlets, booklets, and reports

All-Year School: A Study of the Advantages and Disadvantages of the Twelve-Months Plan for the Operation of the Public Schools of Florida. Tallahassee: Florida State Department of Education, April 1957.

Board of Education Study of Twelve-Month Year. Report. Atlanta, Ga.: Atlanta Public Schools, 1957.

Brief Inquiry into the Four-Quarter School. Report. Cincinnati, Ohio: Cincinnati Public Schools, Cincinnati Board of Education, March 11, 1957.

Full Use of Educational Facilities. Hartford: Bureau of Research and Statistics, Connecticut State Department of Education, May 1957.

Questions and Answers about Year-Round School. Report. Hartford: Connecticut State Board of Education, May 1957.

Year-Round School—Preliminary Study. Report. Adams City, Colo.: Adams County School District no. 14, 1957.

Newspapers

Baker, John. "Coming—School All Year Round." *San Francisco Examiner*, November 4, 1957.

1958

Periodicals

"All-Year Cure All?" *Time*, March 10, 1958, p. 67.

Bailey, Thomas D., and Maynard, Zollie. "Florida Youngsters Like Summer School." *School Executive* 77:85-87.

Clark, Deon O. "Why Not an Eleven-Month School?" *School Executive* 77:61.

Coleman, T. "Full Employment May Be the Answer." *California Teachers Association Journal* 54:234.

Crawford, Robert M. "Advantages and Disadvantages of the Twelve-Month School Year." *Bulletin of the National Association of Secondary School Principals* 42:232-234.

"Double Sessions: The Way They're Being Handled." *School Management*, January 1958.

Fitzpatrick, William J. "All-Year School, Pro and Con." *School and Society* 86:191-192.

Green, Arthur S. "Taking the Hazards from Half-day Session." *American School Board Journal* 137:27-28.

Grieder, Calvin. "Let's Lengthen the School Year." *Nation's Schools* 62:28-29.

Hechinger, Fred M. "Pro and Con—The Year-Round School." *Parents Magazine*, June 1958.

Kalmbach, R. Lynn. "Alternate Day School." *Clearing House* 32:495-496.

"Lengthening the School Year: Superintendent's Opinion." *Nation's Schools* 62:6.

McCarty, Donald J. "Is the All-Year School the Answer?" University of Chicago, *Administrator's Notebook* 6, no. 6, February 1958.

McLeod, June. "Teacher Participations in Meeting Some of the Problems of Double Session." *Educational Leadership* 15:36-62, 396.

Popen, Edward J. "Want to Try It? Rush Henrietta School Did and It Works." *Instructor* 67:105.

Schweickhard, D. W. "More Time in School." *Minnesota Journal of Education* 39:24-25.

Seligman, Daniel. "The Low Productivity of the Education Industry." *Fortune*, October 1958.

"Shall We Change the School Calendar?" *Education Digest* 23:14-16.

Shick, W. "Full Time Education." *Journal of Engineering Education* 48:708-709.

Sternig, John. "Roundup on the Year-Round School." *National Education Association Journal* 47:46-48.

"Summer Schools Get a Face Lifting." *Better Schools* 4:5-6.

Pamphlets, booklets, and reports

The All-Year School. Washington, D.C.: National Education Association, July 1958.

The All-Year School. Report. Urbana, Ill.: Urbana Community Schools, School District no. 116, Urbana Board of Education, January 24, 1958.

Double Session. National Education Association research memo, Washington, D. C., November 1958.

Four-Quarter School Year: A Status Report with Pertinent Applications to Cincinnati. Cincinnati, Ohio: Cincinnati Public Schools, Department of Research, Statistics, and Information, August 1958.

Greater Utilization of School Building Facilities. Madison: Wisconsin Legislative Council, May 1958.

Harbo, Alf F. *A Longer School Year.* Code IX-B-376, Research Project no. 12. St. Paul, Minn.: Minnesota State Department of Education, May 1, 1958.

The High School Principal and Staff Plan for Program Improvement. New York: Secondary School Administration Series, Bureau of Publications, Teachers College, Columbia University, 1958.

How Good are Your Schools? Washington, D. C.: National Education Association, April 1958.

Information on the Twelve Months' School. Sacramento: California State Department of Education, August 1958.

Post, A. Alan. *The All Year School.* Legislative Analyst for the California State Legislature, October 23, 1958.

Report of the Committee to Study the Proposed Twelve Month School. Detroit, Mich.: Detroit Board of Education, December 1, 1958.

Wilson, Lytle. *The All-Year School in Aliquippa.* Report. Aliquippa, Pa.: Aliquippa Public Schools, 1958.

Wright, Grace S. *The All-Year School.* Washington, D. C.: U.S. Department of Health, Education, and Welfare, Office of Education, 1958.

Newspapers

"All-Year School Outlined." Cleveland, Ohio: *The Cleveland News,* March 12, 1958.

Willard, Hal. "New Education Plan is Proposed." Washington, D. C.: *Washington Post and Times Herald,* June 11, 1958.

1959

Periodicals

Boutwell, W. D. "What's Happening in Education? Courses in Summer?" *National Parent-Teacher* 53:20.

"Double Sessions—Double Trouble." *Education Summary,* September 27, 1959.

"Extended Session Schedule." *National Association of Secondary School Principals' Bulletin,* September 1959.

"Four-Term Year." *Times Educational Supplement* 2300:1126, June 19, 1959.

Friggen, Paul. "Year Round Schools." *National Parent-Teacher* 53:7-9.

_____. "Why Not Year-Round Schools?" *Readers Digest,* May 1959, p. 87.

Grieder, Calvin. "Notes on a Revised School Calendar and a More Productive School System." *Nation's Schools,* April 1959.

Imhoff, Myrtle M., and Young, Wayne. "School Organization: The School Year and Day." *Review of Educational Research* 29:160-161.

Koltz, R. R. "How Long Should the Schools' Year Be?" *Pennsylvania School Journal* 107:374-376.

"Let's Look Before We Leap." *American School Board Journal,* October 1959.

Sarner, D. S. "Why 180 Days of School?" *Clearing House* 34:181.

Wenger, Marjorie A. "Glencoe's Summer Program Has Two Aims: Competence and Enrichment." *Nation's Schools* 64:58-63.

Pamphlets, booklets, and reports

The All-Year School. Report. Urbana, Ill.: Urbana Community Schools, School District no. 116, Urbana Board of Education, March 1959.

A Report on the Bard College Pilot Study and Four-Quarter System. Annandale-on-the-Hudson, New York: Bard College, October 1959.

The Summer School Program. Burlingame: California Teachers Association, Commission on Educational Policy, December 1959.

What Price Double Session? Evanston, Ill.: National School Boards Association, 1959.

1960

Books

Gardner, John W. "National Goals in Education." A report of the President's Commission on National Goals. *Goals for Americans.* New York: Prentice Hall, Inc., 1960.

Shane, Harold G., and Polychrones, James Z. "Organization of the Elementary School—Length of Elementary Education." *Encyclopedia of Educational Research.* Third ed. Edited by Chester W. Harris. New York: MacMillan Co., 1960.

Periodicals

"Are Year-Round Schools the Answer to Overcrowding?" *School Management* 4:25-28.

Bruce, William C. "Year-Round Schools." *American School Board Journal* 141:40.

Collier, McDermon, and Cox, Ronald W. "Extending the School Year." *California Schools,* February 1960.

Martin, J. V., and D. Caughey. "Sound Off! Twelve Month School Program Should Be Put into Effect." *Instructor* 69:8.

Nesbitt, W. O. "Extended School Year for Teachers to Plan and Prepare." *California Journal of Secondary Education* 35:257-259.

"Progress in Lengthening the School Year." *Phi Delta Kappan* 42:31.

Pamphlets, booklets, and reports

Bianchi, Evelyn. *Extended Work Year for Teachers.* Research Memo 1960-45. Washington, D. C.: National Education Association, December 1960.

The Community School—What is It? Lansing: Michigan Department of Education, 1960.

Dean, Stuart E. *School Year.* Elementary School Administration and Organization, Bulletin no. 11. Washington, D. C.: U.S. Department of Health, Education, and Welfare, Office of Education, 1960.

Emerging Summer School Practices in the Elementary Schools of California. California Elementary School Administrators Association, 1960.

The Four-Quarter Plan and Other Methods of High School Plant Utilization. Redwood City, Calif.: Citizens' Committee of the Sequoia Union High School District, 1960.

Number of Days in School Year, 837 Urban Districts Over 2,500 in Population. Washington, D. C.: Educational Research Service, National Education Association, and American Association of School Administrators, March 1960.

Recommendation on Length of the School Year. Sacramento: California State Department of Education, January 1960.

Report of the Commission for the Study of a Twelve Months' Use of Public School Buildings and Facilities for Public School Purposes. Raleigh, N.C., December 1960.
A Report on the Possible Operation of the Richmond Secondary Schools on a Four-Quarter Plan. Richmond, Calif.: Richmond Unified School District, January 1960.
The School Year—What Is It? Lansing: Michigan Department of Education, 1960.
Tucson Citizens' Committee Report on the Year Round School. Tucson, Arizona, 1960.
The Twelve-Four Plan. Rockville, Md.: Montgomery County Public Schools, 1960.
The Twelve-Month Tri-Mester School Year. Midland, Mich.: Midland Public Schools, October 19, 1960.
Year-Round School. Washington, D. C.: American Association of School Administrators, National Education Association, 1960. $1.

Newspapers

"Should Schools Keep the Year Round?" *New York Times,* January 24, 1960.

1961

Periodicals

Cammarota, Gloria; Stoops, John A.; and Johnson, Frank R. "Summer Programs for Students and Teachers." *Education Digest* 27:26-28.
Duncan, Ray O., and Carruth, Wincie Ann. "Should the School Year be Lengthened?" *Journal of Health, Physical Education, and Recreation* 32:6.
"Extending the School Year." *National Education Association Journal* 50:55-56.
Kerwin, H. "Should Schools Remain Idle Three Months of School Year?" *California Teachers Association Journal* 57:13-14.
McIntosh, W. R. "Many Faces of the Twelve-Months School." *Illinois Education* 49:393-395.
May, Frank B. "Year-Round School: A Proposal." *Elementary School Journal* 61:388-393.
Shiflet, Earl J. "Twelve-Month Employment for Teachers." *Virginia Journal of Education* 54:13.
Walker, E. A. "Need for Public Co-operation." *The Journal of Higher Education* 32:399-401.
"The Year-Round School." *Education Digest,* February 1961.

Pamphlets, booklets, and reports

Cammarota, Gloria; Stoops, John A.; and Johnson, Frank R. *Extending the School Year.* Washington, D. C.: Association for Supervision and Curriculum Development, 1961.

Chadbourne, Merle B. *Optional Full-Year Professional Employment.* Report. Sacramento, Calif.: Sacramento City Teachers Association, February 2, 1961.

The Glencoe Career-Teacher Plan. Glencoe, Ill.: Glencoe Public Schools, May 1961.

Lawrie, J. D. *The Feasibility of Extending the Secondary School Year in North Carolina.* Dissertation. Duke University, Durham, N.C. 1961. Same, University Microfilms, no. 62-1997, University of Michigan, Ann Arbor.

Ranking of the States, 1961. Research Report 1961-R1. Washington, D. C.: National Education Association, January 1961.

Report of Year-Round School Committee. Tucson, Ariz.: Tucson Public Schools, 1961.

The Twelve-Four Plan. A preliminary report. Rockville, Md.: Montgomery County Public Schools, June 13, 1961.

Newspapers

"Brown-Year-Long Terms a Solution to South Carolina School Problems." Columbia, S.C.: *The State,* December 4, 1961.

Gallup, George. "Parents Veto Longer Terms for Students." *Minneapolis Sunday Tribune,* April 16, 1961.

Mohle, C. B. "Nine Months Is All a Conscientious Teacher Can Take." *Houston Post,* September 15, 1961.

1962

Periodicals

Bullock, Robert P. "Some Cultural Implications of Year-Round Schools." *Education Digest* 28:26-28. Same, *Theory into Practice* 1:154-161.

"Canada: Educational Developments, 1961-1962." *Canadian Education Research Digest* 2:77.

Dunlop, John T. "Automation and Technological Change." *American Assembly,* Columbia University, Prentice Hall, 1962.

Fawcett, Novice G. "New Challenge to Education." *Theory into Practice* 1:125-130.

Gilshcirst, Robert S., and Edmunds, Edwin R. "The Value of an Independent Summer Program." *Theory into Practice* 1:162-165.

Glass, Robert E. "Calendar Possibilities for Year-Round Schools." *Theory into Practice* 1:136-140.

Gorgone, Frederick, Jr. "The Twelve-Month Year for Principals." *National Elementary Principal* 41:42-45.

Hack, W. G. "Year-Round School: A Review Essay." *Theory into Practice* 1:170-175.

Hamann, H. A. "Break-Thru of Tradition." *Wisconsin Journal of Education* 94:15-16.

"If You're Interested in the All Year School." *The National Elementary Principals* 41:46-49.

James, H. Thomas. "Is Year-Round School Operation Economical?" *Theory into Practice* 1:141-147.

Lipson, S. "Dilemma of the Year-Round School." *Theory into Practice* 1:121-124.

Lombardi, John. "Los Angeles Study of Year-Round Operation." *Theory into Practice* 1:131-135.

"Long Vacations Cut." *Times Educational Supplement* 2441:400, March 2, 1962.

McKenna, D. L. "Academic Calendar in Transition." *The Educational Record* 43:68-75.

Oldham, F. H. "Length of the School Day and the School Year." *National Association of Secondary School Principals' Bulletin* 46:194-198.

O'Rourke, J. "Extended School Year: A Teacher's View." *Theory into Practice* 1:166-169.

Rothwell, A. B. "Pity the Poor Teacher." *Wisconsin Journal of Education* 94:12-16.

Sessions, E. B. "Maintenance and Operational Costs Involved in a Year-Round Program." *Theory into Practice* 1:148-153.

"Soundoff: Lengthening the School Day Will Increase Learning Efficiency." *Instructor*, October 1962.

"Summer Activities and Personnel Assignments." *The Defined School Year*, American Federation of Teachers, AFL-CIO, Rochester Public Schools, 1962.

Wallace, Charles E. "Flexible Scheduling for the School Year." *Journal of Secondary Education* 37:132-135.

Pamphlets, booklets, and reports

Administrative Handbook on Summer Secondary Schools. Albany: New York State Education Department, 1962.

All-Year School Study in 1962. Report. Adams City, Colo.: Adams City School District 14, 1962.

Education in Washington. Seattle: Washington State Legislature Interim Committee on Education, University of Washington, 1962.

Full Year—Full Day Plan. Report. Livonia, Mich.: Livonia Public Schools, 1962.

Goldhammer, K., and Hines, C. *The Year-Round School and Building Costs.* A study for the Tucson, Arizona, Public School Districts. Eugene: School of Education, University of Oregon, January 10, 1962.

Guba, Egon E., ed. "The Year-Round School." *Theory into Practice* 1:121-175. Reprint. 249 Arps Hall, 1945 N. High Street, Columbus, Ohio 43210. $1.

Iwamoto, David. *The All-Year School.* Research Memo 1962-2. Washington, D. C.: National Education Association, January 1962.

Jensen, George M. *Let's Update Our School Calendar.* Minneapolis, Minn.: Twin City Federal Savings and Loan, 1962.

The Organization of the School Year: A Comparative Study. Paris, France: United Nations Educational, Scientific and Cultural Organization, 1962.

A Special Study on School Operation. Report. Canton, Ohio: Canton Public Schools, 1962.

Summer School. Des Moines: Iowa State Department of Public Instruction, February 1962.

Summer Science Training Programs for High-Ability Secondary School Students, 1962. Washington, D. C.: National Science Foundation, 1962.

Wright, Grace S. *The All-Year School.* Washington, D. C.: U.S. Department of Health, Education, and Welfare, Office of Education, June 1962.

The Year-Round School. Columbus: Bureau of Educational Research and Service, Ohio State University, June 1962.

1963

Periodicals

Best, John W. "Year Round School Program." *School Executive* 73:56-59.

Caudill, William W. "False Economies in Schoolhouse Construction." *Summary Review*, May 18, 1963.

"Education Developments, 1962-1963." *Canadian Education Research Digest* 3:75-76.

Fleming, Arthur S. "Our Schools Should be Open All Year." *Good Housekeeping*, April 1963, p. 46.

Gage, Kelton. "Longer School Year." *Minnesota Journal of Education* 44:12-13.

McEntire, D. "Academic Year: Nine Months or Twelve?" *AAUP Bulletin* 49:360-363.

Merwin, Willard V. "Trimester Plan." *American School Board Journal* 146:15.

Weaver, A. D. "Trimester Comes to Illinois." *Illinois Education* 51:330-332.

Williams, Robert F. "Lengthening the School Year." *Virginia Journal of Education* 57:7.

Pamphlets, booklets, and reports

Carnine, K. S. *The All-Year School.* Report. Sacramento, Calif.: Sacramento City Teachers Association, April 30, 1963.

"Education for a Changing World of Work." *Decisions for Colorado Progress.* Fort Collins, Colo.: Extension Service, Colorado State University, 1963.

Excerpt from Proposed Salary Policy of the CTA. Burlingame, Calif.: California Teachers Association, June 1963.

Hungate, Thad C., and McGrath, Earl J. *A New Trimester Three-Year Degree Program.* New York: Columbia University, Bureau of Publications, 1963.

Individual Opportunity and Economic Growth in the Denver Metropolitan Area: The Basebook of Key Data and Background Studies. A summary of the findings and recommendations of the Task Group on Post High School Education in the Denver Metropolitan Area. February 1963.

Jensen, George M. *Should Schools Be Used the Year Around?* Horseshoe, N.C.: National School Board Calendar Committee, 1963.

Kosaki, Mildred D., and Makamura, Irene T. O. *Year-Round Operation of Educational Institutions and the Implications for Hawaii.* Report. Honolulu: University of Hawaii, 1963.

Norris, J. A., Jr. *Positions Taken by Governors Pertaining to School Term Extensive as a Factor in the Equalization of Rural and City Educational*

Opportunity in the Public Schools in North Carolina. Dissertation. Duke University, Durham, N.C., 1963. Same, University Microfilms, no. 64-2835, University of Michigan, Ann Arbor.

Project Quality. Report. Canton, Ohio: Canton Local Board of Education, 1963.

Results of Questionnaire on Calendar for Year-Round Operation. Sacramento: California State Department of Education, September 1963.

The Story of the Special Summer Schools. Chicago, Ill.: Chicago Public Schools, 1963.

Summer School Programs. Washington, D. C.: Educational Research Service, July 1963.

Yeomans, Edward. *And Gladly Learn: Summer Enrichment Programs for Urban Children.* Boston, Mass.: National Association of Independent Schools, 1963.

Newspapers

Jensen, George M. "Eight-Month School Is Scandalous." *The Minneapolis Star,* February 26, 1963.

————. "Four-Quarter School Plan Advanced." *The Minneapolis Star,* February 27, 1963.

1964

Books

Schoenfeld, Clarence A., and Schmitz, Neil. *Year-Round Education: Its Problems and Prospects from Kindergarten to College.* Madison, Wis.: Dembar Educational Research Services, 1964. $3.

Thomas, George I. *An Introduction to the Multiple Trails Extended School Year Plan.* Albany: University of the State of New York, State Education Department, 1964.

Periodicals

"All-Year School Can Wait, Two of Three Schoolmen Assert." *Nation's Schools* 73:84.

Allen, D. "Completed School Day Plan." *Education Digest* 29:51.

"Britain and Europe: January Start?" *Times Educational Supplement* 2559:1567, June 5, 1964.

Childress, Jack R., and Philippi, Harlan A. "Administrative Problems Related to the Eleven- or Twelve-Month School Year." *High School Journal* 47:230-237.

Cope, R. G. "Should You Consider Year Round Operation?" *Junior College Journal* 35:20-23.

Frankel, Edward. "Effects of a Program of Advanced Summer Study on the Self-Perceptions of Academically Talented High School Students." *Exceptional Children* 30:245.

Hannah, J. A. "How to Escape from a Three Sided Box." *Michigan Education Journal* 42:8-10.

Hanson, E. H. "What About Twelve Month Schools." *Education* 84:382.

Harshman, Hardwick W. "A Summer Enrichment Program for the Exceptionally Talented." *High School Journal* 47:238-246.

Hickman, Ralph C. "The Dropouts Did Come Back." *California Education* 2:5-9.

Hicks, M. "Stevenson Story: Year-Around Educational Plan." *American School Board Journal* 149:57-58.

Holmes, George W. III, and Seawell, William H. "Extended School Year: Is it Administratively Feasible?" *High School Journal* 47:224-229.

Holton, Samuel M., ed. "Extended School Year." *High School Journal* 47:224-263.

"January to December: Radical Cambridge Plan." *Times Educational Supplement* 2555:1270, May 8, 1964.

Jensen, George M. "Education's Fantastic Coffee Break." *Means Magazine* 3:16-19.

————. "School for Twelve Months?" *Catholic Digest*, September 1964.

Johnstone, R. E. "Wasteful Merry-Go-Round; a January Start for Universities?" *Times Educational Supplement* 2548:741, March 20, 1964.

Moon, J. V. "Extended School Year." *Education* 84:557-564. Same, *Education Digest* 30:35-38.

"Should Schools Be Used the Year-Around?" *The Rotarian Magazine*, June 1964.

Stickler, W. Hugh, and Carothers, Milton W. "The Year-Round Campus: Study Sponsored by the Southern Regional Education Board." *Education Digest* 29:49-51.

"A Study of Crowded Conditions at Southport (Indiana) High School." *Considerations and Proposals*, January 1964.

"Summer School Statistics." *NEA Research Bulletin* 42:18.

"Trimester Plan Makes Nova Novel." *Nation's Schools* 73:84-87.

Tuberville, G. "Sociologist Looks at the Twelve-Month School Year." *Peabody Journal of Education* 42:182-186.

Watson, Eugene R. "Utilization of School Facilities for Adult Education During the Summer." *High School Journal* 47:253-259.

Pamphlets, booklets, and reports

Dye, Emmett C. *Transmittal of a Three Semester School Plan.* Report. 3320-23rd Road North, Arlington, Virginia 22201, March 1964.

Extended-Year Contracts for Teachers. Washington, D. C.: Educational Research Service, September 1964.

Harlan, Hugh A. *The Year-Round School.* Lincoln, Nebraska: School Administration and Junior High Education, Department of Education, 1964.

Jensen, George M. *Another Summer Wasted.* Horseshoe, North Carolina: National School Calendar Study Committee, September 1964.

Lee, Beatrice C. *The All-Year School.* Research Memo 1964-19. Washington, D. C.: National Education Association, 1964.

Report of the Committee for Study of the Twelve Month School Year. Royal Oak, Mich.: Royal Oak Public Schools, 1964.

Salary Policy. Burlingame: California Teachers Association, 1964.

Schoenfeld, Clarence A., and Schmitz, Neil. *Year-Round Education: Its Prob-*

lems and Prospects from Kindergarten to College. Madison, Wis.: Dembar Educational Research Services, 1964.

Sly, John. Taxation and School Support. A report to the Nebraska State School Boards Association, Omaha, Nebraska, November 9, 1964.

Whiteley, Robert. Four-Quarter System Public Survey. Report. Grosse Pointe, Mich., February 1964.

Newspapers

Jensen, George M. "Another Wasted Summer." Minneapolis: Twin Citian, September 1964.

1965

Periodicals

Agger, R. E., and Goldstein, M. N. "Education Innovations in the Community." ED 010 164. 1965.

Bendicksen, Perry. "Extend the School Year?" Instructor 75:98.

Bienenstok, T. "Resistance to an Educational Innovation." Elementary School Journal 65:420-428.

Brown, Douglas M.; Klahn, Richard P.; and Romano, Louis G. "Remediation, Research, Enrichment, Recreation." American School Board Journal, August 1965.

Ellison, Simon. "The Canajoharie Experiment." High Points 47:15.

Healy, G. R. "Extending the Academic Year: The Bates 4/3 Option." Liberal Education 51:361-365.

"Holidays." Times Educational Supplement 2615:29, July 2, 1965.

"Legality of Public Summer Schools." NEA Research Bulletin 43:30-31.

"Length of School Year and School Day." NEA Research Bulletin 43:103-105.

"Let's Update Our School Calendar." The Employer, 1965.

Miller, Marv. "Scholars in Shirt Sleeves." American School Board Journal 150:21.

"School for Twelve Months?" Catholic Digest, January 1965.

"Supervisor Remarks: What is Your Opinion on a Twelve-Month School Year?" Catholic School Journal 65:60.

"Ten Proven Programs to Prevent Dropouts." School Management 9:128.

Westmeyer, Troy R. "Financing Education Grows More Difficult." News in Review 54:45-46.

Whitfield, R. P., and Egger, E. "School Attendance of Swiss and American Children." Schools and Society 93:254-256.

Pamphlets, booklets, and reports

Administrative Standards and Procedures for Implementing State Board of Education Policies for Extended Year and Summer School Programs in School Districts in Utah. Salt Lake City: Utah Department of Public Instruction, March 1965.

Contemporary Issues in American Education. Consultants' papers prepared for use at the White House Conference on Education. Washington, D. C.: Government Printing Office, July 20-21, 1965.

Economy and Increased Educational Opportunity Through Extended School Year Programs. Albany: University of the State of New York, State Education Department, August 1965.

French, William C. *The High School Principal and Staff in the Crowded School.* New York: Bureau of Publication, Teachers College, Columbia University, 1965.

Holmes, George, and Seawell, William. *Summer School Programs in Virginia.* Richmond: Virginia State Department of Education, Division of Educational Research, December 1965.

Thomas, George I. *Descriptions of Some Extended School Year Plans.* Report. Albany: University of the State of New York, State Education Department, August 1965.

What About a Year-Round School? Washington, D. C.: National Education Association, April 1965.

Newspapers

Mindrum, Beverly. "Summer Vacation 'Wastes Time, Money, Teachers.'" *St. Paul Dispatch,* September 21, 1965.

1966

Books

Bauman, W. Scott. *The Flexible System, An Economic Analysis of Advantages of the Quarterly Calendar in Public Schools.* Toledo, Ohio: Business Research Center, University of Toledo, 1966. HC $1.84. Same, ERIC ED 011, 688.

Thomas, George I. *Extended School Year Designs.* Albany: University of the State of New York, State Education Department, January 1966. Same, ERIC ED 020 587.

White, J. B.; Johns, R. L.; Kimbrough, R.; and Myers, R. B. *Year-Round Schools for Polk County.* Gainesville: University of Florida, College of Education, 1966. HC $3.

Periodicals

"Administration: New York City Plans Three-Term High School Year." *Education Summary,* April 1, 1966.

"All-Year High School—Experiment Ends in Failure." *School Management,* November 1966.

"The All-Year School." *School Management,* February 1966, pp. 86-92.

"All Year School Fails." *Texas School Report,* 1966. (Reprint.)

"All-Year School: Time for a New Look?" An interview with James Allen, Jr. *School Management* February 1966, pp. 86-88, 146-156.

Bloom, Arnold M. "Let's Use the 87 Percent That's Now Wasted." *American School and University,* February 1966, p. 9.

Boodnick, Allen. "Educational Stepchild. Secondary Summer School." *Bulletin of the National Association of Secondary School Principals* 50:38.

"California Tries Year Round High School: Idea Gaining Popularity at College Level." *American School and University* 38:80.

"Case for Year Round Schools." *Reader's Digest*, December 1966, pp. 141-144.

Cogswell, J. F., and March, D. G. "System Design for a Continuous Progress School. Iv. Computer Simulation of Autonomous Scheduling Procedures." 1966. ERIC ED 010 564.

Cory, R. T. "Parents Evaluate an Eleven-Month Program." *Education* 87:167-170.

Delaney, A. A. "Information Explosion and the Curriculum." *Education* 86:494-497.

Dickens, R. L., and Ballantyne, R. H. "Year-Round Operation." *The Educational Record* 47:467-473.

Dimon, Stewart. "More Classes—Less Pressure." *Journal of Secondary Education*, March 1966.

Dolan, G. K. "Student Council on a Twelve-Month Basis." *School Activities* 37:7-8.

Engh, Jeri. "Should We Have Year Round Schools?" *Reader's Digest*, December 1966, p. 141. Same, *Saturday Review*, September 17, 1966.

_____. "Why Not Year-Round Schools?" *Saturday Review*, September 17, 1966, pp. 82-84.

Fitzpatrick, Dave. "Why Nova School Switched to Three Seventy-Day Trimesters." *Nation's Schools* 77:30.

Hayward, S. "Traditional and Newly Emerging Approaches to Year-Round Operation." *Liberal Education* 52:218-228.

"How to Get Your Feet Wet." *School Management* 10:146-147.

Johnson, W. T. "Experience for World of Work." *The Agricultural Education Magazine* 38:183.

Phillips, H. F. "Advocating a 12-Month School Year." *Pennsylvania School Journal* 115:74.

Richardson, Joe A. "Winnetka's Learning Laboratory." *Educational Leadership*, March 1966.

Rothwell, Angus B. "What is Meant by Extended School Year?" *Wisconsin Journal of Education* 98:8-9.

Umstattd, J. G. "Summer Programs and Secondary Schools." *Bulletin of the National Association of Secondary School Principals* 50:48.

"Where Do We Go From Here?" *College and University* 41:420-421.

Woods, Bob G. "Evaluating Summer School Programs." *Bulletin of the National Association of Secondary School Principals* 50:38.

Woollatt, L., and Thomas, G. "This is the Extended School Year: Excerpts from Economy and Increased Educational Opportunity through Extended School Year Programs." *School Management* 10:88-90.

"Year-Round School." *School Management*, February 1966.

Pamphlets, booklets, and reports

Advantages and Disadvantages of the Longer School Year. Rockford, Ill.: Rockford Public Schools, 1966.

Bauman, W. Scott. *The Flexible System, An Economic Analysis of Advantages of the Quarterly Calendar in Public Schools.* Toledo, Ohio: Business Research Center, College of Business Administration, University of Toledo, 1966. Same, ERIC ED 011 688.

Extended Summer Segment, Make-Up Segment. Hornell, New York: Hornell Senior High School, 1966.

The Glencoe Extended Year Plan of School Operation. Glencoe, Ill.: Glencoe Public Schools, 1966.

Moon, James V. *The Year-Round School for All?* Paper read at Annual Convention, National School Boards Association, Minneapolis, Minnesota, April 25, 1966.

Number of Days in Regular School Term, 1964-65. Washington, D. C.: Educational Research Service, American Association of School Administrators, 1966.

Parents Reactions to Educational Innovations. Princeton, N.J.: Gallup International, 1966.

Petterson, C. E. *The Extended School Year in the State of Utah.* Salt Lake City: Utah State Board of Education, 1966. ERIC ED 022 267.

Quick, G. L. *The Advantages of Extending the School Year.* Dissertation. University of Nebraska, Teachers College, Lincoln, 1966. Same, University Microfilms, no. 67-3441, University of Michigan, Ann Arbor.

Rochester Summer Activities. Rochester, Minn.: Rochester Public Schools, August 1966.

Shafer, Glen E. *Nebraska's Support of Its Public Schools and the Year-Around School.* Nebraska Public Schools, summer 1966.

Thomas, George I. *Extended School Year Designs.* Albany: University of the State of New York, State Education Department, January 1966. Same, ERIC ED 020 587.

Year-Round Schools for Polk County, Florida: A Feasibility Study. Gainesville: Florida Educational Research and Development Council, College of Education, University of Florida, 1966.

Newspapers

"Expensive Under-Used School Plant." *Seattle Times,* September 12, 1966.

Hoover, Dennis. "Year-Round Classes Seen Around Corner." *Dallas Morning News,* December 19, 1966.

"A Way to Add One Classroom to Every Four." *Louisville Courier-Journal,* March 19, 1966.

1967

Periodicals

Adams, Andrew S. "Criticisms of the Year Round School Can Be Answered." *Nation's Schools* 80:70.

_____. "Philosophy and Goals: Educator Cites Obstacles to Year-Round Schools." *Education Summary,* December 15, 1967.

"All Year Schools Needed." *Chicago American,* October 8, 1967.

"Allentown Classrooms Get Year-Round Decorating." *Nation's Schools* 80:50.

Bauman, W. Scott. "Four-Quarter Plan Uses Schools All Year Long." *Nation's Schools* 80:69.

Borel, William P., and Blackmon, C. Robert. "Year-Round School: Innovation or Trend?" *Boardman* (Baton Rouge, Louisiana), October 1967, pp. 2, 5-8, 22-27.

Cawelti, Gordon. "Innovative Practices in High School: Who Does What—and Why—and How." *Nation's Schools* 79:56.

"A City Prepares to Test Year-Round High Schools." *The National Observer*, November 6, 1967.

"District Offers Teachers Twelve-Month Employment." *Administrative Action Reports*, November 1967.

Eberle, A. W. "Responsive and Responsible Academic Calendar." *National Association of Women Deans and Counselors Journal* 30:138-142.

"Educational Innovation." *Education Digest*, February 1967.

"Eight High Schools in the Atlanta, Georgia, Area Will Begin Year-Round Operations September." *Education U.S.A.*, November 20, 1967.

Frost, J. L. "Time to Teach." *Texas Outlook* 51:34-35.

Grieder, Calvin. "Teachers Don't Get Summer Vacation, They Get Laid Off." *Nation's Schools* 79:4.

Harris, T. L.; Otto, W.; and Barrett, T. C. "Summary and Review of Investigations Relating to Reading." *Journal of Educational Research*, 1967.

Hoover, Dennis. "Year-Round Schools Will Save the Taxpayer Money." *The Mayflower Warehouseman*, May 1967.

"Illinois Joins Trend, A Longer School Year." *Springfield, Illinois, State Journal*, August 24, 1967.

Jensen, George. "Let's Try Year-Round Schools." *Parents Magazine*, September 1967.

"Little Hoover Report Urges School Organization." *Ohio Schools* 45:33-35.

"Ohio Legislature Supports Year-Round School." *School Management*, September 1967.

Ohles, J. F. "Watts, the Schools, and Citizenship Education." *School and Society* 95:256.

Olsen, J. "Needed: A New Kind of School for the Slums." *Changing Education* 2:7-14.

"Revolution in Summer Schools." *Educational Digest*, March 1967.

"School Building Makes a Difference." *Educational Technology* 7:12-15.

"Summer School—Employment for Teachers." *NEA Research Bulletin*, March 1967.

"12-Month Positions." *Michigan Education Journal*, September 1, 1967.

"The Twelve-Month School: Six Possible Arrangements." *Education Summary*, October 1, 1967.

"Year-Round Schools." *Education Age* 4(2):45.

Zachrich, Alvin N. "These Misgivings Make Me Hesitate." *Nation's Schools* 80:69.

Pamphlets, booklets, and reports

Analysis of Termination of PACE Program. Report. Del Campo, Calif.: Del Campo High School, 1967.

Daitsman, Rose. *More Time to Learn.* Report. Middletown: Southwestern Ohio Education Research Council, 1967.

Educational Programs Supported by Federal Funds. Frankfort: Bureau of State and Federal Relations, Kentucky Department of Education, July 1967.

Evening Study Programs. Report. Bloomfield Hills, Mich.: Bloomfield Hills Schools Release, October 1967.

Extending the School Year. Lansing, Mich.: National Education Association Research, December 1967.

Finchum, R. N. *Extended Use of School Facilities.* Washington, D. C.: U.S. Department of Health, Education, and Welfare, Office of Education, October 1967. Same, ERIC ED 018 071.

Gillis, Reid. *A Report of the Plans to Implement the Metropolitan Five-County Twelve-Months School Plan.* Atlanta: Fulton County Board of Education, November 30, 1967.

Report of the Twelve-Month School Year Task Force. Seattle: Seattle Public Schools, December 19, 1967.

St. Aubin, Norman. *Proposal for Year-Around School.* Report. Detroit: Columbus School, 1967.

Teen-Age Opportunity Programs in Summer: A Six-State Study Report. Lansing: Michigan State Department of Education Bulletin, 1967.

Wolf, Robert C. *The Community School Program 1967-68.* Cincinnati, Ohio: The Forest Hills School District, 1967.

Newspapers

"Action Line." *Detroit Free Press,* October 6, 1967.

Angelos, Constantine, ed. "Twelve-Month School Urged by Board President." *The Seattle Times,* May 3, 1967.

Fink, Herschel P. "Eye Twelve-Month Use of Schools." *The Detroit News,* March 9, 1967.

Salsinger, Harry. "Study of Year Round Schools Urged." *The Detroit News,* November 15, 1967.

"School Board OKs $51.7 Million Budget; Summer Enrollment Down 40 Percent." *Cincinnati Post Times Star,* July 14, 1967.

Wax, Judy. "Year Round School Opposed." *Detroit Free Press,* 1967.

1968

Books

Liebman, Mary A. *What is a Twelve-Four Plan?* Horseshoe, North Carolina: National School Calendar Study Committee, 1968.

Thomas, George I. *Setting the Stage for Lengthened School Year Programs.*

Albany: University of the State of New York, State Education Department, March 1968. Same, ERIC ED 020 578. (ED 020 587 is a related document.)

Periodicals

Adams, Andrew S. "Look Hard at This Year Round School Plan." *American School Board Journal* 156:11-15.

Best, Leonard E. "The Twelve-Month Panacea." *Education Summary*, February 5, 1968.

"The Broadening Role of the Classroom Teacher." *Educator's Dispatch* 23(11), February 15, 1968.

"The Case for Keeping Our Schools Going All Year." *Scope Magazine*, June 1968.

"Cleveland Debates Year Round School Proposal." *Education U.S.A.*, April 2, 1968.

"The Concept of an Extended School Year is Receiving Stimulation." *Educator's Dispatch* 23(18), June 1, 1968.

Cotton, Marlene. "The Extended School Year: What's Being Done." *Education Summary*, July 1, 1968.

"Delaware Puts All Year School on Trial." *Education News*, February 1968.

Divoky, Diane. "Schools Go Year Round." *Education News*, August 5, 1968.

"Eleven Month School is Recommended." *NEA Research Bulletin*, May 1968.

"The Four-Quarter Plan for Year-Round Operation." *Michigan Journal of Secondary Education*, spring 1968.

"Four-Quarter Plan in Operation: Year-Round School for Park's Pupils." *PACE Review* 3:1.

Gillin, B. "Twelve-Month Schools Being Studied by Montgomery." *Philadelphia Inquirer*, October 20, 1968.

Gillis, Reid. "Twelve-Month School Year: Plans and Strategy." *Education Summary*, September 1, 1968.

Greene, T. "Georgia's Schools Plan Twelve-Month Year." *Education News*, January 1968.

Hamman, H. A. "Longer School Year?" *Illinois Schools Journal* 48:47-50.

Hartley, Nell Tabor, and Ankrum, Janet L. "Planning an Extended Hours Program." *School Libraries*, summer 1968.

Holmes, George W. III, and Seawell, William H. "Summer School Reappraised." *American School Board Journal*, January 1968, pp. 10-12.

"News Front: An 11-Month School Year is Recommended in a Four-Year Study by the New York State Education Department." *Education U.S.A.*, April 1968.

"Rescheduled School Year: Summary." *NEA Research Bulletin* 46:67-70.

Standa, J. J. "President's Message." *Pennsylvania School Journal* 116:436.

Szuberla, C. A. "Year-Round School Evolution." *American School Board Journal* 155:13.

"Trends and Issues: Bandwagon for the Extended School Year." *Education Summary*, May 1, 1968.

VanHoose, R. "It's a Long, Long Time . . . From June to September." *Kentucky School Journal* 46:12-15.

White, Richard E. "Board Member Looks at the Extended School Year." *Education* 88:245-248.

"Year-Round School Movement." *Educator's Dispatch* 23(13), March 15, 1968.

Zachrich, Alvin N. "Twelve Months School Ahead." *MASB Journal,* March 1968.

Pamphlets, booklets, and reports

All-Year Plan. Stevenson, Wash.: Stevenson Public Schools, March 1968.

Brook, Donald. *Feasibility of Extended Year Operation.* Seattle: Seattle Public Schools, March 1968.

DiBello, Joseph. *One Model of an Extended Year Program.* Lansing: Michigan Education Association, March 1968.

Elseroad, Homer O. *Report on the Twelve-Month Program.* Rockville, Md.: Montgomery County Public Schools, summer 1968.

Evaluation of Trimester Program. Report. Houston, Texas: San Jacinto Senior High School, Houston Independent School District, summer 1968.

"The Extended School Year." Chapter 12 of *The Report of the Governor's Study Committee on the Public School System of North Carolina,* Raleigh, North Carolina, 1968.

The Extended School Year. Richmond: Virginia State Department of Education, 1968.

Extended School Year Seminar. Louisville, Ky.: Jefferson County Public Schools, August 1968.

Extended School Year Study. Report. Winston-Salem, N.C.: Winston-Salem, Forsyth County Schools, June 1968.

Fuller Utilization of Schools. Washington, D. C.: National Education Association News Bulletin, January 1968.

Fulton County Curriculum Study. Report. Atlanta: Fulton County Board of Education, 1968.

Geisinger, Robert W. *The Extended School Year Concept.* Bureau of Research, Administration and Coordination, Department of Public Instruction, Commonwealth of Pennsylvania, 1968.

Introducing the Multiple Trails Extended School Year Plan. Albany: University of the State of New York, State Education Department, 1968.

Jensen, George. *Should Schools be Used the Year Round?* Horseshoe, North Carolina: National School Calendar Study Committee, 1968.

Kehoe, Ray E. *The Four-Quarter Plan for Year-Round School Operation.* Report. Ann Arbor: Bureau of School Services, University of Michigan, February 1968.

Kovalcik, Jerome. *Summer Programs.* Albany: New York Board of Education, April 1968.

Liebman, Mrs. Charles. *The Case: Year-Round Schools.* 410 S. Ridge Road, McHenry, Illinois 60050, 1968.

Martin, John S. *Effective Instruction: A Report on the Four-Quarter Plan of Organization.* Atlanta, Ga.: Atlanta Public Schools, 1968. Same, ERIC ED 028 544.

Martin, John S. *A Four-Quarter Instructional Program.* Report. Atlanta, Ga.: Atlanta Board of Education, 1968.

Materials on Fulton County's Twelve-Month School Plan. Atlanta: Fulton County Board of Education, 1968.

Mitchell, Paul. *Three-Year Extended Project Report.* Commack, N.Y.: Grace L. Hubbs School, Commack Public Schools, April 1968.

1968 Fall Seminar on Year-Round School. Louisville, Ky.: Jefferson County Public Schools, 1968.

Overway, Marvin J. *Organizing Schools for Innovation, Change, and Research: A Year-Round School Proposal.* Hudsonville, Mich.: Hudson Public Schools, 1968.

Page, R. *Survey Report in Lockport, Illinois.* Lockport: Lockport Public Schools, 1968.

Proceedings of Mt. Sequoyah National Seminar on Year-Round Education. Fayetteville, Arkansas: School Study Council, fall 1968. Same, ERIC ED 040 498.

Saxe, Richard. *The All-Year School: Again!* Memos for the *School Executive* 12(1), November 1968.

Scala, Anthony W. *A Survey of the History and Current Status of the Extended School in Selected Public Schools of the United States.* Dissertation. St. John's University, Collegeville, Minn., 1968.

Summer Enrichment Programs. Washington, D. C.: Educational Research Service, 1968.

Thomas, George I. *Setting the Stage for Lengthened School Year Programs—A Special Report for the Governor and the Legislature of the State of New York.* Albany: University of the State of New York, State Education Department, March 1968. Same, ERIC ED 020 578 (ED 020 587 is a related document).

Torge, Herman. *The Year Round School.* Thesis submitted for the Master of Arts Degree, Miami University, Oxford, Ohio, 1968.

Trimester. Report. Houston, Texas: Houston Independent School District, 1968.

The Twelve-Months School: Six Possible Arrangements. Washington, D. C.: National Education Association, January 1968.

Varner, Sherrell E. *The Rescheduled School Year.* Research Summary 1968-S2. Washington, D. C.: National Education Association, 1968. Same, ERIC ED 032 625.

Wehmhoefer, Roy A. *The Twelve-Month School Year—A Study of the Advantages and Disadvantages of the Four-Quarter System.* Chicago: Cook County Educational Service Region, February 1968. Same, ERIC ED 022 252.

Wells, William. *Summer School—School Year Study.* Report. Syosset, N.Y.: Robbins Lane School, April 1968.

Whitney, Howard, comp. *Annotated Bibliography on Year-Round School Programs.* Eugene: University of Oregon, 1968. Same, ERIC ED 023 199.

Witherspoon, Ralph L. *Effect of Trimester School Operation on the Achievement and Adjustment of Kindergarten and First through Third Grade Children.* Washington, D. C.: Department of Health, Education, and Welfare, Office of Education, 1968.

Young, Robert O. *STAY (Start Teaching All Year).* Freeland, Mich.: Freeland Community Schools, November 27, 1968.

Newspapers

Angelos, Constantine, ed. "Educators Hear Call for 'Will to Tax Ourselves.' " *The Seattle Times,* September 15, 1968.

"Area Poll Shows Parents Against Year-Long School." Royal Oak, Mich.: *The Daily Tribune,* July 24, 1968.

"Atlanta, Georgia: System Faces Trouble." Mt. Clemens, Mich.: *Macomb Daily,* August 5, 1968.

"Eleven Month Session in Schools Asked by State Agency." *New York Times,* March 1968.

"The Extended Year Study." Durand, Mich.: *Durand Express,* March 1968.

Hoover, Dennis. "Year-Round School Use May Ease Room Problem." *The Dallas Morning News,* December 18, 1968.

McCormack, Patricia. "Extended School Year May Soon be Reality." New York: UPI, August 9, 1968.

"Shorter but Harder Schooling." *Christian Science Monitor,* March 1968.

"University of Michigan Educator Condemns Extended School Plan." Durand, Mich.: *Durand Express,* March 1968.

"Warren Schools Drop Year-Round Study Proposal." Mt. Clemens, Mich.: *Macomb Daily,* February 15, 1968.

"Year-Round Class Plan Viewed." Pontiac, Mich.: *Pontiac Press,* March 1968.

"Year-Round Schools Being Tried in Durand." Birmingham, Mich.: *Birmingham Eccentric,* March 1968.

1969

Books

Gillis, Reid, and Oldham, Neild B., eds. *The Twelve-Month School: A New Approach.* New London, Conn.: Croft Educational Services, 1969.

Periodicals

"The All-Year School." *Time,* August 15, 1969.

Ames, R. G. "Why One District Rejected Year-Round Schools: Germantown, Wisconsin." *Nation's Schools* 84:94.

"Are We Stuck with a 180-Day School Year?" *Pennsylvania Education* 1(2) (Pennsylvania State Department of Public Instruction), June-July 1969.

Beavan, K. "Eliminating the Long, Hot Summers." *Times Educational Supplement* 2833:14, September 5, 1969.

Beggs, Donald L. "The Summer Vacation—An Interruption in Learning." *Illinois Journal of Education,* January 1969.

Coutts, H. T., and Bergen, J. J. "Modified School Year." *Education Canada* 9:23-27.
Dennard, R. "Twelve-Month Four Quarter School Year." *Journal of Health, Physical Education, and Recreation* 40:40.
Ellena, William J. "Extending the School Year." *Today's Education* 58:48-49.
Higginbotham, James M. "School, How Long?" *Florida Schools*, March-April 1969.
"Increased Interest in Longer School Year." *School and Society*, March 1969.
Jensen, G. M. "Year-Round School: Can Boards Sidestep It Much Longer?" *American School Board Journal* 157:8-12.
Miller, V. "Pondering the Year-Round School." *Illinois Education* 57:381-384.
"Schoolmen Visualize Need for Extended School Year." *Nation's Schools* 83:101.
"Teachers' Views on Pupils' School Day and Year." *NEA Research Bulletin* 47:20-22.
Vacca, R. S. "Can It Be Done in One Hundred and Eighty Days: A Question Rephrased." *Virginia Journal of Education* 62:20-21.
"Year Round School in Atlanta." *ESC Bulletin*, May 1969.

Pamphlets, booklets, and reports

Bauman, W. S. *The School Calendar Dilemma—A Solution for the Approaching Crises.* Eugene: Bureau of Business and Economic Research, University of Oregon, 1969. Same, ERIC ED 033 436.
Bentley, E. L. *Four-Quarter School Year. Results of an Exploratory Study of the Four-Quarter School Year in Metropolitan Atlanta.* Atlanta: Supplementary Educational Center, 1969. Same, ERIC ED 041 382.
Cuddy, E. H. *The Year-Round School or the Rescheduled School Year.* Indianapolis: Warren Township Independent School District, 1969. Same, ERIC ED 041 364.
Elseroad, Homer O. *A Twelve-Month School Year.* Memorandum to members of the Board of Education. Rockville, Md.: Montgomery County Public Schools, March 11, 1969.
Extended School Year. Grand Forks, North Dakota, August 1969.
Extended School Year. Louisville, Ky.: Jefferson County Public Schools, 1969.
The Extended School Year: A Feasibility Study. Frankfort, Ky.: Kentucky Legislative Research Commission, June 1969.
Extended School Year Conference. Tallahassee: Florida State Department of Education, May 1-2, 1969.
Feasibility of Rescheduled School Year Plans for Delaware Public Elementary and Secondary Schools. Dover: Delaware State Department of Public Instruction, 1969. Same, ERIC ED 036 886.
A Feasibility Study Proposal. Ann Arbor: Ann Arbor Public Schools, January 17, 1969.
Finch, Robert H. Remarks presented at the American Society of Newspaper Editors luncheon, April 18, 1969, American Society of Newspaper Editors, Washington, D. C.

First District of Georgia. Washington, D. C.: U.S. Department of Education, January 1969.

"Four-Quarter School Calendar." *Croft Leadership Action Folio 11,* Exhibit A-3. New London, Conn.: Croft Educational Service, 1969.

Gillis, Reid. *Fulton County Schools Four-Quarter Plan.* Atlanta: Fulton County Board of Education, 1969. Same, ERIC ED 049 548.

Glinke, George B. *A List of Annotated Sources Covering Year-Round Schools.* Utica, Mich.: Utica Community Schools, Year-Round School Feasibility Study, October 1969.

——————. *A List of Bibliographical Materials for Year-Round Schools.* Utica, Mich.: Utica Community Schools, September 1969.

A Greater America through Public Education. East Lansing, Mich.: Michigan Citizens to Advance Public Education, March 1969.

Jefferson County Schools' Extended School-Year Seminar. Louisville, Ky.: Jefferson County Public Schools, September 19-20, 1969.

Keith, M. T. *Sustained Primary Program for Bilingual Students.* Paper presented at the International Reading Association Conference, Kansas City, Mo., April 30-May 3, 1969. Same, ERIC ED 030 550.

Liebman, Mary. *How Nine Year-Round Plans Compare.* 410 South Ridge Road, McHenry, Illinois, July 1969.

McLain, John D. *Considerations for Economy and Quality Education through Year-Round Schools.* Clarion, Pa.: Research-Learning Center, Clarion State College, August 1969.

——————. *The Flexible All Year School.* Clarion, Pa.: Research-Learning Center, Clarion State College, 1969.

"Other Extended School Year Designs." *Croft Leadership Action Folio 11,* Exhibit A-1. New London, Conn.: Croft Educational Service, 1969.

Park School Four-Quarter Plan Calendar. Hayward, Calif.: Hayward Unified School District, July 1969.

Perry, I. L., comp. *Post-Conference Report: Extended School Year Conference.* Tallahassee: Florida State Department of Education, Tallahassee Division of Curriculum and Instruction, 1969. Same, ERIC ED 044 811.

A Plan to Lengthen the School Day and Extend the School Program into the Summer Months. Greeley, Colo.: Franklin School, May 2, 1969.

Read, Betty. *The Extended School Year.* Report. Albuquerque, New Mexico, July 1969.

Report on 1969 Summer School Program. Culver City, Calif.: Culver City Unified School District, March 11, 1969.

Report on Year-Round School. National Education Association Task Force on Urban Education, July 1969.

The Rescheduled School Year. Dover, Del.: State Department of Public Instruction, March 1969.

Signs of the Times. Report. Louisville, Ky.: Jefferson County Schools, 1969.

Simmons, J. C. *An Examination of the Socio-Economic Implications of the Adoption of Individually Prescribed Instructional Systems by School Systems. Final Report.* Tallahassee: Florida State University, 1969. Same, ERIC ED 031 801.

Spear, Raymond E. *Opening School Doors.* Northville, Mich.: Northville Public Schools, October 1969.

A Study over Year-Round Schools Possible in Pennsylvania. Harrisburg: Pennsylvania Department of Public Instruction, July 1969.

Superintendent Calendar Committee Report. Omaha: Omaha Public Schools, May 1969.

Superintendent's Committee on Year-Round School. "The Improvement of Instruction by Way of *The Quarter Plan in Secondary Schools.*" Part 1 of a two-part Feasibility Study of the Quarter Plan, Cincinnati Public Schools, December 10, 1969.

Superintendent's Committee on Year-Round School. "More Effective Use of Resources by Way of *The Quarter Plan in Secondary Schools.*" Part 2 of a two-part Feasibility Study of the Quarter Plan, Cincinnati Public Schools, December 10, 1969.

Thomas, G. I. *It's Time to Reschedule the School Year.* Paper presented at the National School Boards Association Meeting, Miami Beach, Florida, April 12-15, 1969. Same, ERIC ED 029 394.

Tri-District Summer Instructional Program, 1969. Report. Okemos-Haslett, East Lansing School Districts, Mich., 1969.

"The Twelve-Month School: A New Approach." *Croft Leadership Action Folio 11.* New London, Conn.: Croft Educational Service, 1969.

The Twelve-Month Use of Schools. Report. Rockville, Md.: Montgomery County Public Schools, January 1969.

"Workable Plan for Year-Round School Sought." *Schools in Action,* Cincinnati Public Schools, Cincinnati, Ohio, January 3, 1969.

Year-Round Education for Public Schools. Dayton, Ohio: Charles F. Kittering Foundation, April 1969.

Newspapers

Aweeka, Charles. "Edmonds Schools Take Long Look at Summer Vacation." *The Seattle Times,* January 26, 1969.

Cisernos, Joe. "Year-Around School Program Would Change Lots of Things." Utica, Mich.: *The Daily Sentinel,* April 13, 1969.

Craig, Dorothy; Kraus, Beth; and Hoyt, Jane. "Year-Round School Policy May Relieve Macomb County." Mt. Clemens, Mich.: *The Macomb Daily,* January 7, 1969.

McCloy, Helen. "County Schools Get Federal Grant for Study on Extended School Year." Louisville, Ky.: *Courier-Journal,* July 31, 1969.

Millius, Peter. "Ugh! Support is Growing Again for Twelve-Month School Year." *The Washington Post,* 1969.

"Rochester Residents Favor State Income Tax for Education Needs." Utica, Mich.: *The Daily Sentinel,* July 24, 1969.

"Rumblings of Action Toward Year-Round Schools Heard." *The Seattle Times,* January 30, 1969.

Schreyer, Lowell. "Wilson Goes to Twelve Month School Year." Mankato, Minn.: *Mankato Free Press,* August 13, 1969.

Shannon, Margaret. "Will Year-Round School Pass the Test?" *The Atlanta Journal and Constitution Magazine*, June 1, 1969.

Stuart, Peter C. "1,100 Students—1,100 Different Curricula." *Christian Science Monitor*, August 14, 1969.

"Summer Time Becomes Vital Part of City Schools Educational Effort." *Sylmar Sentinel*, August 13, 1969.

"Year-Around Schools OKd." Lansing, Mich.: UPI, 1969.

1970

Books

The Impact of a Rescheduled School Year: A Special Report Prepared for the Governor and the Legislature of the State of New York. Albany: State Education Department, March 1970. $8.30. ERIC ED 040 234.

Year-Round School: Is It Feasible? Northville, Mich.: Northville Public Schools, 1970. $6.58. Same, ERIC ED 051 559.

Periodicals

Adams, V. A. "Extended School Year: Status Report." *School Management* 14:13-16.

Beavan, Keith. "Age of the Year-Round School." *Times Educational Supplement* 2885:13, September 4, 1970.

Beckwith, R. M. "Valley View 45-15 Continuous School Year Plan." *American School and University* 43:19-24.

"Exploring the School Year." *Compact* 4:3-48.

Glines, D. E. "12-Month School: Is This the School of the Future?" *Instructor* 80:72.

Glinke, George B. "Experimenting With a Voluntary Program." *Compact* 4:31-32.

Jensen, George. "Does Year-Round Education Make Sense?" *Compact*, December 1970.

Letson, J. W. "Atlanta Schoolman Discusses His Year-Round School Program." *Nation's Schools* 86:12.

Letson, John W., and Spear, Raymond E. "The 12-Month Concept for High Schools." *IASB Dialogue*, December 1970.

McLain, John. "Developing Flexible All-Year Schools." *Compact* 4:7-8.

————. "Major Thrusts for a Flexible All-Year School." *Pennsylvania School Journal* 118:157-163.

National Education Association. "Rescheduling the School Year." *Today's Education* 59:37.

O'Dell, A. M., and Henderson, G. "Becky-David: The Year-Round School: St. Charles County, Mo." *School and Community* 56:13.

"One-Third More School in the Same School." *Educate Magazine* 3(2):4.

Scala, Anthony W. "Year-Round School: Syosset Plan." *Bulletin of the National Association of Secondary School Principals* 54:79-89.

"Success Story at Valley View: School the Year Round." *American School and University*, November 1970.

"The Twelve-Month School Year." *Compact* 4:28-30.

"Why It Pays to Keep School Open All Year." *Parade Magazine*, December 27, 1970, pp. 8-9.

"Year-Round School." *American School and University*, November 1970.

"Year-Round School: Park School, Hayward, California." *Instructor* 79:36-38.

Pamphlets, booklets, and reports

Alam, S. J. *The Four-Quarter Plan and Its Feasibility for the Port Huron Area School District: A Research Study.* Lansing, Mich.: Michigan State Department of Education; Port Huron Area School District, 1970. ERIC ED 046 105.

Beckwith, Robert M. *A Major Step Toward Efficient School Operation: The Valley View 45-15 Continuous School Year Plan.* Chicago: Illinois State Chamber of Commerce, 1970.

Becky-David Year-Round School Plan. St. Charles, Missouri: Francis Howell School District, September 1970.

The Challenge at Romeoville. Chicago: Illinois State Chamber of Commerce, January 1970.

Curriculum Catalogue Quarter Courses. Atlanta: Atlanta Public Schools Publication Center, January 1970.

Feasibility Study of Full-Year Public School Operation—Valley View 45-15 Continuous School Year Plan. Lockport, Ill.: Valley View School District #96, Research and Development Office, 1970. ERIC ED 048 524.

45-15 Meeting the Educational Challenges. Minneapolis: Minnesota School Facilities Council, 1970 Conference Report. $6.

Glinke, George B. *The Extended School Year: A Look at 67 Different School Designs as Proposed by Various School Districts in America.* Utica, Mich.: Utica Community Schools, April 1970.

_____. *The Four-Quarter Staggered School Year: A Feasibility Study.* Utica, Mich.: Utica Community Schools, July 1970.

_____. *The Year-Round Educational Movement: Its Historical Implications on Today's Urbanized Culture.* Utica, Mich.: Utica Community Schools, February 1970.

Hamilton, Charles. *A Financial Evaluation of Becky-David Year-Round School.* St. Louis, Mo.: The Danforth Foundation, 1970.

Henson, E. Curtis. *The Four-Quarter School Year.* Atlanta: Atlanta Public Schools, Publication Center, January 1970.

Illinois School District Initiates 45-15 Year-Round System. Chicago: School Business Affairs, October 1970.

Indepth Study for Freeland Community Schools. Freeland, Mich.: Freeland Community Schools, 1970. Same, ERIC ED 053 438.

Individualized Instruction: The Year Around School Education for the '70's. Minneapolis: Minnesota School Facilities Council, 1970.

Nine-Month School Year Out! Louisville, Ky.: Jefferson County Public Schools, June 1970.

9+ the Year-Round School. Washington, D. C.: American Association of School Administrators, 1970. Same, ERIC ED 040 497.

President Richard M. Nixon. Message to Congress. The White House, Washington, D. C., March 19, 1970.

Proceedings of Second National Seminar on Year-Round Education. Harrisburg: Pennsylvania Department of Education, April 1970.

Providing Year-Round Service for the Commonwealth of Pennsylvania. Clarion, Pa.: Research-Learning Center, Clarion State College, 1970.

Report of the Committee to Study the Extended School Year. Trenton: New Jersey School Boards Association, December 1970.

Selected Bibliography on Year-Round School Operation. Chicago: Illinois State Chamber of Commerce, 1970.

Valley View 45-15 Plan: Problems, Costs, Issues, and Research Designs. USOE #0-0011, grant #OEG-0-70-2642(508), document # ED-047189 ERIC. Bethesda, Md.: Document Reproduction Service, 1970.

What Is the Continuous Learning Year Cycling Plan? Albany: University of the State of New York, The State Education Department, Office of Research and Evaluation, 1970.

Year-Round Operation of Public Schools. Transcript of interim hearing, Assembly Committee on Education, California Legislature, Los Angeles, November 19, 1970.

The Year-Round School. Washington, D. C.: American Association of School Administrators, 1970. Same, ERIC ED 040 497.

Newspapers

"Suburb Turns to All-Year School." *Chicago Daily News*, January 24-25, 1970.

1971

Books

Glines, Don. *Creating Humane Schools.* Mankato, Minn.: Campus Publishers, 1971. $5.

Hermansen, Kenneth L., and Gove, James R. *The Year-Round School: The 45-15 Breakthrough.* Hamden, Conn.: Linnet Books, Shoe String Press, 1971.

Pennsylvania State Department of Public Instruction. *Year-Round School.* Rev. ed. February, 1971. ERIC ED 052 540.

Periodicals

Beavan, Keith. "Open Schools All-Year Task Force Urges." *Times Educational Supplement* 2929:16, July 9, 1971.

Blanton, Jack. "Extended School Year (Texas)." *Compact* 5:16-18.

"Considerations for an Expanded School Year." *Compact* 5:17.

Driscoll, T. F. "School Around the Calendar." *American Education* 7:21-23.

Driscoll, Thomas F. "Year-Round School Meets with Success." *OSBA Journal,* February 1971.
Ernst, Leonard. "The Year-Round School: Faddish or Feasible?" *Nation's Schools* 88:51-56.
"Extending the School Year." *Kaleidescope #4.* Boston: Massachusetts Department of Education, 1971.
Gillis, Reid. "The Extended School Year—It's Now." *The School Administrator,* April 1971.
McLain, John. "Developing Flexible All-Year Schools." *Educational Leadership* 28:472-475. Same, *Education Digest* 36:12-14.
Mallory, Stephen R. "Year-Round School: Coming, Coming, Here!" *School Management* 15:24-25.
Mueller, Ernest H. "Prince William's Year-Round School Plan: How It Was Initiated." *Public Education in Virginia,* 1971.
"The New Trend: Year-Round Schools." *U.S. News & World Report,* July 26, 1971, pp. 35-37.
Rothstein, H., and Adams, R. F. "Quinmester Extended School Year: Dade County Public Schools, Miami, Fla." *Journal of Health, Physical Education and Recreation* 42:30.
"School Around-the-Calendar." *The Enquirer Magazine,* April 18, 1971.
Stefanich, G. P. "Year-Round School Plan with Summer Vacation for Everyone." *School and Community* 57:14-15.
Thomas, Steven C. "Valley View's 45-15 Year-Round School." *Today's Education* 60:42-43.
"What About the 12-Month School?" Teacher opinion poll, *Instructor* 80:17.
"Year-Round School." *South Carolina Schools,* winter 1971.
"Year-Round Schools: Some Questions and Answers." An interview with Charles E. Clear and Dr. Joseph P. Roberts, *Public Education in Virginia,* 1971.
" 'Year Round' Successes Reported." *Education U.S.A.,* March 8, 1971.
Yevish, I. A. "Do We Need a Longer School Year?" *The Educational Forum* 35:193-195.

Pamphlets, booklets, and reports

Authorized Instructional Courses for the Quinmester Program. Miami: Dade County Public Schools, 1971.
Barnes, Jarvis. *Some Internal Problems Associated with a Year-Round Program.* Report. Atlanta: Assistant Superintendent for Research and Development, Atlanta Public Schools, 1971.
Cole, Wilma. *The Year-Round School.* Paper presented at the National Association of Elementary School Principals Annual Meeting, Cleveland, Ohio, April 17-22, 1971. Same, ERIC ED 050 455.
Commissioner's Report: The Extended School Year Project. Providence: Rhode Island State Department of Education, 1971.
The Compulsory Year-Round School. Hayward, Calif.: Hayward Unified Schools, May 3, 1971.

Dade County Public Schools, Department of Program Evaluation. *Evaluation Report of the 1971 Summer Quinmester Program.* Miami: Dade County Public Schools, Division of Instruction, September 1971.

Dade County Public Schools, Division of Instruction. *A Review of the Status and Projections for the Dade County Quinmester Extended School Year Program.* Miami: Dade County Public Schools, April 1971.

"Dear Parents." La Mesa, Calif.: La Mesa-Spring Valley School District, 1971.

Elective Quarter Plan. Louisville, Ky.: Jefferson County Public Schools, Jefferson County Education Center, 1971.

Elementary Education: Operation of the Compulsory Year-Round School. Hayward, Calif.: Hayward Unified School District, 1971.

Fain, James C. *Curriculum Revision Based on Behavioral Objectives for Twelve-Month, Four-Quarter Schools.* Atlanta: Atlanta Public Schools, 1971. $3.29. Same, ERIC ED 051 578.

45-15 Information Packet. Lockport, Ill.: Valley View School District #96, Research and Development Office, 1971. $2.

The Four-Quarter School Program: A Report on the Fourth Quarter. Atlanta: Atlanta Public Schools, September 1971.

Glinke, George B. *Types of Changes and Sample Questions with the Optional Five-Term Year-Round Educational Plan.* Utica, Mich.: Utica Community Schools, March 1971.

Hollingsworth, H. G., Jr. *Extended School Year Possibilities.* Columbia, S.C.: State Department of Education, 1971.

Individualized Education: The Year Around School, Non-graded K-12. Minneapolis: Minnesota School Facilities Council, 1971.

In Quest of Tomorrow Today. North Miami Beach, Florida: North Miami Beach Senior High School, August 1971.

Legislature of the State of California. Act AB 1002. Sacramento: Legislature of the State of California, 1971.

A Major Step Toward Efficient School Operation: Molalla Elementary School, A 12-Month School. Molalla, Oregon: Molalla Elementary School District No. 35.

Modified 45-10 Twelve-Month School Operation. Madison Township, Matawan, New Jersey Schools, 1971.

National Education Association. *Consider a Year-Round School.* Hyattsville, Md.: American Education Week, 1971.

The Optional Five-Term Year-Round Educational Plan: A Step Toward Implementing Plans for Extending the Regular School Year. Submitted to the Michigan State Department of Education. Utica, Mich.: Utica Community Schools, July 1971.

Piele, P. K. *Rescheduled School Year Plans. ERIC/CEM Research Review.* Eugene: Center for Advanced Study of Educational Administration, University of Oregon, 1971. ERIC ED 047 419.

Proceedings of Third National Seminar on Year-Round Education. Cocoa Beach, Fla.: Brevard County School System, March 24-26, 1971.

Teachers' General District Handbook: The Year Forty-Five Fifteen 1970-71. Lockport, Ill.: Valley View School District #96 at Romeoville, 1971.

The Twelve-Month School Plan. Columbia, S.C.: Research Information Unit, Office of Research, State Department of Education, 1971.

Valley View School District No. 96 at Romeoville, Lockport, Illinois. *Planning a Year-Round School Operation—Final Report.* Washington, D. C.: U. S. Office of Education, January 1971. Same, ERIC ED 047 189.

What Does Evaluation Say About the 45-15 Plan? Lockport, Ill.: Valley View School District #96 at Romeoville, 1971.

Year-Round School Background Information. La Mesa, Calif.: La Mesa—Spring Valley School District, 1971.

The Year-Round School Concept. Rockville, Md.: Montgomery County Public Schools, May 11, 1971.

Year-Round School: Districts Develop Successful Programs. Washington, D. C.: National School Public Relations Association, 1971.

Year-Round School . . . for Continuous Education. La Mesa, Calif.: La Mesa—Spring Valley School District, November 1971.

Year-Round School Program Information Packet. Chula Vista, California, city schools, 1971.

Newspapers

Corcoran, Paul. "School Conversion May Be Inevitable." Rock Hill, S.C.: *Evening Herald,* November 5, 1971.

————. "Year-Round School Means Drastic Change." *Evening Herald,* November 4, 1971.

Englert, Lizabeth, and Garino, David. "New Lesson Plan: Year-Round Schools Win Increasing Support of Parents, Teachers." *Wall Street Journal,* vol. CLXXVIII, no. 52.

Fine, Benjamin. "Year-Round Schools Will Soon Be Rule." Columbia, S.C.: *The Columbia Record,* August 1971.

"Greenville District Named Experimental Site." *South Carolina Education News Emphasis,* December 1971. (South Carolina Education Association, Columbia, South Carolina)

Herman, Edith. "Year-Round Schools Are Passing Test." *Chicago Tribune,* August 9, 1971.

Hudson, Ken. "Riles Urges Year-Round Plan." *San Diego Union,* August 1, 1971.

Maeroff, Gene L. "Some Areas Trying Year-Round Plan for School Children." Eugene, Oregon: *Eugene Register-Guard,* July 25, 1971.

————. "Year-Round School Flourishes in Illinois." *New York Times,* July 18, 1971.

Neilan, Edward. "12-Month School Plan May Solve Major Problems." *San Diego Union,* July 25, 1971.

Perrone, Betsy. "Advantages of Year-Round Schools Cited by Vipperman." Rock Hill, S.C.: *Evening Herald,* November 3, 1971.

Sellers, Jim. "Molalla's 12-Month Plan First One of its Kind in State." *Eugene Register-Guard*, July 25, 1971.

————. "Others in Oregon Showing Interest." *Eugene Register-Guard*, July 25, 1971.

————. "Plan to be Studied in Lane Districts." *Eugene Register-Guard*, July 25, 1971.

Triangali, Dot. "12-Month School Talk 'Hot.' " *The Columbia Record*, January 28, 1971.

"U.S. Schools Are Changing." *Know Your World*. Columbus Ohio: American Education Publications, Education Center, December 1, 1971.

1972

Periodicals

Friggens, Paul. "New Impetus for the Year-Round School." *The PTA Magazine*, March 1972. Condensed, *Reader's Digest* March 1972, pp. 115-118.

"Year-Round Schools: Ask Someone Who's Tried It." *Education Daily* 5:3-4.

Pamphlets, booklets, and reports

By-Laws of National Council of Year-Round Education, adopted February, 1972. Dr. Wayne White, president, National Council on Year-Round Education, Brevard County School District, Titusville, Florida.

Faile, James F. *Year-Round Education: A Feasibility Study Report*. Florence, S.C.: Florence Public Schools, Pee Dee Regional Education Center, 1972.

Gayden, Joyce. *The Extended School Year Feasibility Study*. Report. Columbia, S.C.: Columbia Public Schools, Richland County School District One, 1972.

————. *The Year-Round Schools: A Chronological Selected Bibliography from 1907 to 1972*. Columbia, S.C.: Department of Instruction, Richland County School District One, 1972.

Guidelines for the Quarter System. Austin: Office of Program Development, Texas Education Agency, 1972.

Miami Jackson Curriculum Bulletin: A Guide to Course Offerings 1972-73. Miami: Miami Jackson High School, 1972.

Proceedings of Fourth National Seminar on Year-Round Education. San Diego, Calif.: Department of Education, San Diego County, February 23-25, 1972.

Tillotson, John. *Year-Round Education: A Feasibility Study Report*. Spartanburg, S.C.: Spartanburg Public Schools, 1972.

Vipperman, Dave. *Year-Round Education: A Feasibility Study Report*. Rock Hill, S.C.: Rock Hill Public Schools, 1972.

Year-Round School Selected Bibliography. San Diego: Curriculum Library, Department of Education, San Diego County, January 1972.

Year-Round Schools. Report. Washington, D. C.: National School Public Relations Association, 1972. $4.

Newspapers

Krell, Kent. "12-Month School Year Recommended." Columbia, S.C.: *The State*, January 29, 1972.

"Results of Year-Round School Survey." *Tucson Public Schools News*, February, 1972.

"School Effects to be Studied." Columbia, S.C.: *The Columbia Record*, January 24, 1972.

"Year-Round School Term Finally Judged a Success." *Columbia Record*, February 10, 1972.